THE ABERDEEN GUIDE

The Wallace Statue

THE
Aberdeen
GUIDE

RANALD MACINNES

Birlinn

First published in Great Britain in 2000 by
Birlinn Limited
8 Canongate Venture
5 New Street
Edinburgh EH8 8BH

www.birlinn.co.uk

ISBN 1 84158 093 7

The publisher wishes to thank Alison Leslie whose idea this book was

British Library Cataloguing-in-Publication Data
A catalogue record for this book is available on request from the
British Library

Picture Credits
Royal Commission of the Ancient and Historical Monuments of Scotland:
frontispiece, pps 8, 10,14, 18, 28, 31,32,40, 43, 52, 58, 61, 62, 65, 77, 78, 79, 84, 87,
105, 109, 127, 138, 139, 141, 149, 152, 159, 179, 183, 184, 192, 196, 199, 203, 205,
217, 222, 225, 226, 229, 235, 242, 243

Aberdeen Art Gallery and Museums: 13, 85
Aberdeen City Council: 20, 57, 69, 106, 132
National Trust for Scotland: 239,
Historic Scotland: 251
National Galleries of Scotland: 35

Printed and bound in Great Britain by
The Cromwell Press, Trowbridge, Wiltshire

Contents

PART ONE

Introduction	11
1. The City of Aberdeen	15
2. Practical Information	22
3. How to Use the Guide	27
4. Aberdeen's Architects	29
5. Aberdeen's Artists	35
6. Granite City	39

PART TWO

7. The Walks

Walk 1 Union Street	47
Walk 2 Provost Skene's House to the Art Gallery via St Nicholas' Churchyard and on to Rosemount	73
Walk 3 Rennie's Wynd to Castlegate, Gallowgate, Mounthooly and the Lochlands	121
Walk 4 Crown Street to Ferryhill and Duthie Park to the Bridge of Dee	159
Walk 5 Old Aberdeen	179
Walk 6 Footdee and the Harbour, Aberdeen Beach to the Brig o' Balgownie	199
Walk 7 A Sunday Stroll in the West End	217

8. Beyond Aberdeen

1 The Castles of the North-east	236
2 Stonehaven	253
3 Cruden Bay	262
Index	267

Acknowledgements

I am very grateful to many people who have helped in many ways with the preparation of this guidebook. The Urban Fabric section of Aberdeen City Council's planning department, Paul Pillath, Brian Cole and Sandy Beattie have given a lot of help and advice. The city's excellent library service is a model of efficiency and service for the researcher into Aberdeen's past. I must thank Paul Stirton for his insight into Aberdeen's artists, and also Historic Scotland, the National Trust for Scotland, the Royal Commission on the Ancient and Historical Monuments of Scotland and Aberdeen City Museums and Art Galleries.

PART ONE

Aberdeen Town House: the tower

Introduction

Like many Scots from the west of the country, Aberdeen for me was an unexplored place until relatively recently. In other parts of Scotland, you hear plenty about the city: its magnificent Union Street, its honest, if ardently thrifty, people ('Aberdeen Taxi Crash: Twenty Injured', and so on, very tediously). Until you've been there, you cannot imagine how 'different' Aberdeen is from other parts of Scotland and what a marvellous place it is. Many outsiders have noticed this, of course: from Francis Groome in the eighteenth century to John Betjeman and the photographer Eisenstaedt in the twentieth century. What is the Aberdonian response to outsiders pointing out their idiosyncrasies? To stay exactly the same. The attitude is summed up by the motto of George Keith (the founder of Marischal College): 'They haif said: quhat say they? Lat thame say.'

What I have written is a 'hands-on' guide to Aberdeen. I wanted to look very closely at the city and sometimes even to touch it. to feel the astonishing hardness but also the warmth of the place. I cannot agree with Lord Teignmouth, writing in 1836, that 'the opportunities afforded me of making inquiries respecting the morals of the people, in the neighbourhood of Aberdeen, elicited results certainly very unfavourable to them'. Lewis Grassic Gibbon (James Leslie Mitchell) thought the city cold and grey. Fifty years later Paul Theroux was also famously unimpressed with the welcome he was given. I myself am unashamedly a fan of Aberdeen. I have described the things I like in detail; others I only mention in passing. Ultimately, I suppose, the choices I have made are personal ones and they range from sculpture to language.

When I was 12, I became friends with a boy who had 'emigrated' from Aberdeen to Glasgow, bringing with him his wonderful, exotic language, the Doric. Billy's mother was young, dark and pretty like so many of the girls from the north-east. But when she got angry, she got *angry*. Very occasionally, she would let fly a torrent of what I correctly assumed was abuse. 'Awa' wi' your sweirty! Fatty bannocks!' The language of the north-east is a dialect of Scots and visitors to the area should enjoy (if not always understand) the sounds as well as the sights of the city and its huge hinterland. Along with the banter, there is also a thriving folk-song tradition.

For the last thirty years the city has also been connected with the magic word 'oil'. On television night after night throughout the early 1970s we heard about Aberdeen's expanding oil industry. There were overused library pictures of an oil-rig seen from the air and an excited voice-over suggested much was happening up there. But the city itself was rarely shown. What was Aberdeen really like? There seemed to be an insular quality to the place, which is not appreciated by many Scots, let alone visitors from overseas. Finally to see the Silver City about fifteen years ago was a genuine surprise for me, as it is to many first-time visitors. You find yourself suddenly there after miles of travelling by train along the top of a very rugged coastline. The delight on arriving is a bit like getting off the train at Venice railway station and finding yourself right in the very heart of a city you had only ever imagined.

Aberdeen is one of the very few cities in the UK which are actually increasing in size, but it is still delightfully small. This city of 230,000 people is a densely packed, north European type of large town with universities, cathedrals, theatres, bookshops, bars and restaurants. Everything is to hand: the town hall, the art gallery, the museum, the shops – and what shops! The Aberdeen visitor can browse by day in the art galleries and museums, eat very well and go to plays, films and other cultural events in the evenings. The city has plenty of excellent restaurants, many more than places of a comparable size. Aberdeen has far more than its fair share of citations in good food guides.

But what exactly is Aberdeen? I can only give you my answer to that question. I want to use the buildings of Aberdeen to open up the city's secrets to us. *The Aberdeen Guide* tells the city's story through its structures: its houses, churches, offices and bridges. You will soon discover that there is much more to the place than Union Street. It has links with such diverse personalities as William Wallace, Lord Byron, Rob Roy MacGregor, Denis Law and Annie Lennox. The book is divided into seven walks, which take the reader on a guided tour of the city's most interesting parts and some of the surrounding area. To understand the city we need to look beyond its immediate confines – or lack of them, for Aberdeen had no city wall. Historically, this was an unwalled trading community, intimately connected with its hinterland in a way that Edinburgh or even nineteenth-century industrial Glasgow was not.

In this book, hundreds of sites are described and woven into the fabric of Aberdeen's long and illustrious history. The city's famous graveyard of St Nicholas and its celebrated inhabitants are also described. As the 'Granite City', Aberdeen has held its builders and architects very dear, so I have included a section on the city's most famous designers, Archibald Simpson, John Smith and the recently rediscovered firm of Pirie & Clyne who built some of Scotland's most unusual Victorian churches and terraces. I have dealt with some of the issues surrounding architecture – the construction, the styles, the details, and so on – but I have spread these little sections throughout the book wherever a par-

Thirteenth- and fourteenth-century pottery and wooden vessels found in archaeological digs in Aberdeen

ticular building offers a good opportunity. You can find these sections in the index. By looking up 'windows', for example, you will see a reference to a short section on the subject contained within a description of the Gordon Highlanders' Regimental Museum and Sir George Reid's studio on p.232. There is also a short section on the granite industry itself, the vast remains of which are still there to be seen at Rubislaw Den quarry, the biggest man-made hole in Europe. Granite-cutting was by no means the largest industry in Aberdeen, but its products are the most important for the city.

The discovery of oil in 1969 was, of course, crucial for the development of Aberdeen. It affected the people, the buildings and the place. Many of the citizens have talked about the cataclysm of oil, the huge change in Aberdeen that occurred. Changes there undoubtedly were, but what city did not change in the 1960s and '70s? Aberdonians are famously a 'go-ahead' set of people, influencing many areas of world culture, from medicine to the arts. After the successful experiment of Union Street, it was never really likely that things would stay the same.

But how to get at the 'truth' behind Aberdeen's story? In the main, we will look at the buildings by means of a series of walks, but we'll also be in search of the people, both rich and poor, who have made Aberdeen what it is. In dedicating this little book to Aberdonians everywhere, I would say I have done my best to describe your city.

The former General Post Office, Crown Street

CHAPTER I

The City of Aberdeen

More than any other city, Aberdeen owes its existence and development to its strategic economic location. There are plenty of places that have sunk into obscurity after a brief moment on the world stage, but Aberdeen has gone from strength to strength despite being located on the edge of Europe. In fact, the city drew its strength from its position. Hemmed in by spectacular cliffs to the south, Aberdeen's fertile hinterland became a vast garden for the growing town. Many other cities have a great river dividing yet defining them, but Aberdeen has two, the Dee and the Don, known to the Romans as the Deva and the Devona. This is a city of three little hills and two great rivers, its medieval 'ring road' later dramatically sliced through by Union Street at the beginning of the nineteenth century. It is also one of only a few 'beach' cities in the world.

It was within the natural boundaries of the two salmon-packed rivers, flowing fast from the tops of the Grampian mountain range, that the earliest settlement in the area is recorded. The lifestyle remains of hunter-gatherers – the first farmers – have been found concentrated near the medieval settlement of Old Aberdeen: the flint tools which they used to cut down the area's rich woodland, to hunt, fish, cook and to provide shelter. Shelter is the most basic human need and the remains of the area's historic 'shelters' whether medieval churches or twentieth-century office blocks, provide the clearest expression of the past.

What we now think of as Aberdeen is in fact two distinct places, both with the same name. The better known of them is the royal burgh of Aberdeen (or 'New Aberdeen' as it was still being referred to in the early nineteenth century) which grew up around a natural harbour at the mouth of the River Dee. The other Aberdeen (Old Aberdeen) is the very quaint old burgh which was established around the ancient settlements of **St Machar's Cathedral and King's College** (pp.192 and 183). The two places, Old and New Aberdeen, were entirely separate until relatively recently. Even by the end of the Middle Ages, though, New Aberdeen had become one of the wealthiest burghs in the country and the new city continued its growth until it swallowed up Old Aberdeen within its boundaries in 1891. Thankfully, however, Old Aberdeen retains much of its distinctive character.

The burgh of New Aberdeen seems to have taken shape in the **Green** (p.126) and then spread inland up to St Katherine's Hill and Castlegate, where the first market was established. Aberdeen has very extensive civic records and the earliest charter was granted by King William the Lion about 1179. William visited Aberdeen many times, staying in his palace in the Green. Alexander II granted another charter in 1222 which, crucially, established a Merchant Guild, a closed shop of merchant traders who would rule Aberdeen for centuries. As early as 1290 Robert III referred to the market of Aberdeen as a 'forum'. The route north out of the Castlegate was via the Broadgate (on the site of Broad Street, p.57) towards Old Aberdeen, which gave that burgh access to the harbour via the curving street called Shiprow to the south of Castlegate. (The 'gate' referred to in 'Castlegate' and 'Broadgate' are places to walk, rather than a gate in the modern sense of an entry point. Such a thing would be referred to as a 'port', of which Aberdeen had six, as we will see.)

Aberdeen's tidal harbour – or *Gawpuyl* – was defended by a fortification simply called a 'blockhouse', which was built between 1513 and 1542. There is now no trace at all of this vital building except a plaque recording its site in modern Footdee. The story of the improvement of the harbour takes us right up to the twentieth century but the first crucial breakthrough was made in years from 1608 to 1618 when Aberdeen's own Renaissance man, 'Davie dae a'thing' (David Anderson of Finzeauch), removed a gigantic obstruction called Craig Metallan. This was a massive rock which had impeded entry to the harbour for centuries. It is said that he achieved his remarkable feat by borrowing lots of empty barrels and attaching them to the great rock at low tide. When the tide came in, the rock floated to the surface of the water and out to sea.

Like many cities, the origin of the name Aberdeen is much argued over. We know that *aber* means 'the mouth of a river' (Aberystwyth, Aberfoyle, etc) so Aberdeen will be 'mouth of the Dee'. But that would be too simple. Some have said that it actually refers to the mouth of the

THE DEE AND THE DON

The River Dee rises above 4,000 feet (1,250m) in the Cairngorm mountains and flows 90 miles (145km) to the east. The river's headwaters are wild, crashing through rocky glens and heathery moorland, but its latter stages below Aboyne flow through fertile farmland. The River Don rises on the slopes of the Meikle Geal Charn (the great White Mountain) and flows eastwards parallel to the Dee for a course of 82 miles (132km). Like the Dee, the Don tumbles down from the mountains but runs more gently in its later stages through rich agricultural land. Having 'arrived' in the city, the two riversides are quite different. The Dee has gently sloping banks with parks, recreation grounds and walks, while the Don has thickly wooded slopes. Near its mouth at Bridge of Don, the river also powered a number of watermills (p.213).

Looking west from the tower of the Salvation Army Citadel

Den (the Denburn) which flows along the valley bridged by the Union Street viaduct. Old Aberdeen was formerly known as Aberdon ('the mouth of the Don').

In the sixteenth century, Aberdeen became famous as a seat of learning. It was a powerhouse of the new, more 'people-centred' approach to politics and education. The world was shifting from a religious to a secular way of thinking, and Aberdeen was at the forefront of this movement in Scotland. In 1505 Hector Boece was chosen to head the university here, King's College, which had been established by Bishop William Elphinstone in 1495. William Elphinstone was trained in the law and was active in politics before being rewarded with the post of Bishop of Aberdeen in 1483. Elphinstone was a great ally and adviser to James III during his struggle with warring nobles and for this he was made Lord High Chancellor in 1488. In 1494 he petitioned for a Papal Bull (the permission of the Pope) to found a new university at Aberdeen, then referred to as 'New College', which later became known as King's College. Bishop Elphinstone is also credited with introducing the printing press into Scotland.

The intellectual movement begun at Aberdeen by Elphinstone attracted scholars from all over Europe. We can see the magnificent buildings of King's College on **Walk 5**, together with St Machar's, the masterpiece in granite created in the fifteenth century but recalling the much earlier years of the MacMalcolm dynasty of Scottish kings. We can also see the celebrated Bishop Elphinstone's Chapel and his centre for 'patriotic research' along with his beautiful illustrated manuscript, the Aberdeen Breviary, which celebrated the lives of the Scottish saints. These set-piece buildings still exist: St Machar's and King's College are preserved away from the rapid development of the big city of Aberdeen.

Just beyond this little Scottish burgh is **Seaton Park**, one of many award-winning designed landscapes and gardens within this very green city. A reference to the town from 1658 describes Aberdeen as sitting within 'a little garden', and it has kept up this reputation ever since. The best of the parks, **Duthie Park** (p.173), is on the banks of the Dee, very close to the centre of the city. Aberdeen has a justified reputation for cleanliness and good order, which dates back five hundred years.

In the early seventeenth century, Aberdeen was Scotland's third largest town. Its burgesses had a monopoly of trade in foreign goods and exported all types of produce to Europe. The burgesses dominated the town, along with the better-off craftsmen. 'Danzig Willie' of Craigievar (p.241) was a classic example of the merchant burgess: ambitious and adventurous, he made his money in the Baltic trade, exporting wool from Aberdeen's rich hinterland. As soon as he had enough money, like so many before and since, he established a country seat, complete with fairytale castle.

Many of Aberdeen's wealthy burgesses had houses in the city, but only two of these remain today. Both once belonged to the city's provosts or mayors, Provost Skene and Provost Ross, and both are now excellent museums (pp.76 and 130). They survived because they were built of stone. It took a huge effort to demolish a stone building – it was much easier to use the existing structure for some other purpose. In Aberdeen stone buildings were regarded as being the height of luxury and a mark of high status well into the eighteenth century – most houses in the city were still built of wood and thatch. This method of construction led to problems, and a huge fire in 1741 destroyed most of the Broadgate. Following this, the council decreed that all houses should henceforth be built of stone with slate or tiled roofs.

Castle Street in an aquatint of 1812

The seventeenth century was a time of huge urban growth in Scotland. By the late 1680s, the four cities, Glasgow, Edinburgh, Aberdeen and Dundee, had streaked ahead of the rest of the country in terms of the number of inhabitants. Edinburgh reached a population of over 30,000 and the other three had between 10,000 and 12,000 each. In the first half of the century Edinburgh had strengthened its position, but in the second half the others, including Aberdeen, began to catch up. It was the 'burgesses' who ran these communities of burghs, but burgh government was not democratic in the sense we would understand today. Small groups of burgesses held power in the towns, protecting their rights and privileges. These men and a few women built well to broadcast their status, just as they dressed and entertained in style. But they also began to allow for the creation of an urban architecture: buildings in groups and set-piece public buildings. This was the beginning of monumental Aberdeen: the idea that you could create a mile-long street of architecturally linked buildings.

Although it was a large and thriving town, Aberdeen was not such a densely packed place as Edinburgh or Glasgow in the late seventeenth century. Here a smaller scale prevailed, with a constant play between the individuality of gables, turrets and inscriptions. Along with the houses of the rich came the idea that public buildings could form part of an urban whole. Every burgh had its 'tolbooth', its centre of administration and justice, so this was the building, along with the burgh church, which would be most likely to express the ambitions of the population. Significantly, the most ambitious tolbooths in the country were Edinburgh, Glasgow and Aberdeen. In Aberdeen the present **'wardhouse' tower** was formed in the rebuilding of 1616–30, and extended to the rear in 1704–6 to designs by James Smith.

For most European cities, the eighteenth century was a time of very significant change and development, and Aberdeen was no exception. Its population of Aberdeen grew by a third between 1755 and 1775. With

ILLUSTRATION OF ARMS: EXPLANATION

The coat-of-arms of the city consists of a red shield with three triple-towered castles within the double royal tressure. The castles represent the three little hills of the city: Castle Hill, Windmill Hill and St Katherine's Hill. There is an old poem, explaining the origin:

> The three-fold Towres the Castle shews regained,
> From enemies who hit by force maintained,
> The leopards which on each hand ye view,
> The cruel temper of these foes do shew,
> The Shield and Lilies by the King's command,
> As pledges of his great goodwill do stand,
> The colours calls the blood there shed to mind,
> Which these proud foes unto their cost did find,
> And Bon-Accord (which doth safely come
> To Common-Wealth) establisht was at home.

The 'Bastille' at Broadford Works (above); emblazonment of the Burgh Arms, 1674 (left)

the rise of the middle classes came a demand for a more ordered layout with spacious streets and well-built houses. The problem in Aberdeen was how to achieve this. Its geography was hilly and uneven. **Marischal Street** (p.134) was an early example of the city's can-do approach to this problem. A street was constructed seamlessly right across the valley by means of a bridge. It was not until the end of the eighteenth century that modern Aberdeen – the Granite City of Union Street – began to take shape, however. The crossing of the Denburn Valley by an 'inhabited' bridge lined with houses was a massive undertaking for this ambitious city, but it signalled an approach to nineteenth-century development which was at once bold but cautious, intense yet ordered. The money behind the Union Street venture and its later development came from improvements in farming, which became an industry in the nineteenth century as much as any other. With the growth of capital came more industries: from soap-making, comb-making and chemicals to engineering, shipbuilding and the large textile industry harnessing the power of the Don at Grandholm Works or the huge, steam-driven Broadford Works. The Broadford Works' chimney stacks and the gigantic 'Bastille' warehouse still dominate the city in views to the west though the Bastille itself has been converted to luxury flats.

The twentieth century brought with it more change, but none so important as the discovery of oil. On the edge of the city we can see the oil companies offices along with the vital smaller businesses which service the industry. The North Sea oil boom brought more than two hundred new companies to Aberdeen and thousands of new residents from overseas. Some 324 hectares of industrial land were allocated to cope with the boom. Typically in Aberdeen this new development will sit easily alongside older established housing and leisure patterns.

CHAPTER 2

Practical Information

GETTING INFORMATION

Scottish Tourist Board
PO Box 705, Edinburgh EH4 3EU
Tel: 0131 332 2433

Aberdeen Tourist Board
Tourist Information Office (TIC)
St Nicholas' House
Broad Street
Aberdeen
Tel: 01224 632727
General tourist information about Aberdeen and the north-east. This is
a very pleasant and friendly office. Accommodation can be booked at the
office for a small fee.

Newspapers
The *Press and Journal* and the *Evening Express* for news, 'what's on', etc.
These papers are published daily, except Sunday.

Bookshops
There are plenty of bookshops, including two branches of Waterstone's
diagonally opposite one another in Union Street. Other bookshops
include Ottakars on Union Bridge and Bruce Miller's superb music and
book emporium at 365 Union Street. Old Aberdeen has the College
Bookseller and a good second-hand and antiquarian bookshop, Bon
Accord Books, at 69–75 Spital.

Libraries
The main reference library is the excellent Aberdeen City Library (tel:
01224 652500).

TRANSPORT IN ABERDEEN

Aberdeen is an important departure point for travel by road, rail, sea and
air. Dyce Airport is 6 miles (10km) north-west of the city and there are
direct services to the south and north. Aberdeen is also the main ferry

port for Shetland. Full transport information can be obtained from the Tourist Information Centre (TIC). Bus and train stations are on Guild Street.

Most of central Aberdeen can be easily reached on foot but for journeys further afield the buses are excellent and speed along designated bus lanes. The bus station for journeys beyond Aberdeen is situated close to the main railway station

Taxis are plentiful. A taxi can be called on 01224 595959 or you can pick one up at various stances, the main one of which is at Back Wynd.

ACCOMMODATION

There is a wide choice of places to stay in the city ranging from good-value bed-and-breakfast establishments offering huge cooked breakfasts for hungry oil workers to extremely refined and expensive hotels with superb restaurants. There are also a number of short-stay apartment hotels, which offer good value in central locations, especially at week-ends. The same is true of many of the more expensive hotels. It is always worth asking for a rate rather than simply relying on the published price. You can park a caravan or pitch a tent at Aberdeen's lovely Hazelhead Park which is on a hill to the west overlooking the city (tel: 01224 321268). There is also a youth hostel at 8 Queen's Road (01224 646988).

EATING AND DRINKING

For such a relatively small city, Aberdeen has a large number of restaurants, pubs, clubs and coffee-houses. There is a thriving nightlife and it is dominated neither by youths nor by SAGA tourists. During the day many pubs provide meals or sandwiches. Aberdeen also has a legendary fish-and-chip shop at Holburn. Most of the restaurants and pubs are concentrated in the city centre. The walks will lead you past several of these and I have described those I know personally but this book is not a restaurant guide.

SPECIAL EVENTS AND PUBLIC HOLIDAYS

The calendar below gives details of public holidays and special events. Nowadays the majority of shops and restaurants remain open on holidays but it is best to check. Be warned that the super-efficient Aberdeen traffic wardens never take public holidays!

FACILITIES FOR THE DISABLED

Aberdeen was 'flattened out' in the nineteenth century for the convenience of wheeled transport among other things. Consequently, much of the city is remarkably accessible for wheelchair users. Nevertheless, with their almost obligatory flight of imposing steps, many of the city's nineteenth-century public buildings and hotels still present difficulties. Visitors should ask at the TIC for details.

PUBLIC TOILETS

There are not many public toilets in Aberdeen. You should make the appropriate preparations, particularly on the longer walks away from the central area.

SHOPPING

Aberdeen's famous shopping street was traditionally Union Street, but its pull is gradually being eclipsed by the city's incredible acreage of covered shopping at the St Nicholas Centre and the Bon Accord Centre which together (as they practically are) make the largest mall in the UK. There are many other smaller independent shops, which you will pass on the various walks.

SAFETY

Aberdeen is traditionally a very safe city, but it is still a large and populous place so the usual precautions should be taken. Visitors should always take the greatest care when crossing roads. Aberdeen has wide straight streets, which lend themselves to high speed, particularly the bus lanes. Also, like Paris, Aberdeen is a major centre for pavement cycling so beware.

OPEN CHURCHES AND CHURCHES PARTICIPATING IN 'SCOTLAND'S CHURCHES SCHEME'

The Cathedral of Our Lady of the Assumption
Huntly Street
Open daily, summer 8 a.m.–5 p.m., winter 8 a.m.–4 p.m.
Roman Catholic

Church of St Nicholas
Back Wynd
Open 1 May to 30 September, Monday to Friday, noon–4 p.m., Saturday 1–3 p.m., other times on application to the church office, 10 a.m.–1 p.m.
Church of Scotland

Ferryhill Parish Church
Fonthill Road
Open weekday mornings during school term times (details from TIC)
Church of Scotland

Gilcomston South Church
Union Street
To view, telephone Mr John Glibborn on 01224 873919
Church of Scotland

Greyfriars Church of Scotland
Broad Street
Church of Scotland

King's College Chapel
King's College
University of Aberdeen
Old Aberdeen

Newhills Church
Bucksburn
Open Monday to Friday, 9 a.m.–1 p.m.
Church of Scotland

Rosemount Church
120 Rosemount Place
Open Monday to Saturday, 10 a.m.–noon
Church of Scotland

St Andrew's Cathedral
King Street
Open May to September, Monday to Saturday, 10 a.m.–4 p.m.
Scottish Episcopal

St Columba's Parish Church
Braehead Way
Bridge of Don
Open by arrangement by telephoning Mr Thomson on 01224 702753
Church of Scotland and Roman Catholic

St Machar's Cathedral
The Chanonry
Old Aberdeen
Open daily 9 a.m.–5 p.m.
Church of Scotland

St Mark's Church of Scotland
St Margaret of Scotland
Gallowgate
Open Tuesday mornings. For other times, telephone Canon Nimmo on
01224 644969
Scottish Episcopal

St Mary's Church
Carden Place

Open by arrangement by telephoning the Rector on 01224 584123
Scottish Episcopal

The Chapel of the Convent of St Margaret of Scotland
17 Spital Street
Open by arrangement. Apply at front door of convent. The chapel may
be viewed through grille in west porch
Scottish Episcopal

St James the Great
Arbuthnott Street
Stonehaven
Open Easter to the end of September, Monday to Friday, 2–4 p.m.
Scottish Episcopal

St James Church
Chapel Hill
Cruden Bay
Open daily
Scottish Episcopal

DOORS OPEN DAY

If your visit coincides with this day, which usually takes place in September, you are in for a special treat. Arrangements are made to open to the public buildings which they might not otherwise easily see, including **Robert Gordon's College** (p.100), the **Town House** (p.53), **St Nicholas' Church Carillon** (p.95), and the delightful **Tivoli Theatre** (p.157).

CHAPTER 3

How to Use the Guide

The main part of the guide is a series of walks around Aberdeen. I have recommended a different day of the week for each walk. I suggest Union Street for a Monday, for example, since it is very crowded on a Saturday. The walks can of course be undertaken at any time. By following these walks you will see the great majority of the city's interesting sites. Each commences with a description and a map. The walks also cross-refer to avoid duplication of description.

Archibald Simpson (1790–1847): in the background is his Triple Kirks

CHAPTER 4

Aberdeen's Architects

Most cities of any historical worth will tend to hold their architects in high regard. Aberdeen has a special devotion to the way it looks: its planned streets of granite buildings, its church spires dominating the city centre and its impressive works of engineering which tamed an unpromisingly difficult topography. Building in Aberdeen has never been especially easy, so the city's architects deserve special praise.

The Capitol in Washington DC is one of the world's best known buildings, but few people know that its architect came from Aberdeen. **William Thornton** (1759–1828) was an architect-inventor who began his working life as an Aberdeen doctor, receiving his medical degree from the University of Aberdeen in 1784. Five years later he won a competition to design the library at Tortola in the Virgin Islands – without having received any formal training in architecture. It was not long before Thornton had graduated to winner of the competition to design the Capitol at Washington, the most important building in the United States. Could Thornton's design have been inspired by the cool severity of Aberdeen granite? It would be good to think so.

The city has produced many very good architects but the most important of these is **James Gibbs** (1682–1754), who has a strong claim on the city as a formative influence. He was born at Fittysmire near St Clement's Church (p.202), the son of William Gibb, a merchant, and Ann Gordon. Gibbs was educated at the Grammar School and Marischal College. Like William Thornton, he had not initially chosen architecture as a profession. He left Scotland to study for the priesthood in Rome but soon left that calling and joined the celebrated Italian architect Carlo Fontana. Excelling in the art of design, Gibbs set himself up as an architect in England and designed many celebrated buildings, including the Radcliffe Camera at Oxford, King's College in Cambridge and St Martin in the Fields Church in London. James Gibbs and his compatriot Colen Campbell represented new practical tendencies in British architecture. Previously it had been one of the liberal arts, a part of a gentleman's education, but Gibbs contributed to the growing idea of the architect as a professional man.

Among the architects of Aberdeen's later expansion, two men in particular stand out: John Smith and Archibald Simpson. The two were great rivals. **Archibald Simpson** (1790–1847) worked in London with Robert Lugar and David Laing until 1813 when he returned to his native Aberdeen after carrying out a study trip to Italy. In 1813 he began a series of largely Grecian public buildings, beginning with the Ionic-porticoed Medico-Chirurgical Society's Hall, King Street (1818) and the similarly porticoed Assembly Rooms (1820–22). His Athenaeum or Union Buildings (1822–23) rhetorically addressed the square around the Mercat Cross. Elsewhere in the city, the colossal façade of the New Market (1840–42) brought shopping under cover for the first (but certainly not the last) time in the city. The need to build churches in a hurry increased dramatically, of course, when the Free Church broke away. Simpson's Triple Kirks (1843), a superb complex of largely brick buildings, was built in a matter of weeks to house three congregations displaced from St Nicholas' Kirk.

John Smith (1781–1852) was born into the world of building as the son of a contractor-architect, William Smith. The elder Smith built several houses in Marischal Street (p.137) and young John trained with his father before working in London, possibly with James Playfair, at the age of just 13. Returning to Aberdeen, Smith was the first to hold the public office of City Architect and from that position he supervised all the important public projects of the day and advised on many private works through the Dean of Guild Court. He was therefore very influential in the shaping of modern Aberdeen's architectural consciousness. His first major piece of work was the layout and design of King Street, where he himself lived in a villa tucked away behind the main terrace. He had a large private practice as well as his public office and he built many country houses in the north-east. His most celebrated design is that for the Screen at St Nicholas' Kirkyard (1829). From 1845 onwards Smith was in partnership with his son **William** (1817–91), the architect of Queen Victoria's Balmoral.

The office of City Architect has continued in one form or another right through to the present day, but the Planning Department of the city council has taken over the role of arbiter of taste. William Smith took over the role of City Architect from his father. **Alexander Ellis** (1830–1917) was William's apprentice and specialised in church commissions. His best design was for St Mary's Church (1877), and his partner **R.G. Wilson** (1844-1931) designed the steeple. Wilson had worked with Alexander 'Greek' Thomson in Glasgow but returned to Aberdeen and retired in 1896 due to ill health. **Dr William Kelly** (1861–1944), one of Aberdeen's most important designers and architectural historians, took over from William Smith as City Architect. Kelly, too, had been Smith's pupil. His first design was one of the best of its day, the Aberdeen Savings Bank on Union Terrace (1893–96), but he is best remembered for 'Kelly's Cats' – the diminutive leopards on the extended Union Bridge parapet of 1905. As Kelly continued his researches into historic architecture, he began to become more involved in conservation work, notably in Old Aberdeen.

One of the city's most important architects is not an Aberdonian at all but a designer from Haddington near Edinburgh. It was **James Burn** (died 1816) who first cut granite into the precise smooth blocks we associate with the city. This was done for the Aberdeen Banking Co. (1801) at their offices in Castlegate.

Most professions produce dynasties and Aberdeen managed one in architecture that equals the best of them. The Mackenzie architects span the years from Smith and Simpson to the present day. The first of them was **Thomas Mackenzie** (1815–54) who trained and worked in Aberdeen before going to work with the neo-classicist William Robertson in Elgin. Thomas formed a partnership with **James Matthews**, who had been his assistant in the office of Archibald Simpson. Matthews had worked in Gilbert Scott's huge office in London. Together they designed Christ's College (1850) and St John's Episcopal Church (1849–51), although they seem to have collaborated very little on projects for individuals. **J. Russell Mackenzie** (died 1889) was in partnership with **Duncan MacMillan** (1840–1928) and the firm built several churches around the city. Mackenzie emigrated to South Africa in 1888 after becoming bankrupt and died there the following year. The most important member of the Mackenzie clan to enter the architectural profession was **A. Marshall Mackenzie** (1847–1933). He had been trained by James Matthews and worked for the immensely successful Edinburgh architect-businessman David Bryce. Mackenzie came back to the north-

Balmoral Castle, Aberdeenshire, designed by William Smith with Prince Albert

MR. A. M. MACKENZIE, A.R.S.A.
Architect of the New Buildin s

A. Marshall Mackenzie (1847–1933)

east and set up in Elgin. In 1877 he entered into partnership with his former employer James Matthews. During the later years of their partnership Matthews, who retired in 1893, had become an important local politician, eventually becoming lord provost in 1883. This connection could not have hindered the firm's progress. Matthews' municipal and architectural ambition was behind the huge Rosemount Viaduct project of the 1880s. By far the most celebrated of Marshall Mackenzie's individual designs was the extension to Marischal College (1893–1906). It was he who extended the firm's affairs and opened a London office. It was to this office that the next Mackenzie, **A.G.R. Mackenzie** (1879–1963), was sent as manager in 1904. Among other fashionable projects, the firm built the Waldorf and Astoria hotels. Back in Aberdeen after the First World War, A.G.R. Mackenzie adapted the new streamlined Modernism to the local conditions and built a series of small masterpieces in that style. These include Jackson's Garage (1937), St Mary's Church, King Street (1937–39), and the Northern Hotel (1937–38). Later he turned his attention to conservation and the listing of buildings for protection in the post-war years. He conserved Provost Ross's House for the city in 1954.

James Souttar (1844?–1922) was one of the most intriguing architects in a city that produced its fair share of individualists. He was Mackenzie & Matthews' apprentice from the age of 12 but left that firm to train with another architectural dynasty in London, that of the Wyatts. He worked on prestigious buildings such as the Durbar Court of the Foreign Office. However, Souttar wasn't content with this and moved to Sweden where he married, designed one of that country's most celebrated churches at Stockholm and wrote a history of English Gothic Architecture in Swedish. Souttar then returned to Aberdeen with his assistant A.E. Melander. There he designed, among other buildings, the Congregational Church in Belmont Street (p.63), the Imperial Hotel (p.128) and the huge Salvation Army Citadel (p.144) in Castlegate (1893–96). It is thought that Souttar may have been in some kind of professional or business partnership with a local builder and granite merchant named **William Leslie** (1802–79). The connection between building and architecture was very strong, of course, and there was no absolute demarcation between the two. For a long time Leslie, who built all over the north of Scotland, was credited with the design of the masterful Congregational Church in Belmont Street but it seems far more likely now that Souttar was the architectural mind behind Leslie's plan.

John Pirie (1852–90) and **Arthur Clyne** (1852–1923) formed Aberdeen's most intriguing creative partnership. Their professional relationship was cut short by Pirie's tragic death from tuberculosis but it is thought that his main inspiration came not from Clyne but from the eccentric businessman and contractor John Morgan for whom the firm built Argyll Place, Hamilton Place and Morgan's own fantastic house at 50 Queen's Road (1886). The firm's masterpiece is Queen's Cross Church (1881).

Another, more prolific, Aberdeen partnership is that of **Alexander Brown** (1852–1925) and **George Watt** (1864–1931). Watt had worked with the brilliant Glaswegian architect James Sellars and, as a consequence, their work has a suave cosmopolitan quality. The best of it is to be found at Rosemount Viaduct. Aberdeen's most mysterious architect is **George Coutts**. Very little is known about him, but his houses, particularly the half-timber and granite masterpiece at Rubislaw Den North (see p.226), are extremely good. **Sir John Ninian Comper** was born in Aberdeen, the son of an Episcopalian clergyman. He studied art at Edinburgh and the Royal College in London. He designed the chapel of the convent of St Margaret's, Gallowgate, in 1891 and took the lead in the Seabury Memorial Restoration of St Andrew's Cathedral (see p.148). Another influential Aberdeen architect was in fact not an architect at all but a painter. **James Giles** specialised in landscapes with tower houses and castles and also advised on the composition of modern Romantic buildings such as Rubislaw Terrace (see p.222) or designing the landscape of Haddo House (see p.248).

T. Scott Sutherland (1899–1963) was an important local architect and one of Aberdeen's great modern-day characters. Although disabled and getting about on one leg, Sutherland was a motorbiking prominent local politician who was convener of the council's housing committee. He was behind many of the council's housing projects, including the garden suburb of Kincorth (p.175). During the 1960s, the Scott Sutherland School of Architecture was established in his house at Garthdee, which he had donated for this purpose. One of Aberdeen's recent award-winning buildings, the Maritime Museum (p.130), was the work of the council's architect, **Trevor Smith**.

CHAPTER 5

Aberdeen's Artists

Aberdeen has a very fine tradition in painting which first came to national notice in the work of **George Jamesone** (c.1588–1644). Histories of Scottish art often begin with Jamesone, the Aberdeen-born portraitist who spent most of his career in Edinburgh. He did, however, begin his practice in Aberdeen, painting the professors and burgesses of the city before attracting the attention of Sir Colin Campbell and members of the Royal Court in Edinburgh. Jamesone is often described as 'the Van Dyck of Scotland' but this is little more than a convenient tag: his work has none of Van Dyck's swagger. Like the older painter, however, his portraits and temporary decorations, such as those for Charles I's entry into Edinburgh in 1633, provided a genealogical gallery of royal likenesses stretching back to the mythical origins of Scotland, that defined the House of Stuart.

William Dyce (1806–64), one of the leading painters of the early Victorian period, was born in Aberdeen and studied at Marischal College before taking up art in Edinburgh. Dyce is most famous for pioneering

George Jamesone: Self-portrait

the revival of early Italian art and, in the 1820s and '30s, he made several trips to Italy to study the technique of true fresco, the medium which Giotto, Masaccio and Piero della Francesca had used. This stood him in good stead when, in 1836, he was appointed director of the new Government Schools of Design in London. From this position he was able to advise on the decoration of Barry & Pugin's new Palace of Westminster (Houses of Parliament). Following a competition, Dyce was one of several artists invited to execute murals for the interior but, since most of the others were technically incompetent at this sort of work, Dyce himself produced most of the murals. Favouring an early Renaissance style, he soon found that he was in the vanguard of the new taste in Britain for 'Italian Primitives' and he found kinship with the younger generation of Pre-Raphaelites who emerged after 1848. In fact, Dyce became a close associate of this new group and his later work, notably *Titian's First Essay in Colour* in Aberdeen art Gallery, has the intense pure colour and precise details that one associates with the Pre-Raphaelite Brotherhood. His most famous picture of this period, however, is the atmospheric *Pegwell Bay* in the Tate Gallery, a picture whose fresh, naturalistic lighting is often thought to have been inspired by photography.

John 'Spanish' Phillip (1817–67) began his career as the protégé of Lord Panmure when he was sent to London in 1837 to train in the Royal Academy. There he became a leading member of the group known as The Clique, which included Augustus Egg, William Frith and Richard Dadd. Unlike the others in this circle, Phillip became a painter of Scottish rural scenes in the manner of David Wilkie and he achieved considerable success in this vein. In 1851, however, owing to ill health, Phillip visited Spain for the first time and this marked a watershed in his career. Impressed by the culture of Spain as well as Spanish artists such as Velazquez and Murillo, he painted *The Spanish Gypsy Mother* which was bought by Queen Victoria as a present for Prince Albert. This began a great series of pictures of Spanish life and customs which were immensely popular in Britain. Of those in Aberdeen Art Gallery, *La Bomba (The Wine Drinkers)* of 1863, *La Loteria Nacional* and *The Spanish Flower Seller* are among his best. There is also a sketch for *La Gloria: a Spanish Wake*, his greatest work, painted in 1864 after his final visit to Spain, which is now in the National Gallery of Scotland in Edinburgh. This large picture reveals not only Phillip's interest in the picturesque aspects of Andalusian life but the loose handling of paint and rich colour that was associated with the Spanish School. Phillip was one of Queen Victoria's favourite artists and the royal family kept up the pattern set in 1852 buying many of his best pictures as family presents. As a result, there are many works by Phillip in the Royal Collection, including a portrait of the Prince Consort.

George Paul Chalmers (1836–78) was born in Montrose and, like many other Aberdeen painters, at first followed a tradesman's career path.

He was apprenticed to a ship's chandler before taking up painting at the Trustees Academy in Edinburgh. Following his teacher, Robert Scott Lauder, Chalmers developed a loose, painterly technique and a lively sense of colour typical of his generation. His most popular subjects were vernacular narrative paintings, such as *The Legend*. This was felt to be very progressive in the 1860s and '70s, since many of these effects were associated with the modern French school.

Sir George Reid (1841–1913) was, like Chalmers, trained at the Trustees Academy in Edinburgh in the manner of Robert Scott Lauder. Following this, however, he took an interest in contemporary Dutch painting, notably the work of Josef Israels and the Hague School, which favoured greater naturalism and looser handling of paint. This is apparent in his atmospheric landscapes but Reid showed an early facility for portraiture and this proved to be the mainstay of his career as an artist. By the 1880s he had become one of the leading portraitists in Scotland, and in 1891 was elected President of the Royal Scottish Academy. In this position he was a bastion of conservatism, ensuring that the academy remained out of touch with new developments in art both in Scotland and abroad. Reid's house and studio are open to the public as the Gordon Highlanders Museum (see p.232).

James Cadenhead (1858–1927) was born in Aberdeen and studied at the Trustees Academy in Edinburgh although, like many of his contemporaries, he completed his art education in Paris. Cadenhead was a distinctive and atmospheric painter, linked with several tendencies in British art (he was a member of the New English Art Club) although he never achieved the success which his early landscapes promised.

Robert Brough (1872–1905) continued the tradition of Jamesone into the twentieth century. He was born in Invergordon and studied at Aberdeen Art School and in the studio of Constant in Paris before returning to Scotland in 1894 where he practised as a portraitist and figure painter. Widely regarded as one of the most promising young artists in Scotland at the turn of the century he was, unfortunately, killed in a railway accident at Sheffield.

Robert Douglas Strachan (1875–1950) was the finest Scottish stained-glass designer of the twentieth century although he came to this activity relatively late. Trained in Edinburgh and abroad, he made his name from two mural cycles in Aberdeen, the first for the Trades Hall in 1898 and slightly later for Aberdeen Town House. Strachan's stained-glass designs adorn many of the most important churches and public buildings in Scotland, notably St Giles Cathedral in Edinburgh, St Machar's Cathedral here (see p.192) and the Scottish National War Memorial, but he was also commissioned to produce windows in England and abroad, including the windows for post-First World War Palace of Peace at The Hague in the Netherlands.

James McBey (1883–1959) is the artist most closely associated with

Aberdeen. He is one of the finest printmakers of the early twentieth century. His greatest success was in the field of etching which was a hugely popular and highly regarded medium before and after the First World War. He was particularly noted for his views of North Africa, where he lived for much of his life, and which he depicted in prints, watercolours and oil paintings. He is also known nowadays for a remarkable autobiography, simply entitled *The Early Life of James McBey*, which he was encouraged to write by one of his American patrons. This book recounts a childhood of almost unrelieved poverty and hardship as the illegitimate son of a village woman in Newburgh, near Aberdeen. Despite the difficulties of this situation, which resulted in his mother's suicide, the book shows no trace of self-pity or bitterness. Instead, McBey describes rural life in Aberdeenshire in a simple, unaffected way, going on to recount his first job as a bank clerk and his gradual discovery of art. The story of how he made his first etching on his grandmother's mangle is a gem. The book ends in 1911 when, having won a drawing competition, McBey gives up his job at the bank to devote himself to art. This proved to be a wise move as, within a few years, McBey had held a successful exhibition of his etchings in London and was embarked on a career as a major artist in Britain and the USA. Despite his tough upbringing, McBey did not abandon his native city. After his death in 1959 he bequeathed a large collection of his own work to Aberdeen Art Gallery and the funds to build what is now known as the McBey Print Room.

Duncan Grant (1885–1978) one of the leading figures of the Bloomsbury Circle, was born at Rothiemurchus in Aberdeenshire although he spent most of his life in England and France. Charleston, the house he shared with Vanessa Bell in Sussex, has become something of a pilgrimage centre for devotees of the Bloomsbury Group.

James Cowie (1886–1956), one of the finest figurative painters in Britain in the twentieth century, was born in Monquhitter, Aberdeenshire, although he is more frequently associated with Glasgow where he studied and worked. His finest paintings, such as *Two Schoolgirls* (1937) which is in Aberdeen Art Gallery, depict the pupils from his class when he taught at Bellshill Academy in Glasgow and subsequently at Hospitalfield in Arbroath.

CHAPTER 6

Granite City

'The houses are large and lofty, and the streets spacious and clean. They build almost wholly with the granite used in the new pavements of the streets of London, which is well known not to want hardness, yet they shape it easily. It is beautiful and must be very lasting.'

DR JOHNSON, 1773

Aberdeen and granite are inextricably linked in people's minds. The devotion to granite as the local building material is quite extraordinary and carried right through to the middle of the twentieth century. The huge Foresterhill Hospital complex was built of granite in the late 1930s after a public outcry against the use of more 'modern' materials. It was only in the 1950s and '60s that the city wavered in its affection towards granite as thousands of council-houses were put up to accommodate the post-war boom. However, even Aberdeen's monumental high-rise blocks were often faced with shards of granite in order to 'fit in'. As the interest in conservation and heritage has grown, granite is once again the preferred material for all new buildings. Old buildings are also carefully protected. Quite rightly, the local council nowadays has a policy to prevent the demolition of any granite building.

Throughout the world the main stones used for building are sedimentary stones such as limestone and sandstone. But granite is an igneous rock, formed from cooled molten matter. It is an exceptionally hard material containing feldspar, mica and quartz, giving granite its marvellous sparkle. Granite comes in a wide range of colours. You can see a broad range built as columns in the atrium of Aberdeen Art Gallery (see p.101). The main types of granite used in Aberdeen are Loanhead, Dancing Cairns, Sclattie and, by far the most common, Rubislaw. These are all local types (other sources of UK granite are Cornwall, Devon and the Island of Mull – Ross of Mull granite). As in the rest of Scotland, stone is the basic building material, from the tenement to the palace. In Aberdeen it is given local character by the distinctive material, eventually arriving at one of the most astonishing granite buildings in the world – Marischal College. The material has even made its way into the title of a Scottish literary classic, Lewis Grassic Gibbon's *Grey Granite*. At its

Aberdeen Town House

peak, there were more than 20 granite works in the city but the industry went into decline in the 1930s and the last working quarry, at Rubislaw, closed in 1971.

Granite was important in giving the city its character, but it also took on an economic importance when the material began to be exported in the later nineteenth century. Scandinavian and North American architects were particularly keen to use the material.

Before granite and oil, Aberdeen's wealth was founded on its vast hinterland of newly improved farming. From the start of the nineteenth century, this money paid for a series of bold schemes which followed the Edinburgh example of long straight streets and 'bridge streets', that curious hybrid. The first example of the bridge street, Marischal Street (see p.137), was built down to the harbour in the 1760s, but the Aberdeenshire County Road Trustees surveyor, Charles Abercrombie, with local ratepayer support, successfully pressed for a far larger scheme for an inland road gateway: a new, axial street running south-west from the old centre for a mile, on a series of arches, with a bridge at the Denburn. Following the passing of special legislation in 1800, the new street (later named Union Street to celebrate the union of Ireland, England and Scotland in 1800) was built between 1801 and 1805 at a total cost of £114,000.

Monumental classicism could have been invented for Aberdeen and for granite – the local material previously considered too hard for decorative work. The city's first fully dressed ashlar granite building (James Burn's Aberdeen Banking Company office) was built in 1801–2 at the east end of Union Street, in the Castlegate. Slightly later, by the 1830s, the cutting of granite was revolutionised by the introduction of steam-powered technology. The north-east granite industry expanded and even began an export drive. Aberdeen granite was exported all over the world, but it was particularly appreciated in Scandinavia where it was considered especially suitable for the new 'national' style of architecture in the 1880s and 1890s. The Swedish architect Lundholm visited the city and reported back favourably to his government. The Aberdeen architect James Souttar, who had lived in Sweden and built the English church in Stockholm, was at the forefront of this interest in the material. Aberdeen granite-cutters became well known for their hard work and ingenuity. In 1886 a North American employer's agent recruited 86 of them to work on the building of the state capitol at Austin, Texas. What the agent did not tell the men was that they were to be strike-breakers. The men had no option but to complete the job but they were blacklisted and could get no more work in the USA. In the 1890s, in time for the building of Marischal College, pneumatic tools were invented which made the cutting of granite significantly easier.

From the 1810s to the 1830s, the grand axis of Union Street, along with streets and squares, was embellished with new public buildings and flanking residential areas, including the beginning of curved layouts in the Edinburgh manner. As in the Scottish capital, two rival architects were responsible for the evolution of Aberdeen's granite classicism, John Smith and Archibald Simpson. The dominant architectural theme in Aberdeen's civic developments was neo-Greek from the start. The style suited the material, the place, and perhaps even the people. Working in the city from 1804, Smith set the standard with his so-called 'Façade': the colonnaded, arched St Nicholas' Graveyard screen of 1829. He designed a succession of Grecian public and ecclesiastical monuments like the North Church (1830), a powerful mixture of several sources including a steeple based on the Tower of the Winds in ancient Athens. He also designed the single-storeyed Town's School (1840) which would not look out of place in Prussian Berlin. There is sometimes an icy severity about the architecture, which can also be quite thrilling. Aberdeen is not a 'cosy' place of half-timbering and narrow lanes but for the most part a boldly executed town of straight streets and sharp angles. In King Street, which is the unflexed forearm of Union Street, Smith's North Church formed part of a second landward axis, opening up the route to the north-west. He also designed severe blocks on the east side of King Street (1825–30).

It was the much-celebrated local hero Archibald Simpson who made the most distinguished contribution to the shaping of classical Aberdeen. Returning from his travels in Italy in 1813, Simpson began a series of largely Grecian-style public buildings, beginning with the Medico-Chirurgical Society's Hall in King Street (1818) opposite his Gothic St Andrew's Episcopal Church (1816–17), and the Assembly Rooms (Music Hall), Union Street (1820–22). Simpson's Athenaeum or Union Buildings (1822–23) pioneered a new type of multi-purpose building in Aberdeen: a simplified version of Robert Adam's multi-level idea, which he had introduced to Edinburgh and elsewhere. Simpson's building is on a steep, narrow site at the east end of Union Street; its great Ionic porticoed entrance front jutting into the square around the Mercat Cross in Castle Street (newly restored by John Smith, 1820). Other Simpson commissions further enhanced the new monumental ensemble at the junction of King Street, Union Street and Castle Street: the Northern Insurance Company's office at 1–4 King Street (1839–40), and the adjacent North of Scotland Bank (1839–42), whose porticoed corner was crowned by James Giles's terracotta statue of Ceres, symbolising the triumph of agricultural improvement in the north-east.

Elsewhere in the city, Simpson's Royal Infirmary (1832–40) on Woolmanhill, an 'H'-plan block with a dome and three pedimented temple fronts, provided both a romantic object in the landscape, looming over the Denburn Valley, and an essay in understated Grecian architecture in monumental granite. This huge hospital was also a great symbol of Aberdeen's progress in medicine for which the city was becoming famous. There was also the colossal façade of the New Market (1840–42), accompanied by the laying out of the new Market Street, which accorded an unprecedented monumentality to the act of shopping.

As in Edinburgh, the construction of public buildings in Aberdeen was matched by residential development, along the great, straight Union Street axis (and its continuation, from 1820, into Albyn Place). The most severely monumental of these new schemes was the sheer curve of Simpson's Bon Accord Crescent (1823, Walk 4) built with adjoining streets (Bon Accord Square and West Craibstone Street).

Aberdeen's building boom came to an end later than Edinburgh's did with a local commercial slump in 1848. It was not until 40 years later that the city again attempted anything as bold in terms of town planning, when it built the Denburn and Roseburn viaducts (Walk 2) to further regularise and 'flatten' the topography of the city. Simpson also built prominent classical monuments in other north-east and northern burghs: in Elgin, St Giles' Church (1827–28, with Lysicrates tower above a portico) and Anderson's Institution (1830–33).

Marischal College

PART TWO

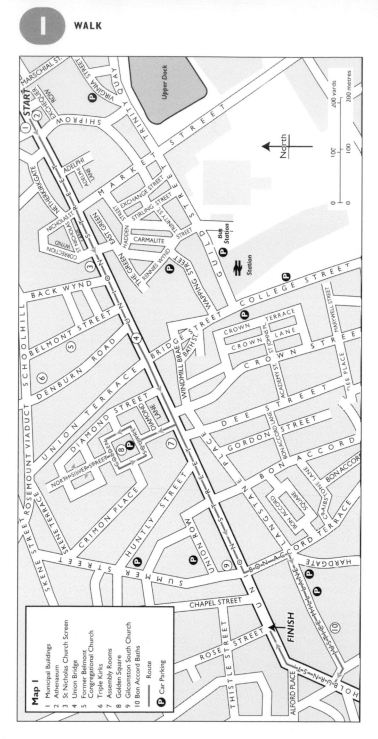

WALK

I

Upper Dock

North

0   100   200 yards
0   100   200 metres

Map I

1 Municipal Buildings
2 Athenaeum
3 St Nicholas Church Screen
4 Union Bridge
5 Former Belmont Congregational Church
6 Triple Kirks
7 Assembly Rooms
8 Golden Square
9 Gilcomston South Church
10 Bon Accord Baths

— Route
P Car Parking

Union Street

A walk that explores Aberdeen's famous shopping street

The former Congregational Church in Belmont Street, as seen from Union Terrace

Main places of interest	The Town House, The Tolbooth, Union Bridge
Circular/linear	Linear
Starting point	The Town House
Finishing point	Holborn Junction
Distance	1½ miles
Terrain	Pavements
Public transport	Buses along Union Street
Sections	Bus to Union Bridge. Return bus to Town House from Holburn Junction
Architects	Archibald Simpson (Athenaeum, Assembly Rooms, Triple Kirks), John Smith (St Nicholas' Graveyard Screen)
Nearby walks	7, 2 (return section), 3
Refreshments	The Grill public house and many other cafés and pubs
Notes	Try to avoid midday on a Saturday and the rush hour

*'Could there be such a thing as a great city with tramcars,
electric lights, hotels, and cathedrals so far away among empty
fields so near the North Pole as we were going?'*
SIR JOHN BETJEMAN

The walk begins at the Town House, goes straight along Union Street and then takes a detour among the exclusive squares of nineteenth-century Aberdeen. First, a short introduction to Union Street.

The English poet Sir John Betjeman was a famous admirer of Aberdeen's architecture and idiosyncrasies. He delighted at the 'busyness' of Union Street, at encountering a city of such size and consequence after travelling through so many miles of what he considered to be 'wilderness'. Betjeman's attitude probably sprang from a Home Countries world-view. In his time, the south-east of England had become more or less one massive suburban conurbation, with only token strips of green belt separating the various centres of population. But, as Betjeman saw, in spite of all its mountains and moorland, Scotland is nevertheless one of the most urbanised countries in the world and Aberdeen is a great example of the desire to create a place of importance, a great northern city.

Scotland has rather specialised in new towns and has occasionally spread this tendency to Europe, to the countless new towns of Catherine the Great's Russia and even to North America. Generally speaking, Scotland could be said to have a culture of renewal and that is one of the reasons why it has specialised in new towns and new solutions: the burghs of David I; Edinburgh's New Town; Inveraray; the five new towns

Union Street, 1878, in a photograph by George Washington Wilson

around Glasgow in the second half of the twentieth century, and count-less planned villages here in the north-east. Scotland's municipal improvers did not lack ambition. Especially after the start of the eigh-teenth century and the union with England and Ireland, Scotland's was a culture of change and improvement. But this love of the new was strangely mixed with ancestor worship and a love of the old represented in front of us here by the massive 'Scotch Baronial' **Town House.** Although perhaps reluctantly at first, Aberdeen dramatically contributed to the improving side of this tradition with an incredibly bold but simple idea. That idea was **Union Street**.

The key to Union Street as a concept is of course the Union Bridge. This magnificent structure linked two hills and provided a level – if certainly not flat – platform for housing and commerce and to facilitate wheeled transport. It was constructed at a crucial time in bridge design, when the engineer was beginning to take over from the architect as the chief consultant in these matters. In the past, bridges had been seen as frameworks for applied architectural details such as columns and stone swags. For example, when Robert Adam designed bridges he did not even include construction details – he left such incidentals to the con-tractor. Now, at the beginning of the nineteenth century, bridges were seen as a completely separate branch of design and the specialist began to emerge. This specialism accompanied an economic theory which argued that wealth could be stimulated by improving what we now call the 'economic infrastructure'. The argument was associated with so-called 'Scotch philosophy', a rationalist way of thinking which stemmed from the works of David Hume, Adam Smith and the counter philoso-phy of the Aberdonians Thomas Reid and James Beattie, who place the emphasis on the practical. Along with all of this came a national obses-sion with monumentality in architecture, which produced the great bridging schemes of the late eighteenth and early nineteenth century.

Union Street is also a 'great street' in the same tradition as Grey Street in Newcastle or Regent Street in London, which was planned as a royal progress to Regent's Park from Buckingham Palace. The crucial differ-ence here is Regent Street's picturesque winding as opposed to Union Street's straightness. (It seems that from an early date, Aberdonians could not really abide a meandering street.) Union Street is strictly 'neo-classical' in that it recalls the unending straight Roman roads of the ancient world, but the materials and the idea of an infinitely long monu-mental street is also in keeping with a Scottish tradition of town plan-ning. Like Edinburgh, Aberdeen decided on grandiose town planning and stuck to it.

To many outsiders, of course, Union Street *is* Aberdeen. It has developed an iconic quality like Berlin's Unter den Linden or London's Oxford Street. Union Street has stood, many would say very appropri-ately, for Aberdeen: a straight, clean, uncomplicated idea made real. But it seems from looking at its history that Aberdeen did not invent Union Street, but to some extent had Union Street thrust upon it by outsiders, the powerful Roads Commissioners. During the second half of the eighteenth century Aberdeen had improved its harbour but was in need of an inland gateway, to the south and to the north. Out of this came the County Road Trustees' commissioning of its engineer, Charles Abercrombie, to weigh up all the options. Abercrombie had worked on many roads in Aberdeenshire but none on the scale on which he was about to embark. Abercrombie's 'feasibility study' offered three possibilities: a road from Bridge of Dee which followed the banks of the river to the foot of Marischal Street; a road continuing the earlier 'bridge street', Marischal Street, over to Torry via a new bridge over the Dee; and the final option which was Union Street with its mighty bridge over the Denburn. This was a huge project which required not only wholesale demolition but also the slicing-off of the top of St Katherine's Hill. We should think for a moment of the work involved in removing a hilltop and carting away the spoil by the cartload. It was the type of ambitious exercise for which Baron Haussmann, many years later, became famous as superintendent of works in Paris.

The town council were famously 'dumbfounded' by the audacity of Charles Abercrombie's proposals. Some smart houses along with a large and imposing but run-down tenement in Castlegate had to be compulsorily purchased only to be demolished. It seemed like an enormous expense for the sake of a street of houses. Nevertheless, the ordinary ratepayers of Aberdeen were impressed. Estimates were obtained which proved to be outrageously wide of the mark (Abercrombie had estimated £6,493 for building the bridge and between £30,000 to £40,000 for acquiring property; the eventual cost was not far short of £225,000). The citizens nevertheless loaned their money in large amounts and on 12 February 1799 Aberdeen New Streets Act was passed and trustees appointed to supervise the work. The result of the operation is that half of the street from what is now Adelphi Court to Diamond Street is actually an artificial creation raised at the lowest level of the ground and carried on a series of arches with a bridge at the Denburn. The design was by Thomas Fletcher. Work to construct the street began in 1802 and was finished in three years later. Laying out the ground cost £114,000, bankrupting the burgh. And still there were no buildings. In contrast to Edinburgh's South Bridge scheme, which Union Street emulated, all the buildings in the path of the bridge were demolished. People said that Aberdeen had been a city with no entrance, but now it was an entrance with no city! The destruction and the disruption must have been a foretaste of what was to come in the huge construction schemes of the nineteenth and twentieth centuries. Some things never change. On top of everything else, this was an act of faith in the city's greatest natural resource – granite.

The Tolbooth steeple

The Glasgow architect David Hamilton had won the original Union Bridge competition. Everything was going fine – until the bridge collapsed. Hamilton was the most important Glasgow architect of his day, the Father of the Profession indeed, but he never set his foot in Aberdeen again. Such a catastrophe of collapse was not unusual in those days, however. Engineering was still very much a matter of trial and error. Edinburgh's new North Bridge had fallen down during its construction, killing five people. In any event, the city of Aberdeen decided to take no more risks and called in the experts, including the great Thomas Telford, to advise. Hamilton had proposed a three-arched, fairly traditional bridge, but Telford suggested a daring single-arch structure. For many years it was one of the wonders of engineering, much talked about and illustrated in guidebooks, the way we would think of Sydney Harbour Bridge or San Francisco's Golden Gate. Hamilton was almost certainly a former assistant or surveyor of Robert Adam in Glasgow and the west and, although he failed as bridge builder, he brought some of Adam's entrepreneurial flair north. Although other surviving schemes do not include shops, the earliest Union Street buildings allow for them, and this too was the key to some of Robert Adam's great speculative work and also to the future of Aberdeen. Union Street was designed as an exclusive residential area but it became one of the most celebrated shopping streets in Britain. Today, I suppose, even the most proud Aberdonian would accept that Union Street is no longer the fantastic continuous bazaar of beautifully presented shops of every description that it once was. However, times change and perhaps Union Street too must change.

As well as the shops, here and there Union Street breaks out of its linear bonds and enters the side streets with important public buildings and churches such as the beautiful **Cathedral of Our Lady of the Assumption** at St Mary's, Huntly Street. Probably the best example is at **Crown Street** where the huge general post office addresses Union Street from its position a couple of hundred yards away. Union Street is, of course, a long straight walk, a mile long. It has the dubious distinction of being the only street in Britain outside London with two McDonald's on it. It was the premier shopping street and justly famous throughout the country until the opening of the covered shopping of the **St Nicholas Centre** (see p.88). When the Queen opened the St Nicholas Centre in 1990 she asked what would happen to Union Street. This prompted action by the city council who immediately set about beautifying the centre and implementing policies which were designed to keep the street alive and looking well cared for. The results are good. Of course, the style and quality of the shops have changed, but that has happened in every city. Union Street is still a very pleasant walk with plenty of diversions along the way.

The walk begins at the centre of Aberdeen's municipal power. The **Town Buildings** were the administrative centre for modern Aberdeen in the nineteenth century. The architects of this shining new granite masterpiece were Peddie & Kinnear from Edinburgh. They specialised in banks and courthouses, many of which were designed in the Scotch Baronial style as it began to spread from country houses to urban public buildings. The greatest of these was undoubtedly their enlargement here of **Aberdeen Town House** between 1866 and 1874. Its turreted main tower was for several decades by far the most prominent landmark in the city. This tower echoed, in a hugely amplified form, the old Schoolhill mansions of Aberdeen which had been illustrated by the antiquarian architect Robert Billings. Billings had brought some fame to Aberdeen in the 1850s by publishing examples of the 'street architecture' of the city, paving the way for the adoption of this style by Peddie & Kinnear for Cockburn Street in Edinburgh, the world's first entire street of Romantic buildings. The metal sundial on the front of the Town House was relocated here when the old front of the Tolbooth was removed.

The Town House has an entrance hall with a marvellously geometric staircase framing a statue of a young Queen Victoria. This statue was moved here from St Nicholas' Place to protect it from the weather. In its placed there was installed another 'older' version of Her Majesty, which in turn was later moved to Queen's Cross (see p.225). At the head of the stair is a magnificent hall at first-floor level, with a double-height space and tall windows. The hall has important paintings and a ceiling with heraldic decoration in the manner of St Machar's Cathedral (see p.192).

Behind the new façade of the Town House is Aberdeen's original Town House or Tolbooth. This was the old centre of administration and punishment in Aberdeen. The **Tolbooth** was the most important building of the seventeenth-century burgh and it survives to this day although partially demolished and, of course, hidden by the later Town Buildings. The original Tolbooth collapsed in 1589; Thomas Watson, a mason from Old Rayne, was ordered to build a new one after James VI had decreed that all burghs were to have 'sufficient and sure prisons'. This Watson did with some panache. It is a massive, imposing structure for its day, bristling with corbels and crenellations. Like the 'new' Town House, this was to suggest history and modernity at the same time. As was common with such buildings, the steeple was added later, around 1629.

The Tolbooth is one of Aberdeen's oldest buildings and has survived because of its important public function. It was here that tolls and customs taxes were collected and where the burgh council held their meetings. Bailie Alexander Skene of Newtyle in 1685 published *Memorials* for the government of the royal burghs in Scotland. This was a sort of manual for the magistrates, charged with keeping the city dwellers under control. He advised: 'It concerns all Magistrates to be careful that no gross sin be indulged amongst them, such as Whoring, Drunkenness, and Swearing, these are the most common Scandalls unsuitable to the Gospel and such as profess it, that are to be found in Cities and Towns. These are sufficient to provoke God to withdraw his mercies, and to send sad Plagues and Rods, and confound all your Counsells and blast your Endevours: for suppressing whereof, I know no better outward mean than a conscientious, faithfull, and diligent Court of Justice keeped by well principled Magistrats assisted by pious, honest and zealous Constables weekly.'

To get inside the Tolbooth we go in at a ground-floor entrance created between 1818 and 1820 when the external staircase to the first floor was removed. The mason-contractor Watson was ordered to build 'ane massive wall of fyve futes in thikness' at ground level with an arcade at first-floor level. We can still see the remnants of the arcade inside the building. The Tolbooth was a complex of civic buildings, including a prison, but now most of what remains is the 'wardhouse' or jail. The cells on view are of great interest since most contemporary work of this kind has long disappeared. There is a variety of themes on view, such as 'Crime and Punishment', 'Great Escapes' and the 'Jacobite Cell' which give a very lively history of the building. Public punishment of an almost medieval kind survived well into the eighteenth century. An account of 1750 records that: 'On Saturday last, James Aberdein, having been found guilty of cutting a young birch tree, which was growing in the enclosures of Hilton, by the Justices, they ordained the said Aberdein to be returned back to prison in the Tolbooth of Aberdeen, and to remain for the space of four months, and to be publicly whipped through the town of Aberdeen by the hand of the common hangman upon the last Friday of each of the said four months between the hours of twelve and two, and thereafter to remain in prison till he find sufficient caution for his good behaviour for the space of two years.'

Visitors can also see excellent scale models of seventeenth-century Aberdeen. These are based on the famous views drawn by Parson Rothiemay.

Behind the Town House, along Concert Court entered off Broad Street, is the **Advocates' Hall**. This was erected in 1869 when the advocates 'hid away' here after moving from Union Street (see p.62). It is a very sober building, designed by James Matthews in 1869. Advocates are the élite of the Scottish legal profession. Only they are licensed to appear in the High Court in the most serious of cases. The reputation of the Aberdeen-trained lawyer is legendary. Sir Walter Scott recounted the story that 'Some English lawyer expressed to Lord Elibank an opinion that at the Union the English Law should have extended all over Scotland. "I cannot say how that might have answered our purpose," said Lord Patrick who was never nonsuited for want of an answer, "but it would scarce have suited yours since by this time the Aberdeen Advocates would have possessed themselves of all the business in Westminster Hall." '

The name of Alexander Cruden (1701–70) is celebrated here at Cruden's Court, which is off Concert Court. He devised the idea of a concordance or companion volume to the Bible. His book systematically explained and interpreted the Bible, the first time this had ever been attempted. There have been many concordances produced since but Cruden's is still available and remains the basis for all later works.

Opposite the Town House on Union Street is the **Athenaeum**, which is part of the Union Buildings created by Archibald Simpson from 1819. The building creates a 'gushet' (a building at a 'V' junction) between Exchequer Row and Union Street. The first building in the group was 19 Union Street, designed for Baillie Galen. This very plain but distinguished design, a model of good taste, was a kind of template for the rest of the street. Simpson then extended the building and in 1822 added the Athenaeum, a subscription library behind the superb front on Castlegate. So this is a very clever building with two faces, one public and the other residential. The great space of the library was later converted into a famous Aberdeen restaurant, Jimmy Hay's, but the whole place was burnt out in 1973 and has since been converted into offices.

At the top of Shiprow, Union Street was formerly restricted by a tenement which faced Castlegate. The way through to what is now Union Street was via a passage called Narrow Wynd. The whole area of Castlegate was therefore a very large enclosed square. Looking over to Broad Street on the other side of the road, we are seeing a much-widened and altered version of the seventeenth-century precinct that contained town houses, Greyfriars Church and Marischal College. Looking at the shop on the corner, you can see that a whole side of the street, between here and Guest Row has been demolished. The name 'Guest Row' is an unusual one. It is the only example of such a name in existence and there has been much speculation as to its derivation. The most romantic explanation is that it refers to the ghosts of the churchyard of St Nicholas who were to be seen out on their nightly constitutional. Broad Street fell into disrepair and degradation in the nineteenth century and became the scandalous 'canker' at the heart of the city, like the High Streets of Edinburgh and Glasgow at the same time. Grandiose solutions were considered over a lengthy period, including the pipedream of building of a magnificent Episcopal cathedral (see p.148). The extension of Marischal College (see p.79) was used as a planning tool for clearing the east side of the street and the rest was reorganised as a municipal plaza as part of a plan dating back to 1952.

On the opposite side of the street is one of Aberdeen's oldest department stores (or 'warehouses' as they were known) still in existence, Esslemont & Macintosh, or 'E&M's'. Peter Esslemont, a nineteenth-century lord provost of the city, founded the store. Nos. 26–30 were designed by Ellis and Wilson in 1892, while R.G. Wilson, Ellis's former partner, designed the next block, nos. 32–38, in 1897. Both buildings are in the busy, north European 'free style' then popular for commercial and some domestic buildings.

Union Street, c.1900; notice 'the Queen' on the left of the picture – the statue was later removed to Queen's Cross

As the only shopping centre for many miles around, the city had a huge catchment area and Aberdeen was able to build up a collection of celebrated stores. One of them, Isaac Benzie's, was in a film made in the 1920s: a fascinating 'advertising feature' which demonstrated how the whole family could enjoy a day out in one shop. The department store building replaced another famous shop, that of the celebrated 'hatter to the people', Samuel Martin, who was a kind of McGonagall of hat-making. Martin seems to have been the original mad hatter. On the marriage of the Prince of Wales to Princess Alexandra of Denmark, he appeared in his window above the shop, 'dressed *à la* Garibaldi, lustily blowing loyal tunes out of a bugle'.

Between Esslemont & Macintosh is St Catherine's Street, which leads to Guest Row. Between Guest Row and Broad Street was another strip of buildings which was entirely demolished in the widening of Broad Street and behind this, via Netherkirkgate, is Flourmill Lane. This was the site of an unusual watermill, which was powered by the stream that had fed the 'Loch of Aberdeen'. The loch's stream was dammed at Netherkirkgate. When the loch (which was little more than a piece of boggy ground) was drained, the stream was diverted underground and continued to power the mill until 1865.

The north side of Union Street is mostly made up of the original buildings; many of these have been altered, however, at least at ground-floor level for commercial purposes. On the other side of the street is Union Chambers at nos. 46–48 which is a replacement of 1895 of an original Archibald Simpson building, much in the same spirit, and no. 40. At no. 50 is McCombie's Court, a very old 'passage' or arcade which, as

The Wallace Tower in Netherkirkgate: it was taken down in 1967 and removed to Seaton Park

the sign temptingly announces, leads through to Marks & Spencer's. The court was named after Thomas McCombie, a bailie of Aberdeen and snuff manufacturer whose house was in Netherkirkgate where the passage leads.

Tucked in behind Union Street, just beyond Shiprow, is the **Adelphi**. This was a centre for the city's papermaking industry with the premises of the brothers Pirie being situated at the end of the cul-de-sac. Since *adelphi* means 'brothers' in Greek, the classical scholars of Aberdeen have long assumed that the name referred to the Piries, but it was more likely in recognition of another Scottish engineering feat carried out by the Adam brothers and proudly emulated here in Aberdeen: the first embanking of the River Thames at the Adelphi in London. In that case the Adelphi *did* refer to the Adam brothers, John, Robert, William and James. Have a look into this other-worldly little court with its old-fashioned harled (rendered) buildings and then carry on along Union Street.

We now reach Market Street with St Nicholas Street opposite. On the corner diagonally opposite you will see the massive, monumental bank designed by Jenkins & Marr for the Royal Bank of Scotland. This great essay in granite classicism was built as late as 1936. The area directly in front of the bank was formerly (and by some still) known as 'The Queen'. This was because of the statue of Queen Victoria which stood on a spot opposite it before it was moved to Queen's Cross (see p.225). The Queen stood just in front of some railings protecting the drop into Carnegies Brae which has now been decked over. That statue was itself a replacement for the beautiful marble example which was moved to the Town House, where it still stands in the entrance hall (see p.54). Statues, and even buildings, were always on the move in Aberdeen. It must have been quite disorientating for the inhabitants. The whole subject was a matter for prolonged public debate. And where there was an issue at stake as there was in 1864, Samuel Martin, 'hatter to the people', felt the need to address the public:

> *Up with the Statue to Britain's loved QUEEN;*
> *Let it be handsome, complete and well seen.*
> *Let the site be well chosen, the best that's in town,*
> *For a more beloved QUEEN ne'er wore a crown.*
> *Somewhere in Union Street would be the best place,*
> *If about there could be got a good space;*
> *But it must be conspicuous and easy to view,*
> *Without these essentials it may please but a few.*

Martin suggested St Nicholas Street corner, which was fine, but he did have a problem with a rhyme for 'marble'.

> *And tho' not made of Granite there's no need to garble,*
> *T'will look very well of Sicilian marble,*
> *THE QUEEN, God bless her, is a nice canty bodie,*
> *And the Statute may please if done by A. Brodie.*

At the end of the truncated St Nicholas Street is the St Nicholas Centre (p.88). Opposite the bank at nos. 60–62 Union Street is the farmers' bank, the Clydesdale, designed by James Matthews in 1862. Comparing the two banks we can get a sense of the intense competition that existed between the various financial institutions in the nineteenth century. The banks used architecture in a way to broadcast a powerful message of opulence. Marks & Spencer's in St Nicholas Street is on the site of the so-called **Wallace Tower**, although it had nothing to do with the Scottish patriot. The building was moved from its site here in the centre of the city at Netherkirkgate to a new home in Seaton Park (p.195). The work was supervised by the historian Douglas Simpson who lived in the house until his death in 1968.

Market Street, another long straight street, was cut through in 1840, in this case to give direct access to the harbour from Union Street. It continued the straight line of St Nicholas Street through to George Street and on to the Inverurie Turnpike. It was laid out by Archibald Simpson and named after his magnificent covered 'shopping mall' (p.127), which was demolished in 1971.

All the way from Adelphi Court we have been walking not on a road but on a bridge: an artificial creation raised on arches. We become aware of this for the first time at Correction Wynd. On the north side of the street some steps lead down to the Wynd on the side of the churchyard. This is on the site of a 'House of Correction' which was founded in 1637 on the initiative of Provost Jaffray and stood near by until 1711. It provided lodging and employment in the cloth industry for 'vagrants and delinquents'. If you wish, you can experience this subterranean pleasure by going down these steps and cutting under Union Street to the Green, picking up on Walk 3 at p.126.

On the Union Street walk we limit our interest to noticing this broad 'polite' staircase of granite. Just look at these beautiful great slabs and imagine them being cut, brought to the site, manoeuvred into position. It's too easy to think of features like these as part of the landscape. Every stone laid was part of a complex decision-making process involving a chain of command going back to a master of works and ultimately an architect. It is an easily gained stair, with turned balusters of cast iron imitating wood. The steps are a good example of the care that Aberdonians have taken to preserve their city. The simple rough staircase was improved and recast into three flights in the 1890s. On the north side opposite Correction Wynd there are no steps, just railings. At no. 113 there is a little balcony set high over Correction Wynd. At one time you would have walked out on to the balcony to look in the side shop window which is now blocked; notice where the railings were cut to give access. This section of Union Street, from Market Street to Correction Wynd, was the most difficult to develop owing to the great amount of underbuilding required to anchor any buildings down below in the Green. Consequently, a rough wall of granite protected the drop until such time as new buildings would be constructed. In the meantime,

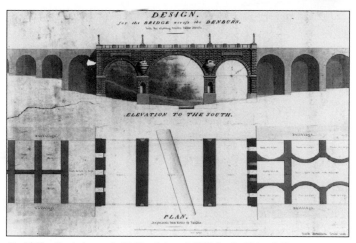

David Hamilton's three-arched bridge design of 1800 for the Union Bridge

the proprietors of houses on the Green built wooden gangways out of top-storey windows to gain direct access to the new viaduct. Soon commercial activity was taking place here. Signboards were put up and customers made their perilous way on these little bridges over the Green.

The scientist James Clerk Maxwell (1831–79), who developed the concept of electromagnetic radiation, lived at 129 Union Street. His intellectual contribution was described by Einstein as 'the most profound and the most fruitful that physics has experienced since the time of Newton'. Another celebrated Aberdeen professor, Colin Maclaurin (1698–1746), had earlier developed some of Sir Isaac Newton's ideas.

We now reach a major architectural diversion on our route. This is the superb architecture of John Smith's screen or 'façade' to **St Nicholas' Churchyard**. The idea of erecting an architectural screen wall derives from the French *hôtel* (town house). The screen was popularised in the UK by Robert Adam at the Admiralty in London (1760–61). Smith was the town architect and his screen puts a polite distance between Union Street and the town's church St Nicholas' West. The screen is a version of a more elaborate one designed for the council by Decimus Burton after the success of his example at Hyde Park in London. The churchyard was extended towards Union Street in 1819 with the fine railings extending the enclosure to Back Wynd. The ground had previously been used to hold the sort of travelling shows of which councillors and magistrates did not approve. These were the fire-eaters, sword-swallowers and jugglers – exactly the kind of colourful entertainers who have recently been welcomed back onto the city streets. Smith's majestic colonnade also maintains the continuity of architecture on Union Street.

Union Bridge and the Triple Kirks, c.1875; note the pantile-roofed cottages in the foreground

He designed the building immediately to the south on Back Wynd, too, the **Advocates' Hall** (later the Queen's Cinema). The Union Street frontage was remodelled by A. Marshall Mackenzie in 1898. The Back Wynd façade is very sober and reminiscent of the capital, reminding us of the Edinburgh architect James Gillespie Graham's one and only Aberdeen building at 7–9 King Street (p.148). At Belmont Street there is a charming sign strung between two buildings which says: 'Art Gallery at end of this Street'. This is quite true; if you wish to break off at this point, go straight to p.98 for a description of Belmont Street followed by the art gallery.

Opposite now is the **Trinity Hall** of 1844 by John and William Smith. This was the first building in Union Street to break the unwritten neo-classical law by going Gothic. The architect got the nickname 'Tudor Johnnie' for his trouble, but the building is reputed to have impressed Prince Albert, who thereafter gave William Smith the job of designing Balmoral Castle. Trinity Hall was built for the Seven Incorporated Trades of Aberdeen. The Trades had formerly regulated the activities of their members but that function had long since ceased by the 1840s, by which time the Trades had become a charitable and social organisation.

The redevelopment of Smith's buildings for the Littlewood's department store was a blow for conservation in Aberdeen, but some of the interiors were kept in the new scheme, including a very impressive and elaborately detailed hammerbeam roof which you can see in the restaurant.

We have now arrived at **Union Bridge**. Imagine the thrill of being confined within the tight geometry of Union Street and the gorge suddenly appearing below with a view to your left right out to sea. Television and travel have dulled our ability to appreciate this kind of experience, but that is how it was conceived: a dramatic interface of the rational and the romantic. The original bridge of 1805 has been widened twice, once in 1905 and again in 1963. This work has been added to the bridge so it's still possible to see the original structure from below with its later metal projecting 'balcony'. The 1905 work to the bridge was overseen by Dr William Kelly who added the additional steel arch and a parapet topped by diminutive leopards, a reference to the city's coat-of-arms (p.20). For years these have been known as 'Kelly's Cats'. The figurative panels are the work of Sidney Boyes.

It was in 1963 that the row of shops on the other side of the bridge was added. This was undoubtedly a mistake but we should not judge this work by the heritage-conscious standards of today. In those days progress was the thing, and heritage was fine – in its place. Within the general terms of redevelopment, Aberdeen chose to preserve certain isolated monuments such as Provost Skene's House and Provost Ross's House along with the whole of Old Aberdeen.

Looking back in the direction we have just come over the parapet of Union Bridge, we see the rear of Belmont Street which finishes with the ruin of the **Triple Kirks.** At the centre of our view is James Souttar's wonderful building for the **Congregational Church**. This is a building whose rear elevation is designed with a long view in mind, its four tourelles (little towers) overscaled to give them even greater presence.

Although we will come to the Triple Kirks on Walk 2 (see p.104), it was actually designed to be seen from the platform of Union Bridge where it was historically most admired. The celebrated conservationist and diarist Lord Cockburn wrote of the Triple Kirks when it had just been constructed that he 'was struck with the view from the bridge towards the Infirmary of a rude Cathedral-looking mass, which contains three Free Churches'. Looking from the bridge this is the unmistakable group of brick buildings which we can see in the distance to the right above the roadway of the Denburn. The complex of three churches known as the Triple Kirks came into existence as an immediate result of the Disruption of the Church of Scotland in 1843. This was a major event in Scottish history, and is discussed in more detail on the churches walk at p.219. The issue at the heart of the crisis was the 'establishment' of the Church, that is its affiliation with the state. The 'Free' Church was to be entirely free from patronage and therefore much more suited to the new independent-minded city dweller. The churches in the complex are the East, West and South Churches. The East and West Free Churches were for the dissenters from the East and West Churches of St Nicholas along with the only recently built South Church in Belmont Street (now Slains, p.97). The site had previously been home to a handloom weaving factory which had gone out of business with the introduction of steam power. The site had romantic potential, which the architect Archibald Simpson used to great effect, clustering the buildings to make them appear more complicated and larger in size than they actually were. Simpson was very pleased with the result and included a view of the buildings in the background to his portrait (p.28). Of course, the most controversial aspect of the design was the architect's use of brick, which was associated with industrial buildings. Time was very short (the whole thing was constructed in the amazingly short period of six weeks) and the historic brick churches of the Netherlands offered the best model for Simpson's design. There would not have been enough time to dress the granite required for such a large structure, and although that stone is used for the core of the building complex, this is of the easily available rough-hewn type not intended for display.

Crossing now over Bridge Street we should bear in mind that we are on a bridge and that any new street joining it would have to be a linking bridge itself. Bridge Street is therefore exactly that: a street formed out of a bridge connected to Union Bridge. The scheme was worked out by the engineer John Willet in 1865–67, the plan being to take traffic over Windmill Brae, the pre-Union Street entrance to the town, and down to Guild Street to link with the harbour and the railway station. You can see the arch of the bridge exposed at its meeting with Windmill Brae (see p.163). Every town has its local peculiarities of behaviour, and Aberdeen is no different. The junction of Bridge Street, Union Terrace and Union Street is the best place to see one of its most curious. The time to witness this spectacle is midday, when the streets are at their busiest. Pedestrians are waiting patiently for the signal to cross. Then it happens. The people scurry diagonally across the road, meeting others coming directly at them, towards them at an angle and yet more from the left and right. Watching this, you half expect a monstrous pile-up, but the whole operation is carried out with military precision, like the band of the Grenadier Guards on display. This immediate area is known as 'The Mat'. 'Walking the Mat' on a Saturday night was part of the mating ritual until relatively recently.

Opposite Bridge Street is **Union Terrace**, which in its original form was part of the Union Street scheme. Note the similarity with Princes Street in Edinburgh, which is also a prestigious one-sided street facing gardens. In Aberdeen's case these are Union Terrace Gardens. The wonderfully restored and gilded **statue** of Edward VII on the corner was made from Kemnay granite and was designed in 1910 by the celebrated advocate of the 'New Sculpture', Alfred Drury. The statue itself is not particularly 'new' but the bronze panels around the plinth are very interesting. The figure of 'Peace' is shown breaking a sword. The statue replaced a memorial to Prince Albert which was shunted to something of a backwater, in the shadow of the huge Wallace statue (p.108). The Edward VII statue was originally intended as the centrepiece of the Cowdray Hall quadrant (see p.104). Aberdonians argued interminably about the placing and composition of statues. The architect Arthur Clyne objected quite strongly to the use of granite for the monument.

A. Marshall Mackenzie designed the superb building at no. 1 Union Terrace in 1885. Mackenzie designed the building for the Northern Assurance Company after winning the commission in competition. For some reason the building is universally known as the Monkey House, possibly because of the 'monkey business' at the Mat. Next to this is an attempt to please the growing heritage lobby of 1979: Lloyds Bank, designed by the long-established Aberdeen firm of Jenkins & Marr. There then follows the excellent Caledonian Hotel, again by Mackenzie, some original town houses and then Dr William Kelly's beautifully detailed Trustee Savings Bank of 1896. The scheme was won in competition in 1896, with the Glasgow architect Sir John James Burnet as the assessor. Kelly was famously a very hard taskmaster and also a very large man, who frightened the life out of his contractors with his close scrutiny of their work. Beyond are three more of these great classical blocks, the last a scheme of 1906 by the famous Edinburgh architect Sydney Mitchell for the County Offices. We can see that by the late nineteenth century, Union Terrace had all but lost any remaining residential character and had become an extension of the commercial centre of Aberdeen.

Back on Union Street itself, you can see where this process of commercialisation has been at work on the north side. Presumptuous office buildings thrust upwards over the imposed three-storey form of the

Union Street, c.1900, with the Assembly Rooms on the left

Union Street buildings. The idea of the late eighteenth-century scheme of improvement was to bring some order to the chaos then existing there, but this order had no sooner been established when it was broken down by the forces of nineteenth-century commercialism. In the 1950s conservationists began to worry about the preservation of Union Street as a complete entity. The infill block at no. 150 on the corner with Diamond Street is actually a design of 1956, by the conservationist A.G.R. Mackenzie.

Just on our right here is Diamond Street. This was a fanciful name, which has nothing to do with the gemstone. In 1937 Diamond Street was the scene of the death during a visit to Aberdeen of Alfred Adler, the controversial Austrian psychiatrist who clashed with Freud and also developed the notion of 'inferiority feeling', which was later altered to the more scientific-sounding 'inferiority complex'. Here on Union Street we are perhaps witnessing a kind of architectural inferiority complex: a tiny version of the New York battle of the skyscrapers with each building attempting to outdo the other.

We should now be at Crown Street, where we take a right into South Silver Street. Just before that, we have in front of us the **Assembly Rooms**, one of the most celebrated buildings of monumental Aberdeen. Archibald Simpson designed the Assembly Rooms in 1820. The exemplar for a building of this sort would be the Assembly Rooms at York of 1749, but many more had been built since then. The model for the Assembly Rooms was based on the aristocratic idea of a country-house party brought into the genteel public realm. The ever-growing numbers of middle-class town dwellers could safely mix for cards, dancing and conversation. Entry was by subscription. Inside the very grandiose façade to Union Street is the saloon with its large statue of a young Queen Victoria. On the other side of this is the promenade. There was also originally a ballroom on the east side of the building. In 1858 James Matthews added a music hall to the rear but the main entrance to this is from Diamond Street.

South Silver Street takes us into one of the stately backwaters of Aberdeen at Golden Square. The name follows the theme of gems and precious metal but it may also have been named after its namesake in London. On the way towards the square, the imposing entrance on the left is the separate entry to the music hall. Aberdeen's Golden Square was laid out as a speculation on what was known as the Longlands by the Hammermen Corporation of the Incorporated Trades. It was planned in 1807 as part of Abercrombie's Further Improvements (the first 'improvement' being Union Street). The houses of Golden Square are a rather reduced version of the Union Street prototype. They are broad and very well finished, but they do not have drawing-rooms occupying the whole of the first floor, as is the case elsewhere in the UK. Nevertheless the space available between the plot widths set down by the feuars was rapidly taken up. The remaining rooms were squeezed into the house, including the roof space. The following reminiscence of life in one of these houses, which reminds us of the sanitary arrangements at the time, was written as recently as 1935: 'The decorations might run to green-and-gold wallpapers, drop-crystal chandeliers and other embellishments, but there was no bathroom in my father's house and the domestic servants' quarters were dark and limited. There was no hot water in the kitchen and no cold water above the first floor. Strange to say, there was no sewer, and in our house the sewage passed into two cesspools in the sunk area at the rear and immediately under the back windows.' (MacKinnon Recollections, 1935).

Not long prior to that, water was obtained from a well in the middle of the square. (In July 1821 the 'essay' prescribed for a candidate for entry to the Hammermen Craft, with its overtones of Masonic secrecy, was 'a key to the well in Golden Square'.) The well has since been removed and can now be seen in the entrance hall of Trinity Hall (p.62).

Legal proceedings were threatened against the original owners of the houses to make them pay for their share of the railings around the communal 'pleasure ground' in the middle of the square. Unusually, the railings are set in a circle. Today, unfortunately, the square is full of cars. The area became a centre for business as long ago as the turn of the century and it has remained so ever since. In front of us in the middle of the square is the first granite statue in the world. It represents George, fifth and last Duke of Gordon (1770–1836), and stood originally in the Castlegate where it was put up in 1844. This is the famous Gordon memorably dubbed the 'savage noble' by the writer Frank Walker, the same Gordon who romanticised Fyvie Castle (see p.247). He was a very early exponent of the romantic in architecture, and was helped in this by the fact that he already owned one of the best castles in the country. There is a superb painting of the man at Fyvie, in the vibrant colours of the Gordon tartan. The duke is standing on a cannon and has a sword in his hand so there's no mistaking his heroic credentials. He was the first colonel of the 92nd Highlanders, and first raised the regiment the famous 'cocky wee Gordons', the Gordon Highlanders. There were doubts over the choice of the site and material for the statue, but the granite, from the Dancing Cairn quarry, proved a success. The duke did not last long in his position in the Castlegate. The town council asked the War Office to take the statue but they declined the offer and so the the statue was taken down. Much debate then ensued over where the duke's last resting-place should be. Golden Square was finally agreed upon.

The inhabitants of Golden Square were very handy for the Assembly Rooms and here we can begin to imagine the polite world of Aberdeen 'society'. As in all towns during the period, strenuous attempts were being made to segregate the 'mechanics' from the upper strata of society.

There is a nice 'survivor' at no. 11 North Silver Street. This is the Bon Accord Auction Saloon with the wittily named basement pub, Under the Hammer, next door. The street becomes more residential at the end. There is a striking contrast between the very grand **Migvie House** (c.1810) with its boundary walls and gate piers, and the little cottage in the backland at 31 Diamond Street. Aberdeen specialises in a very nice mixing of the quaintly domestic with the commercial and powerful. Closing the end of the street is Brown & Watt's huge tenement at 1–27 Rosemount Viaduct (see p.112). We should now leave this little enclave by the way we came in and go back on to Union Street. The tall gable of St Mary's Presbytery House closes the other 'exit' from the square at Crimon Place.

Back on Union Street from this point west the street is ten feet wider. This was the result of a deal arrived at between the new Streets Trustees and the Hammermen who were developing the area south of Crown Street (see p.162). At no. 213 Union Street is a famous old bar, The Grill. This is probably the last of the 'real' pubs on Union Street. It has resisted being 'Victorianised' in the last twenty years. The bar was fitted out by Jenkins & Marr in the 1920s with a mixture of clean lines and exuberant plasterwork. The interior is worth a look and features an American-style long bar with Art Deco lighting. The bar offers snacks of traditional stovies or mince and tatties along with an amazing selection of malt whiskies.

A little way along Huntly Street there is a good view of **St Mary's Church**. This is Aberdeen's Catholic cathedral. St Mary's was designed in 1860 by Alexander Ellis. Its very tall spire was added by Ellis's partner R.G. Wilson in 1877 in celebration of the church's elevation to cathedral status. The spire is beautifully lit at night. The building is best appreciated by walking slightly beyond it and looking back. Rather oddly, perhaps, the church does not 'address' Union Street but rather turns its back on it. Nevertheless, it is a superb building, and was Aberdeen's first Roman Catholic cathedral since the Reformation of 1560. There is a good interior with a daring scissors beams roof and important stained glass. It is open all day. The church also has a very good peal of bells.

Spires and towers are vital to Aberdeen. They give the impression that the city is sitting on a level plain but they also tend to be overscaled so that they appear closer together than they actually are. In certain slightly misty conditions and with the church bells ringing, the city has an intimate and slightly eerie quality. The poet Iain Crichton Smith called it 'a town of pure crystal'. The very air has a hard crystalline edge, which gives a unique clarity to the Aberdeen's light. Just beyond St Mary's is the former **Royal Blind Asylum**, designed in 1840 by John Smith. In the absence of large 'palace-fronted' groups of houses in the style of Edinburgh, Smith made do with this very handsome classical block. The trees give a very welcome break to the regularity of the surrounding streets.

Back on Union Street, opposite is **Langstane Place Church**. It is immediately apparent that the present-day church is the only building on Union Street which is set back, allowing a view of the next gable, which is built of Seaton brick. The brick gable strikes quite a startling note amongst all the granite. The Langstane Kirk was built in 1869 with the proceeds of a lawsuit against a railway company for undermining the West Kirk as it cleared a path for tracks through the Denburn. The railway companies were desperate for land and were often a soft touch for aggrieved landowners. Fears about structural damage to the West Church proved groundless and most of the congregation soon returned. Lang-

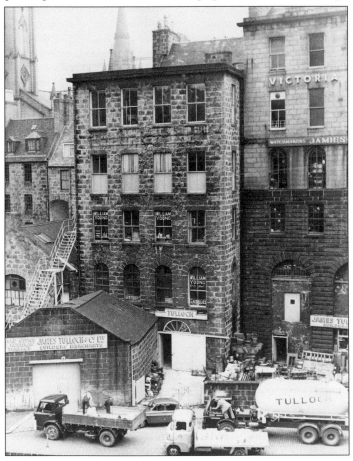

The former Victoria Hotel and the back of Belmont Street as seen from the Union Bridge, c.1963; notice the change in architectural detailing below the level of Union Street

stane was designed by James Matthews with daringly slender spires in imitation of the 'Mither Kirk', St Nicholas.

The next notable building worth a look is **Gilcomston South Church** on the south side of the street on the corner with Summer Street. A few years ago its steeple suddenly developed a structural problem. It was proposed to bring it down but the people of the city and many others, including the Prince of Wales, could not abide the idea, and the entire steeple was completely rebuilt so as to preserve Aberdeen's famous cityscape.

Church-going and cinema-going are two of the most popular pastimes in Aberdeen. In 1939 the city had 39 cinemas. At no. 443 Union Street is the **Capitol Cinema**, the city's largest ever. It was designed by A. Marshall Mackenzie, son, & George, architects. In locations like Union Street even something as modern and flashy as a cinema was made of granite. The very large auditorium can seat 2,100 people within an 'atmospheric' scheme of decoration which included patent Holophane colour lighting as an integral part of the design, the first theatre in the country to do so. The building replaced a smaller picture-house on the site and still has its built-in organ, which rises dramatically through the stage.

We should cross over Union Street here and go down Bon Accord Terrace and down the short way to Justice Mill Lane. Just opposite, built into a wall, is the 'Crabstone'. This is the boundary stone of John Crab, who gave his name to nearby Craibstone Street. Crab was originally from Flanders, there being historically an easy connection and relationship between Scotland and the Low Countries. Crab was a military engineer and helped the Scots in their perennial battles with their southern foe. At the siege of Berwick in 1319, the English had constructed a 'sow', which was a very heavy transportable wooden building in the shape of a sow's back. The idea was that defensive walls could be mined under the protection of the wooden canopy. Crab's achievement was to devise a crane capable of lifting stones heavy enough to break the back of the sow and thereby confound the besiegers. For this action he was well rewarded and eventually settled in Aberdeen. He bought up much of the property on what was then the outskirts of the town and lending his name to the district of Crabstone (Crab's Toun) near Bucksburn.

Along Justice Mill Lane on the left is the Hardgate. This was a kind of medieval motorway whose name simply records the fact that it was a proper road rather than a muddy track. The street was widened in 1885. The granite wall is all that is left of a terrace of houses called Strawberry Bank. Into this wall is built the Hardgate Well which is supposed to have 'run red' with the blood of the victims of the Battle of Justice Mills in 1644 (see p.167). On the right is the astonishing brick box of the Capitol Cinema: granite and polite at the front but totally functional at the rear and rather a blight on the street. Previously, businesses on Union Street, such as The Grill, for example (see p.68), would create a double entrance, front and rear, and this gave interest on both sides. From the 1930s as the scale of shops and cinemas got ever greater, this was no longer possible.

On the left now is the monumental grandeur of the Bon Accord Baths, which was designed by Alexander McRobbie of the City Architects Department in 1937. The building looks as if it has a much more serious purpose than swimming; indeed, they were proudly described in contemporary advertising as 'the most artistic and up-to-date in Britain'. For the City Architects and the council, the health, strength and, especially, cleanliness of the citizens was not a subject to be taken lightly in Aberdeen or anywhere else in the country. The interior with its original streamlined chrome fittings and 'ripple sycamore' timber panelling is also worth seeing if you are a '30s enthusiast.

In the area you will see a signpost for the 'Satrosphere'. This is an excellent 'hands-on' science centre, mainly aimed at children. Among the attractions are various mind-expanding experiments and a sunflower which stays in bloom all year.

Next door to the Baths is rather an antidote to all the strict granite precision of its neighbour. This is the gaily polychromatic granite and red-tile Odeon Cinema, designed by the architect-entrepreneur T. Scott Sutherland (1899–1963), one of Aberdeen's great modern-day characters (p.34). Sutherland was a prominent local architect and politician who was convener of the council's housing committee. He was behind the 'improved' garden-city-style housing of the Kincorth housing scheme (p.175). During the 1960s, the Scott Sutherland School of Architecture was established in Sutherland's house at Garthdee, which he had donated for this purpose. There is a sudden burst of exuberant design at the delightful Art Nouveau **ventilator** at the end of Justice Mill Lane where it meets Holburn Street and the curved granite Granary pub. The ventilator marks the end of a cable subway running from here under Crown Street to the former Electricity Works and Tramcar Depot in Millburn and Crown Streets. As a fully tunnelled subway, the cars had to use a cable rather than steam, which could not be properly ventilated. The style for the ventilator was perhaps suggested by the contemporary Paris Metro.

Holburn Street passes over the Howburn, hence the name. Looking down Holburn Street, on the corner with Union Grove diagonally opposite is the former St Nicholas' United Free Church at no. 50. R.G. Wilson, a member of the congregation, designed it. One of its most celebrated members was Dr Robert Laws of Livingstonia, who defended the rights of Africans against the colonialists. Directly opposite the end of Justice Mill Lane is the Holburn central parish church of 1891. Since there is no way of exploring the mile-long Union Street on a circular tour, we now find ourselves at the end of the walk. Your choice here is to go straight back down Union Street or to follow Rose Street, which is opposite, down to Skene Street and to pick up on the inward half of Walk 2: Denburn and Rosemount at Aberdeen Grammar School (p.117).

Provost Skene's House to Aberdeen Art Gallery via St Nicholas' Churchyard and on to Rosemount

A walk exploring old 'New' Aberdeen, St Nicholas' Churchyard and the Art Gallery

Upperkirkgate with Roland Piché's sculpture Moon Table *in the foreground*

WALK

Main places of interest	Provost Skene's House, Marischal College, St Nicholas' Church, Aberdeen Art Gallery
Circular/linear	Circular
Starting point	Provost Skene's House
Finishing point	Union Terrace
Distance	2 miles
Terrain	Gentle incline on pavements and steps on the way out
Public transport	Bus
Sections	Bus to Rosemount Viaduct
Architects	William Adam (Robert Gordon's Hospital), A. Marshall Mackenzie (Marischal College, Art Gallery, Cowdray Memorial)
Nearby walks	Walk 1
Refreshments	Kirkgate Bar, Littlejohn's, Academy cafés and bars
Notes	The walk is in two parts. If you visit the museums and galleries of the first part, the second part of the walk, in Rosemount, can be left for another time. Looking at the exteriors only, the walk can be done in about one and a half hours at the most.

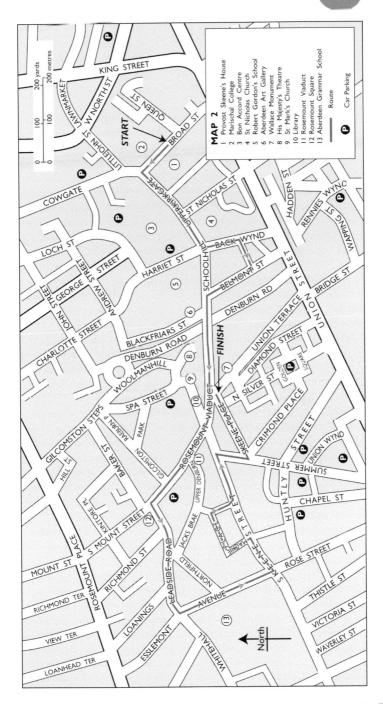

MAP 2

1 Provost Skene's House
2 Marischal College
3 Bon Accord Centre
4 St Nicholas Church
5 Robert Gordon's School
6 Aberdeen Art Gallery
7 Wallace Monument
8 His Majesty's Theatre
9 St Mark's Church
10 Library
11 Rosemount Viaduct
12 Rosemount Square
13 Aberdeen Grammar School

— Route
P Car Parking

> *'Aberdeen is reputed the seminarie of so many quho are*
> *remarkable for wisdom, learning, gallantrie, breeding, and civill*
> *conversatione.'*
>
> JAMES GORDON, 1660

We start our walk at **Provost Skene's 'Lodging'**, which is Aberdeen's oldest surviving house. It has a remarkable story. The increasing interest in preserving Aberdeen's heritage was less dramatic than elsewhere since the city had always maintained a high regard for its old granite buildings. Aberdeen's 1952 City Plan had recognised the need to preserve the 'authentic old-world atmosphere' of Old Aberdeen along with certain historic buildings throughout the city such as Provost Ross's House (p.131) or Provost Skene's House. But it was not always thus. As we can see, Skene's House has been designed into the municipal piazza around the dramatic 1960s podium and tower of St Nicholas' House, but the original plan was to demolish the building along with the slums which hemmed it in on all sides. As it stands, the scheme shows how the concept of heritage was viewed in the 1950s. The assumption was in favour of redevelopment, if necessary building around the identified heritage site.

Dating from 1545, the building has housed several distinguished Aberdonians. Over its long history, it has been converted into two houses, converted again into a boarding-house and then commandeered by the Duke of Cumberland's troops on their way to the battlefield of Culloden. It was known for a time as 'Cumberland House'.

The house is now named after Provost George Skene, who was a wealthy merchant who lived there in the seventeenth century at a time when Aberdeen's trade with northern Europe was flourishing. As well as being a very important local politician, Skene was also one of the earliest writers of the city's burgh history. In his book of 1685, he traces the story of the burgh interestingly (but rather improbably) far back beyond medieval times. It seems his purpose was to present the burgh as an ancient and independent one, free from outside interference.

Matthew Lumsden, who lived there before Skene, added the celebrated Painted Gallery (see below). Skene himself made additions and alterations, including the corner stair tower.

Since the nineteenth century Provost Skene's House had become a very poor slum called the Victoria lodging-house. The initial plan was to sweep the whole thing away and this was only reversed after a comment by Queen Elizabeth (now the Queen Mother) in 1938 who expressed an interest in the building's fate. For many years Skene's House sat on its own. During the eighteenth and nineteenth centuries the district became very congested: a typical inner-city area of slums and lodging-houses. The slums were cleared from the 1890s until the 1930s and again the building sat in isolation. The area was afterwards reinhabited, this time as a council precinct with New York-style tower and podium of St Nicholas' House fronting Broad Street and lower buildings on Upperkirkgate to the rear of Provost Skene's House. The plan in the 1950s was to put an art gallery next to the house where the open square now exists. A straight street was to be cut right through to St Nicholas' Church on the space now occupied by Marks & Spencer's.

Very appropriately, the Queen Mother returned to open Provost Skene's House to the public as a museum in 1953. (It is open Monday to Friday, 10 a.m.–5 p.m., and Sundays, 1 p.m.–4 p.m.) This very interesting and attractive period museum has rooms containing furniture dating from the seventeenth, eighteenth and nineteenth centuries. These pieces did not originally belong to the house but they are an accurate reflection of what such an interior would possess. There is also a costume gallery, which is situated in the west wing of the house, halfway up the spiral staircase. Monthly exhibitions of costume and textiles featuring fashionable dress are selected from a wide-ranging collection of local costumes. There are also temporary exhibitions on the top floor relating to Aberdeen's social history. This latter exhibition includes finds from recent archaeological excavations, which have changed opinions on the history of the burgh.

Perhaps the most fascinating part of the museum is the wonderful Painted Gallery. When renovations were being carried out in 1951, workmen discovered the most marvellous scheme of painted decoration which had lain undiscovered for centuries. The work was all concealed behind later ceilings and panelling of three small rooms off the west staircase. As the later work was stripped out, it became clear that a major discovery had been made: a piece of archaeology had suddenly been

Provost Skene's House when it was in use as a lodging-house

Marischal College

brought to light. Now restored by Historic Scotland, the Painted Gallery ceiling shows an unusual cycle of religious painting. The life of Christ is depicted in ten tempera panels from the Annunciation to the Ascension. The ceiling also includes a number of symbolic emblems which make reference to the biblical story. You will see, for example, the cock, which is referred to in the story of Peter's denial of Christ. No one knows when or by whom the paintings were commissioned. There are strong Flemish and Germanic influences which might indicate that the work was carried out by foreign craftsmen, or that the images were copied from books or tapestries. Some of the armorial devices which appear on the ceiling may be those of Matthew Lumsden, who lived in the house between 1622 and 1644.

The Nursery has a wonderful collection of Victorian and Edwardian toys, dolls and paintings from the Art Gallery and Museums Collection. Visitors get a rare glimpse of how children in comfortable circumstances were cared for a hundred years ago. In the attic you will see a marvellous doll's-house made for a lucky Aberdeen girl in 1912. With its kitchen, dining-room, sitting-room and attic bedrooms, the house is packed full of interesting pieces of miniature furniture and fittings. The passion for collecting miniature objects and doll's-houses began in the eighteenth century when they were seen as costly playthings for adults.

Leaving Provost's Skene's house, we now walk back up the few steps to Broad Street across the piazza. As we pass the gable of the house, notice the hideous **gargoyle**. This was moved here when the building it originally adorned was demolished in 1959. The grimacing face had

Marichal College c.1885, prior to its extension and the removal of the McGrigor Obelisk

been on the shop of one George Russel and it unflatteringly represented his neighbour with whom he had been involved in a long-running dispute.

We now have **Marischal College** straight ahead of us. This is an astonishing piece of work by any standards. What we can see dates from relatively recently but the university itself is very old. Marischal College was founded in 1593 at a time when there was increased emphasis on the teaching of language, literature and mathematics. King's College (p.182), founded in 1495, had been dedicated to the teaching of Latin and Greek and, of course, theology and law. There was no mention in the university's foundation charter of theology, law or medicine, for which the institution has become famous worldwide. Until 1860, when the two universities were combined, Aberdonians would point out that their city had two universities, the same number as in the whole of England!

The founder of Marischal College was George Keith, the fourth Earl Marischal of Scotland. The new university was a breakaway from King's College, which was under severe pressure from the Reformers. In broad terms, King's was seen as the guardian of the old religion, Catholicism, and Marischal as the standard-bearer for Protestantism. The original institution was a small foundation in the buildings 'formerly belonging to the Franciscans'. The buildings were made redundant by the Reformation and were gifted to the college. None of these buildings remain. They were replaced by the first expansion of the university in 1837–41. You will see these buildings in the courtyard beyond the main front when we go through. They were carried out in a Tudor Gothic style by

Looking west from Upperkirkgate

Archibald Simpson. Alterations and additions were made by the government architect Robert Matheson in 1873, but most of the work visible
from the exterior today is that of A. Marshall Mackenzie which was
carried out between 1893 and 1898. Mackenzie raised the central tower
as the Mitchell Tower, created the huge Mitchell Hall and added the
great Gothic wall of buildings to Broad Street to enclose the new work.
This wall itself is over 400 feet long and 80 feet high. The tower is named
after Dr Charles Mitchell, the Newcastle shipbuilder who was born in
Footdee, graduated here at Marischal College and became consultant to
the Russian government in the building of St Petersburg docks.

In preparation for the huge work of extending the college in the
1890s, the whole of the north side of Broad Street and the west side of
Queen Street was pulled down along with one of the country's most
historic collegiate churches, Greyfriars. This was a massive undertaking
and one that caused huge controversy at the time, almost akin to that
surrounding the construction of the shopping centre on George Street
sixty years later. An Act of Parliament, passed in 1893, was required for
the work to be carried out. There was much humming and hawing over

the loss of the church, but in the end, in a *fin-de-siècle* spirit of reconstruction and renewal, the church was completely demolished apart from its east window, which was inserted as a fragment into Mackenzie's new building for the church. The university would have preferred to move the church from the site altogether but no agreement could be reached. In the end Mackenzie designed the church as well as part of the overall composition. Greyfriars John Knox Church (as it is now called) was originally founded in 1471 by the grey-robed followers of St Francis of Assisi. The church formed the centrepiece of Marischal College, part of the post-Reformation gift to the college when it was founded.

The glory of Mackenzie's scheme is of course the incredibly spiky Gothic style of the building. The use of Gothic architecture outside of churches was very rare in Scotland, but the greatest example is to be found here in Aberdeen. It is one of the most exuberant designs of the nineteenth century. Its 'Perpendicular' style echoed Archibald Simpson's existing college buildings, which Mackenzie extended both outwards (including the new Mitchell Hall) and upwards (in the 260-foot-high Mitchell Memorial Tower). The soaring tower and the incredible filigree-like intricacy of the new Broad Street façade amazed everyone who saw it, including the celebrated English poet John Betjeman. He wrote that it is 'bigger than any cathedral, tower on tower, forests of pinnacles, a group of palatial buildings rivalled only by the Houses of Parliament'. This was an astonishing climax to Aberdeen's adventure in granite building, which was then enjoying its heyday. In his history of the city's granite industry (1949), W. Diack boasted that Marischal College was (after the Escorial, one of Madrid's royal palaces) the world's second largest granite building; it was 'a testimony to the superb durability of our Aberdeenshire granite, and the pride of our silver city by the sea'. Mackenzie's building is of Kemnay granite which can be contrasted with Simpson's Rubislaw granite buildings.

We can now enter through the passageway to the left of the building. Above are painted heraldic panels summarising the history of King's College and Marischal College from 1495 to 1906. The coats-of-arms are, from left to right: Lord Strathcona, chancellor and benefactor of the extension; the boat refers to his Hudson's Bay Company connection; the burgh of Old Aberdeen; Bishop William Elphinstone, founder of King's College; the University of Aberdeen; George Keith, fourth Earl Marischal, founder of Marischal College; the burgh of (new) Aberdeen. Painting of this type was common in prestigious Scottish buildings and this is the tradition which Mackenzie was reviving. The medieval painters also belonged to the Incorporation of Wrights and Builders. There is a beautifully cut stone panel with raised lettering commemorating Mackenzie's work on the left as you enter.

The **quadrangle** was formerly dominated by a gigantic obelisk to the memory of one of the most famous Aberdeen doctors, Sir James

2 WALK

McGrigor. With the extension of the university the column was moved to Duthie Park (p.173). The quadrangle is the setting for student 'battles' during the election for rector, who is the students' representative on the University Court. In recent years the role has become more symbolic, with celebrities elected to the post. We should go straight across the quadrangle, through the Mitchell Entrance and up the stairs to the Museum and Picture Gallery on the first floor. On the right of the quadrangle you will see the Seabury memorial, a plaque commemorating the establishment of the American Episcopal Church. This is discussed in more detail at St Andrew's Episcopal Cathedral (see p.148).

The university has a very fine anthropological museum, whose exhibits were donated largely by graduates over many years. The natural history museum was transferred to the department of zoology at Old Aberdeen and is also open to the public. The picture gallery has many paintings, chiefly of local interest and concentrating on celebrated graduates. The university also houses the MacBean Stuart and Jacobite Collection which consists of more than 1,300 engravings and drawings, and 4,500 books and pamphlets covering every aspect of the Jacobite Uprisings, the causes and effects and the personalities both national and local. William M. MacBean donated the collection to the university in 1919. The superb interior of the Mitchell Hall has a very striking commemorative stained-glass window designed by T.R. Spence of London.

We should retrace our steps and come back out onto Broad Street, turn right and cross over at the traffic lights to the top of **Upperkirkgate** on the left-hand pavement. From its name we can easily see that Upperkirkgate is on the site of one of the city's ancient gates. (As mentioned previously, this was not a 'gate' in the modern sense but in fact a walkway or a passage. It is in the sense we still mean when we say that someone has a peculiar 'gait', which is the original spelling. An entrance gate would be referred to as a 'port', as in Justice Port (p.145). A 'kirk', as we know, is the Scots word for a church, so Upperkirkgate means 'upper church walk'. The church is, of course, St Nicholas, whose spire we can see just in front of us to the left.)

Most of what is visible in Upperkirkgate derives from the late eighteenth and nineteenth centuries, but it is a very old street with much of the work of previous centuries built into the late fabric. The south side of the street was completely swept away from the 1930s onwards in a tide of improvement and slum clearance. Under the terms of Aberdeen Corporation Act of 1881 many buildings were declared unfit for human habitation and closed up by order. Most of the buildings on this side of Upperkirkgate fell into this category. On the corner with Gallowgate and turning into Upperkirkgate is the student union building, a comprehensive remodelling to create a Romantic building, more so even than the original street. Inside are murals by the artist Alberto Morrocco. Conveniently close to the union is the Kirkgate Bar at 18 Upperkirk-

Robert Barclay was born in 1648 at Gordonstoun in Moray and was educated in Aberdeen and Paris where his uncle was rector of the Scots College. After his return, he joined the Society of Friends (the Quakers) in 1666 and in 1675 published the key propositions of the Quaker faith, the Theses Theologicae. Three years later he published his famous Apology for the Quaker faith. Barclay eschewed both Protestantism and Catholicism and defined Quakerism as a faith of 'inner light'. He and his partner William Penn (who gave his name to Pennsylvania) were persecuted but Barclay found an influential ally in the Duke of York, who later became James VII. The Duke of York's influence saw Barclay installed as the governor of the foundling state of East Jersey, New York, from 1662 to 1668. Barclay then returned to Aberdeen, dying at Ury in 1690. The former Scots College in Paris is still in existence and contains the tomb of James VII who died in exile in 1701.

gate, where, traditionally, the victorious rector after the university's election for the post must buy his supporters a drink.

Now we enter **Upperkirkgate** itself. At nos. 6 and 8 we have a building of 1899, designed by R.G. Wilson, which incorporates fragments of the previous building on the site. During the second half of the nineteenth century, as the technology of construction and demolition improved, and the Victorian can-do mentality grew ever more in scope and scale, huge numbers of buildings were demolished. This in turn fostered the beginnings of a consciousness that a sense of history was disappearing from ancient towns and burghs.

Old buildings had always been 'recycled' as rubble for new ones, but now decorative features of seventeenth-century buildings started to be kept and built into new structures. Here we can see a cornice and dormer heads, one dated 1680, along with a doorway copied from the Scots College in Paris. The rather odd result of this copying is that the building appears to have two doorways, one stacked on top of the other. This had been copied literally from Robert Barclay's college in Paris even although the composition there had been the result of a lowering of the street, thereby leaving the entrance stranded in mid-air. There is reused corbelling (elaborate projecting brackets), almost certainly from one of the demolished buildings illustrated in Robert Billings' *Baronial and Ecclesiastical Antiquities of Scotland* (p.84). There is also a moulded doorway and armorial panel dated 1730 recording the marriage of Alexander Robertson and Jean Strachan. This would have come from the house of Provost Robertson, which stood on the site. At no. 18 the earlier Loanhead granite is evident, indicating a late eighteenth-century date, which is also the period in which the building's tall brick chimney stacks were constructed. These would have been unthinkable later in the century as granite refinement and appreciation of architecture grew.

At nos. 24–26 Upperkirkgate there is an original building of 1694 built of sandstone rubble. It has recently been rendered, concealing the

George Jamesone's House in an engraving by R.W. Billings, c.1855

sandstone. It has large corbelled skews (the sloping stones which finish a gable) with sundials. Between nos. 24 and 30 is a passage called Drum's Lane. This was the site of Lady Drum's hospital 'for poor widows and aged virgins' which by 1721 also accommodated the daughters of burgesses of guild. It was built in 1671 and demolished in 1798 when the street was being redeveloped in line with the burgh's many improvements around that time.

A little further on, at no. 42, we have an even older structure, probably dating from the earlier seventeenth century, and still with its gable facing the street like the medieval 'burgage'. Although the medieval town imported agricultural produce from its hinterland, the citizens still needed to cultivate land within the town; Aberdeen was therefore laid out in long 'burgage' plots the size of each of which was generally related to the width of the house. Towns therefore took on a shape like a comb, with plots running quite a distance back from the street. (It was only when communications and markets improved that city blocks in the modern sense could be created.) No architects or planners seem to have been involved at this stage. Most of the houses around this time would have been made of timber with plaster infill. The houses that followed in the late sixteenth and seventeenth century were much better built and more comfortable, as you might expect. But what did the town houses of the rich look like? They were in fact

The destruction of Jamesone's House, from a cartoon entitled The Vandals at Work

usually very similar to country houses; the largest were like miniature royal palaces and others were castles, complete with turrets and battlements. This was not peculiar to Aberdeen: the two best surviving examples in Scotland can be found in Stirling and Edinburgh, Argyll's Lodging and Moray House respectively. Provost Skene's House (where we started this walk), built between 1622 and 1641 and enlarged later, is the best example in Aberdeen.

Close to this spot, in Schoolhill, stood a very large house with a tower flanked by wings, all in finely cut stone. It was occupied in the early seventeenth century by the celebrated painter **George Jamesone** (1588–1644) who had studied in the atelier of Peter Paul Rubens before returning to build a highly successful career in Scotland. He was born into a dynasty of painters, something that was by no means unusual at this time; entry to crafts – and painting was a craft like any other in those days – was through a family connection. Jamesone may have been related through his mother, Marjory Anderson, to the man who was his master, John Anderson. (Although Anderson trained in Edinburgh, he was an Aberdonian.) Jamesone was chiefly an artist for the new middle class that was a product of the increased prosperity to be found particularly in flourishing trading communities like Aberdeen. In 1625 Jamesone married Isobel Tosche in Aberdeen. Four years later he completed one of his most celebrated paintings, for Mary Erskine Countess Marischal. You can see something of the Dutch interest in personality combined with a minute attention to costume detail in the portrait. With his great gift for painting portraits, Jamesone became a wealthy man and built up property in the city. His house here at Schoolhill, built originally by his father Andro Jamesone in 1586, was very large and imposing, turreted and bartizaned to convey his social position. There was a public outcry at the destruction of the house towards the end of the nineteenth century. When we look at a house like this we can see how much society was changing. For an artist to acquire such wealth and social standing had been quite unheard of. The painter's fame soon spread far beyond Aberdeen. He was asked by the millionaire Earl of Glenorchy to complete a series of portraits of kings as well as an elaborate family tree. Perhaps his greatest honour was the call to Edinburgh to decorate a triumphal arch for the entry of King Charles I in 1633. Jamesone's job was to paint the semi-mythical 119 kings of Scotland from Fergus I to Charles I and to hang these from the temporary arch through which the king would pass.

In George Jamesone's self-portrait (see p.35) we see a very respectable man who knows his place in society. He is inseparable from his craft as an artist. Even in a contemporary family portrait he is shown with his palette in his hand. In the self-portrait he proudly displays his work, but in the foreground there are reminders in the hourglass and the skull that all life comes to an end.

St Nicholas' Church

Jamesone was something of a hero both locally and nationally. When, at the end of the nineteenth century, the council decided to demolish his much dilapidated and converted house because it was considered unfit for human habitation, there was a public outcry. The 'work of vandalism' nevertheless went ahead. Jameson's house had become the haunt of 'mendicants', including a forceful character called 'Thunder and Lightning'. This blind beggar had been a seafaring man and every day he told the tale of how he lost his sight at Kingston, Jamaica, after 'a flash of thunder and lightning'. Boys making their way to or from school would throw him a penny just as he reached the climax of his story so that he would have to interject a 'God bless, you young man – with a flash of thunder and lightning!'

Where the hill flattens into a little valley we have reached George Street, or at least a tiny section of this very long street. George Street was laid out in the early nineteenth century as a subsidiary to the Union Street–King Street scheme, coming off Union Street at a right angle. Having made its brief appearance, however, George Street is temporarily lost within the huge Bon Accord shopping mall. The original street began as a small affair of compulsory purchase in 1754. The council bought some run-down buildings in order to construct a street coming off Upperkirkgate and Schoolhill to the loch. The street attracted business in the form of a tannery who paid the council £27 a year to operate there. It was thereafter known as Tannery Street but was given the more grandiose name of George Street when it was extended in 1808. Providing access to a whole new area of development, this street soon became the focus of property speculators and the area was feued in the normal way to individual proprietors according to a preordained plan. That is how regular streets were created. It was a mixture of lease conditions and control by the council Dean of Guild court, which was a kind of planning authority dealing with building heights, materials and the all-important building line: the boundary beyond which the structure must not go. Adherence to building line allowed for the creation of regular streets and 'planning' in the modern sense of the word. This was a potent mixture of town-council speculation, Dean of Guild and feuing restriction that was developed in Edinburgh and carried through in Glasgow, Aberdeen and elsewhere. Eventually the line of George Street was carried through, all the way to the Inverurie turnpike (toll road to Inverurie) and on its east side it was connected with Union Street through the creation of St Nicholas Street, now on the other side of the St Nicholas Centre.

The St Nicholas Centre and the Bon Accord Centre face each other across the remnant of George Street, providing an almost uninterrupted sequence of covered shopping. Building work on the St Nicholas Centre began in 1967. It has two levels of shopping with an upper deck of quite intimate gardens and giving direct access to the graveyard of St Nicholas' Church. In one corner of the garden deck you will see all that remains of the Grammar School (see below) which stood on the site until the 1860s. Raised on a deck above St Nicholas' Churchyard, it's a very pleasant place in fine weather. There are some very good pieces of sculpture on the raised piazza, all of them commissioned in 1985. They are *Moon Table* by Roland Piché; a relief panel entitled *Two* by Gavin Scobie; and the stone sculpture *Trumpet Leaf* by Paul Mason.

The Bon Accord Centre is a later and much larger piece of work: a vast shopping mall almost on the same scale as its massive Canadian exemplars. The beauty of it is that it's in the heart of the city, not in a soulless out-of-town shopping mall. And it's extremely popular: since its opening in 1990, the 'footfall' has amounted to 20 million visits. Of course the developers have arranged things so that if you park your car there you must exit via the mall – but who can blame them? The two shopping centres have between them created a huge indoor town held in the benign grip of two 'magnet' stores at either end of the supermall: Marks & Spencer's and John Lewis. Whether we love or loathe shopping malls, we must admit that this is something remarkable. A gigantic modern *agora* has been created right in the centre of the city, recalling Aberdeen's roots as a free market town. And the shopping mall is not really a new invention. Aberdeen had a covered arcade as early as 1840 (see p.127). But can these shopping malls ever have the character of a 'traditional' city street? The answer is probably yes. The first North American shopping malls are protected 'landmark' buildings, unique in their own way. There is no reason why Aberdeen's malls, which have already acquired a degree of fame, cannot do the same.

For the moment, let's put off the shopping till a rainy day and walk up the gentle brae of Schoolhill towards St Nicholas' Church. The buildings opposite are Victorian versions of the houses which used to line the street, although not quite on this line. These are tenements, very much in the manner of Edinburgh's Cockburn Street, which have been designed in homage to the buildings illustrated by Robert Billings. That street was very old. Schoolhill was not, as you might think, named after Robert Gordon's School at the top of the hill. The school in question is the Sang (Song) School which taught music to be played in church. After the Reformation, when music was banned, the school switched entirely to teaching the singing of psalms. The Sang School took this art to its highest degree in the *Aberdeen Psalter* of 1637. This was a song

St Nicholas' Churchyard

book of psalms arranged as four-part harmonies.

On the left is the little lodge-house guarding the graveyard from bodysnatchers and acting as the centre for the administration of the city of the dead. The city architect John Smith designed both the gates and the lodge in 1830. In spite of its pioneering researches in medicine, Aberdeen does not seem to have produced graverobbers after the fashion of Burke and Hare in Edinburgh to provide subjects for anatomy students. There are no caged 'mortsafes' in the graveyard, which were so necessary in Glasgow or Edinburgh. Perhaps because of its very central position in the city, the graveyard has always acted as a kind of public square, thoroughfare and garden.

St Nicholas' Church and its **graveyard** are among the glories of Aberdeen. The latter has a rich collection of monuments, most notably those of Mowat of Logie (c.1622), Davidson (1663), Rickert (1699) and Guild (1699). These are all baroque mural monuments, which would have fared better indoors. (One of the many consequences of the Reformation in 1560 was that monuments were banished from churches, and were not permitted to return until the eighteenth century.) Burial aisles and funerary monuments provided an obvious way to display wealth and status. Funerary monuments increasingly adopted an upright form, like grand entrances. The greatest concentration of the latter was in Greyfriars in Edinburgh, but the Riccarton monument (1696) at St Nicholas's Churchyard here in Aberdeen is one of the most elaborate in the country.

When you look at the inscriptions in the graveyard, you can see that many people's occupations are given. This is a practice that has only recently been discontinued and for historical researchers at least this is a pity. Many of the occupations here are, of course, the same as those that exist everywhere but there are also many examples of Aberdeen's own specialities. We have 'William Walker, Railway Manager', 'Alexander Innes, Joiner in Aberdeen', along with 'Alexander Christie, Deputy Inspector General of Hospitals and Fleets' and, sadly, a large number of victims of drowning. One example is the stone in memory of an 18-year-old man who was drowned in the wreck of the ship *Oscar* on 1 April 1813. The *Oscar* was a 'whaler of this place who was bound for the Greenland fishery and was totally wrecked on Grey's Head [Greyhope] twixt this harbour and Girdleness' (St Clement's Churchyard, p.202). In contrast to the men, the women buried here are defined not by occupation but as the wife, daughter, widow of a man.

There has been some dissatisfaction expressed over the years that Aberdeen has a graveyard stuck in the middle of the town and a very tired joke has circulated about the graveyard being the dead centre of Union Street. There have been various attempts to deal with this 'problem', including John Smith's beautifully detailed architectural screen of 1829. A recent proposal suggested cutting the area back to create a public square behind the screen, but I for one am glad this plan was never carried out.

The modern world has developed a misunderstanding of the function of a graveyard. Of course, we tend to think of them as creepy, but they're coming into their own again as receptacles of history. In a strange way, the fact that this graveyard is centrally placed keeps the history of Aberdeen alive. There are monuments here to most of its important citizens, because this was also a place to express public gratitude. It was a kind of Westminster Abbey of Aberdeen. Pirie & Clyne's Hamilton Place (p.228) was named after the civic improver Professor Robert Hamilton (1742–1829), and further honour was given to him here at St Nicholas'. His is a very elaborate monument, a testimony to the importance placed on scientific research and its community benefits at a time when diseases such as cholera were still rife. Hamilton was a professor of mathematics who also gained international fame with his theory on the national debt. His monument was raised by public subscription and is by far the grandest of the nineteenth-century monuments, a reminder of the growth of meritocracy over aristocracy.

We should spend a while just wandering around admiring all the tremendous tombs and enjoying their inscriptions. There are a large number of table tombs. This is a development of the stone slab simply laid into the ground. This type was vulnerable to the elements and could quickly become illegible. The table tombs vary in complexity; some are simple, while others have carved legs. These are, of course, indicators of wealth and status. The stars of the graveyard are the earlier walled tombs set like triumphal arches against the perimeter on the left-hand side, like gateways to heaven. Some of the most important people to have been born or lived in the city are buried here. Others must just have been passing through, such as 'James Groombridge, Commercial Traveller from London died 24 October 1832 aged 46 Years' – in those days all but the most wealthy were buried where they fell. There are also a number of cast-iron monuments, even in the Granite City.

Aberdeen is a relatively small place in its interlinking of people and business and St Nicholas' is a good place to appreciate this. There has been less coming and going in Aberdeen and perhaps more continuity than elsewhere. Nevertheless, there were some false starts. The family burial place of 'William Allan, Mile-End 1852' has not a name on it. This was clearly the unsuccessful start of a dynasty. Another notable stone is on the west of the churchyard. It reads: 'Here also rests the above John Anderson, the Wizard of the North, died 3 Feb 1864 aged 60.' Anderson was an Aberdonian, born at Craigmyle on 14 July 1814, who became a very popular music-hall entertainer. He described himself as 'Professor Anderson, the Wizard of the North', a play on Sir Walter Scott's famous sobriquet when he was still writing anonymously. Anderson's performance was part science, part magic. He employed a huge range of strange devices and appeared to risk death in the pursuit of sensation. His most famous trick, performed for the first time in the USA, was to catch a bullet fired by a member of the audience. On returning to the UK he gave a royal command performance for Queen Victoria at Balmoral. (Some rowdier audiences in those days gave as good as they got. On one occasion, at a riotous performance in Covent Garden, Anderson attempted to calm things down by lowering the gaslights. Instead of helping matters, he set fire to the theatre and the building was completely destroyed, creating a lot of publicity for the Wizard in the process.)

We should enter the church itself (or, correctly, churches) from the east side, going past the granite (from Queensferry!) front of the West Church. It is open every day, 10 a.m.–4 p.m. St Nicholas' Church or 'Kirk' dates from the twelfth century. It was founded in 1151 and has since that time been known as the 'Mither Kirk'. It was one of the largest medieval churches in Scotland. Of the earlier buildings on the site, two pieces survive: the late twelfth-century Collison's Aisle and St Mary's Chapel of 1438, which became the crypt of the present church. There was excellent timber work carried out by John Fendour from 1495 onwards. This was similar to the ceiling of King's College Chapel (p.183) and was probably sponsored by Bishop William Elphinstone, but it did not survive the nineteenth century.

At the Reformation, as happened to many of the larger churches, St Nicholas' was split into parts. The ministers drew lots to see who would get what. In the end, the nave of the church became the West Church and when this fell into disrepair it was recast by Aberdeen's greatest architect, James Gibbs. The East Church was remodelled around 1835 by Archibald Simpson. During the execution of Simpson's work the remains of an earlier choir were found and the congregation decided to showcase this piece of archaeology by means of a gas chandelier called a 'sunlight'. This was a modern marvel, but a bit experimental also: it consisted of gas jets under a reflector, cooled by water to avoid an excessive build-up of heat to which gas lighting was always prone. It seems that the experiment did not work. The lighting proved defective and started a terrible fire, which destroyed the ancient timber spire of the church.

In 1790 the magistrates generously allowed the city's growing Gaelic-speaking population to fit out St Mary's Chapel under the East Church as a place of public worship. Services continued there until 1795 when a new chapel was built in Belmont Street (p.98). St Mary's Chapel is now a lovely little shop called the Third World Centre. It can be reached by going out of the church and down the steps to the north at Correction Wynd.

Let us look first of all at the West Church. Take a left turn inside the church. This is one of Aberdeen's most important buildings, for a number of reasons. Late seventeenth- and early eighteenth-century churches

St Nicholas' Church prior to the fire which destroyed the steeple

were firmly attuned to a reformed tradition of plainness and modest size, although burgh churches, as this is, could express burgh aspirations. For the most part in Scotland, church designers employed an austere classicism, occasionally with Gothic elements, as at Edinburgh Tron Kirk, but this was later reduced to a very simple but grand monumentality, as here at Aberdeen. Larger churches might have a steeple, but this was by no means considered as essential as it did later, in the nineteenth century. The growing cities produced church designs of temple-like proportions. St Andrew's Parish Church in Glasgow (1737–59), designed by Allan Dreghorn, has a giant portico, matched with a Gibbs-inspired steeple. James Gibbs, the master architect himself, returned here to Aberdeen to design St Nicholas' West, in 1752.

As the town's church, St Nicholas' West had great civic importance. As mentioned above, the nave had become the West Church at the Reformation in 1560, but it became dilapidated after the 'Glorious Revolution' in 1688 when many Aberdonians turned to non-conformist religion. The congregation of the West Church went with their minister to the Trinity Church near the Green. Gibbs was made a burgess of the city and in his gratitude he designed the church for the city free of charge. We should remember that by this time Gibbs was the premier architect in Britain, with the sublime Radcliffe Camera at Oxford and the King's Quadrangle at Cambridge as well as St Martin in the Fields Church in Trafalgar Square to his credit. Although the council had been given the design for no cost, they did not have the money to realise the architect's plans – they were not executed until 1752, when sufficent funds had been raised. In the meantime, the church was used as a store-house by the invading Hanoverian army. After the defeat of Prince Charles at Culloden, the 'Butcher' Cumberland showed his more sensitive side by donating money for the rebuilding of the church, and this went into the pot for Gibbs' design.

The lithograph on the left shows the East Church before the rebuilding of 1837 and the fire of 1874 which destroyed the steeple. To the right of this picture is a depiction of the situation prior to 1837. Inside Gibbs' church is a superb example of original furniture and also some very interesting later pieces clearly influenced by the Greek revival. The pulpit is especially good. At one end is the provost's loft with its elaborate baldacchino or canopy. Here we have physical evidence of the growing power of the town over the country. As the towns and cities grew, the landowners' power was matched by that of wealthy citizens. There are fine effigies of Margaret Liddell and Gilbert Menzies, brought from Maryculter Church. These two were husband and wife. (The Scottish tradition was that once a married woman was dead she would be referred to by her maiden name.) There is also an etching of Jamesone's House (see p.86) which was formerly the manse of the West Kirk. There is a series of interior views of the church drawn by Sir George Reid, who studied in Edinburgh, Utrecht and Paris and introduced Dutch land- and seascapes to Scotland via his home town of Aberdeen. Reid moved to Edinburgh in 1885 but he kept a house and studio in Aberdeen which today is the Gordon Highlanders Regimental Museum (see p.232).

In the central space is the Collison Aisle, the remains of the much older crossing of the undivided church. There are important memorials, including that of a local hero, Provost Davidson, who performed the traditional role of leading the citizen army into battle. Davidson was killed at the decisive Battle of Harlaw in 1411, when the rising power of the Highlands was dealt a critical blow in the creation of 'imperial' Scotland. In front of us is a chapel donated in 1990 by the oil companies after the disastrous Piper Alpha oil-rig accident, which claimed so many lives. The victims' names, together with those of others who have died in the pursuit of North Sea oil, are in the Book of Remembrance. The beautiful stained-glass window is by Shona McInnes and represents the Dee and the Don with their leaping salmon, the dark slabs of Aberdeen granite, the ploughed field for the farming community, the roses for the city's famous flowers, the spires of the city, Marshall College, King's College and the Townhouse. The black 'fingers' represent the basins of Aberdeen's harbour. There is also a fishing-boat, the Girdleness lighthouse, a red oil supply ship, two oil-tankers and two production platforms. The green arrow coming ashore from the platform represents oil and the red arrow represents gas. The flare off the burner represents the Holy Spirit in the shape of the dove of peace; there is also St Andrew, patron saint of fishermen; the three gold balls of St Nicholas; and the eagle of St John, patron saint of oil-refiners, with an oil-drum in its talons. The timber screen is the work of artist Tim Stead.

Listen out for the bells of St Nicholas'. A peal of bells in the form of a carillon was installed in the church in 1893 by M.E. Michiels of Malines. A carillon is a set of chromatically tuned stationary bells that are usually played from a keyboard. The bells are hit with hammers rather than swung. There are 48 bells, making up four octaves. These were cast by Gillet & Johnson of Croydon. The carillon is played every Sunday from 10.30 a.m. until 10.55 a.m. Aberdeen has lovely church spires, which figure prominently in views of the city. The church's bells also ring out very atmospherically, especially through the early morning 'haar', the chilly mist that spreads inland from the sea. The best of the other bells is at St Mary's Church in Huntly Street (p.68).

We now leave St Nicholas' Church by Schoolhill as we entered. The buildings directly opposite, which cover the area from Harriet Street, up the hill and as far as the 'square' in front of Robert Gordon's and the art gallery, were all designed in 1885 and 1886 by Marshall Mackenzie, architect of the new Marischal College – except the block on the corner, Littlejohn's. This was the work of James Rust (1897). It is hard to believe that this group was designed at different times by different architects, they are so much in sympathy. This is quite typical of Aberdeen: the aim of the architects as a professional group was to design a whole city, not a collection of individual monuments. It is a superb piece of urban infill which defines the new improved municipality of the nineteenth century and turns the corner into the space in front of **Robert Gordon's Hospital**. Here there is a very unusual use of highly polished granite window surrounds of contrasting colour. The main building is of Tilliefourie granite and the surrounds are of pink granite from Corennie. The granite from Corennie is still quarried. The building facing the 'square' is an apartment block of large flats.

The gentle incline of Schoolhill led not to the long-lost Sang School (p.89) but to Aberdeen Grammar School which stood on the site until the 1860s when it relocated to Rosemount (p.117). The school has had many celebrated former pupils, but none has quite reached the superstar status of George Gordon, Lord Byron, poet, 'childe of passion' and national hero of Greece who supported that country's struggle for independence. Byron's mother was Catherine Gordon of Gight, the only child of Sir George Gordon after whom her son was named. Byron fell heir to his title in a very roundabout way. He was the son of a nephew of the 'wicked Byron' who had tortured two wives and been thoroughly bad. Young George's own father, 'mad Jack' Byron, was not all that much better. He met and married Catherine Gordon during the 'season' at Bath for her supposed wealth – only to be very disappointed.

So Byron was born in London in 1788 to a runaway father and a dispossessed mother. His father quickly spent what little was left of the Gight 'fortune' and fled to France. The hapless mother made her way back to Aberdeen to lodge first at 10 **Queen Street** (see p.149) and later

Robert Gordon's Hospital prior to the 'straightening' of the pediments

68 Broad Street, only to be later pestered by 'mad Jack' who had made his way back in secret from overseas. Little George, the future poet, was sent to school in Aberdeen and must have walked this short road from Queen Street to Schoolhill every day. The little boy had been born with a clubfoot and was extremely sensitive about his disability. In 1798 he unexpectedly fell heir to the title and estates of his great uncle William, the fifth Baron Byron, and his mother took him to claim his birthright. What they encountered was the half-ruined Newstead Abbey near Nottingham, which set the ten-year-old's Romantic imagination alight. The contrast with the down-to-earth common sense of an Aberdeen education must have been considerable.

In Byron's day Queen Street wound its way up from the Denburn Valley to Marischal College by way of Robert Gordon's School (see p.100) Schoolhill was widened in the 1880s in order to improve the setting and amenity of St Nicholas' Churchyard. As part of this work the sexton's office had to be moved and re-erected as a kind of gate-lodge to the churchyard. (The sexton is the church officer in charge of ringing the bell, digging the graves and generally overseeing the graveyard. He or she has a list of all the 'occupants' of the graveyard and the owners of the lairs.)

By now we are at Back Wynd which is the narrow street with the churchyard wall on one side. There are two very good shops, a toy shop and a pencil shop, just on the other side of Back Wynd on Schoolhill. Back Wynd itself is a very old street which used to lead right down to the Green (p.126) prior to the construction of Union Street. The Wynd continues over Union Street in set of steps. The buildings which you now see facing the churchyard date mostly from the eighteenth century.

Robert Gordon's College

In Back Wynd, the public building on your right is the church hall of St Nicholas' Church. Next on the left you will see the separate entrance to St Nicholas' West Church. In Little Belmont Street further on we find ourselves at a famous old Aberdeen bar, **Ma Cameron's**. It has many interesting old prints of Aberdeen, so purely in the interests of historical research we may step inside. Since we are here anyway, we might have some refreshment.

If you would prefer something a little less stimulating, carry straight on to the coffee shops of Belmont Street, which is directly ahead. On our right is the **Old Town School**, designed in 1840 by John Smith, and now converted to a very lively pub. The building has some of the almost sinister quality we associate with Prussian buildings of the period in the work of Karl Freidrich Schinkel. It is Aberdeen's *Neue Wache*, Schinkel's brooding classical guardhouse in Berlin, but it had a purely educational purpose. The German education system was, of course, much admired in nineteenth-century Britain so there may be a connection there. Archibald Simpson's High School for Girls (1837–39) is another Aberdeen example of this tendency (p.221), but there is also a strong Greek 'academy' tradition in Scotland which meshed well with a worldwide interest in 'pure' Greek architecture in the first half of the nineteenth century.

The church on our left at the junction with Belmont Street is renamed Slains Castle, which is the former South Church of 1830 by John Smith. It seems that a chain of bar-restaurants called Eerie Pubs Ltd was looking for a suitably ghoulish local poisoner or general evil-doer and couldn't find one in Aberdeen to match Edinburgh's infamous Deacon Brodie. They decided instead to call the place after Slains Castle at Cruden Bay (see p.263), where the writer Bram Stoker got the inspiration for his novel *Dracula*.

Belmont Street was feued (leased) for building in the 1770s, a very agreeable hillside spot well above the Denburn, which is below to the rear. You can reach the (now subterranean) Denburn itself by an Edinburgh-style wynd at Patagonian Court, which is opposite Gaelic Lane, on the other side of the South Church.

Gaelic Lane was named after the Gaelic Chapel which stood on the site. The church was founded in 1795 for the many first-generation Gaelic-speakers who had been making their way to Scotland's cities in their thousands in the aftermath of the Uprising of 1745 and later the Great Famine of 1845. Large numbers of Highland labourers had been coming to the city from 1758 onwards when a London entrepreneur called Adams opened new granite quarries and carried out a recruiting drive in the north. In addition, there were many Gaelic-speaking students at Aberdeen University, a tradition which continues to this day. Most of the Highlanders were described in prejudicial terms as being 'extremely ignorant of the principles of the Christian religion'. What this in fact meant was that the Highlanders could not speak English. Gaelic services were held in the East Church of St Nicholas from 1758 until St Mary's Chapel (below the East Church) was made available in 1790. 'By assistance of voluntary contributions from benevolent individuals', the congregation was able to build a very neat chapel in Belmont Street. The Gaelic Chapel had a long sloping garden down to the Green. We should bear in mind that all this existed before Union Street was built.

Now continue up Belmont Street. Immediately on our left is the **Congregational Church** by James Souttar (1865) which is best seen from Union Bridge, where I have described it (p.63). The pioneering 'genteel' house in Belmont Street is at no. 37 (now Lizar's with its super later shopfront). This was the house of Menzies of Pitfodels who had fled the Castlegate (p.134) for a country retreat on the edge of town. Compared to his old, rambling home, this spanking new house in Belmont Street was a square-cut sensible box of a building with all mod cons. There were originally two pavilions (low wings) to either side of the building. These were gobbled up as commercial activity grew in the nineteenth century. As the city grew and the business centre of the town spread after the building of Union Street, Belmont Street was gradually completely commercialised.

The rest of the buildings on this side of the street are either social clubs or commercial premises but the best of these is the former **Aberdeen Trades Council** building which makes no impression on Belmont Street itself, being a building sited in the back yard and entered through a passage at no. 51. It was built in 1896 by Alexander Ellis and R.G. Wilson. The building was to be used principally for the meetings of the newly formed labour movement in the city. A plaque commemorates

Robert Gordon's College showing the statue of its founder

James Leathan (1865–1945). Leathan was a great socialist and advocate of free speech. His particular target was the press, which were more and more being brought under the control of the establishment. Leathan's answer was his own paper, *The Worker's Herald*. Inside the building, the ceiling of the main hall had panels by Strachan illustrating themes of class solidarity but these have been covered over as the years have passed. Ironically enough, the building has now been converted to a media

WALK

centre which will have editing facilities and also a small cinema.

On the other side of the street is the fairly recent redevelopment of Aberdeen's Italian Centre, the Academy. The new development of the site for a shopping and restaurant complex was the work of the Edinburgh architecture firm of Percy Johnson-Marshall and Partners (1998). The main block, Aberdeen Academy, the former Central School, was designed by J. Ogg Allan in 1901. It is very elaborately detailed and makes a very effective group on the irregularly shaped square in front of Robert Gordon's School. Like other Aberdeen city schools, the Academy followed the London example of E.R. Robson in putting a playground on the roof. As a former Glasgow schoolboy, common sense would tell me not to attempt this, but they seem to have been quite successful in Aberdeen. The Glaswegian architectural critic J.J. Stevenson did not like the idea at all. In any case the schoolchildren have all gone now, to be replaced by the bars, bistros and shops of Aberdeen's own Italian Centre. This was a big development, taking over a whole city block, which has added a great deal to the Aberdeen leisure scene.

We now find ourselves back on Schoolhill. The meandering street was straightened in the 1880s when the Schoolhill viaduct was built to line up with the immense Rosemount Viaduct, cancelling out Mutton Brae, which had led down to the Denburn Valley, and replacing it with steps.

In front of us is Aberdeen Art Gallery with its statue of Gordon of Khartoum in front. The statue was designed by T. Stuart Burnett in 1884 with a plinth of Corennie granite, matching the window surrounds of the overlooking buildings.

The Robert Gordon's complex of buildings is immediately adjacent to the gallery. The school was built in 1731–32 by William Adam, the father of the famous Scottish architect Robert Adam, and was originally named Robert Gordon's Hospital. The word 'hospital' was used in the sense of offering charity to the underprivileged, as George Heriot had famously done in the creation of his Edinburgh school, George Heriot's Hospital. Later, the status of the school changed from being a charitable institution to a private school and was renamed Robert Gordon's College. Gray's School of Art was also established here at the site, but later grew to such an extent that it became a college in its own right and now has a separate building at Garthdee. Also on the same site is the well-known Robert Gordon's Institute of Technology (now Robert Gordon's University), a technical university for the training of architects, engineers and other specialist professionals. RGIT also has an extensive campus at Garthdee, including the Scott Sutherland School of Architecture, which was established in that architect's house after his death.

Standing in front of the courtyard entrance to the complex of buildings, just to the right, is a stone marking the existence on the site from 1757 to 1863 of the Grammar School, Byron's *alma mater*, which was removed to Gilcomston (p.117). Through the pend or passageway and into the courtyard, there is a superb vista of the original school building. The buildings which close the courtyard to the left and right were built later for RGIT.

On the 'Auld Hoose' itself is a statue of its founder, Robert Gordon, by John Cheere. The placing of such statues was normal practice in 'donor' buildings of this type. Robert Gordon was the son of an Aberdeen lawyer and the nephew of James Gordon of Rothiemay who drew views of Edinburgh and Aberdeen in the seventeenth century. Gordon made a fortune in the Baltic trade; he never married and on his death he left a huge sum for the education of the less well-off boys of his native city. Fortunately, a scheme to replace the school in the 1820s proved too expensive and the masters made do with alterations. The attic storeys and straight pedimented wings were added by John Smith in 1830–33, replacing the original, more baroque curved pediments. This was a strange alteration to make in a city which rather specialised in this type of baroque gable. Note the lead-covered flèche (decorative roof feature). As you walk back now to School Wynd, if you look at the original school, then the block on the right and then that on the left, you can see the development of architecture. As time went by, ornament has been stripped away

During the Uprising of 1745, the Duke of Cumberland took over the building and its grounds. Cumberland's troops waited a long time in Aberdeen as they prepared for their final assault on Prince Charlie's army. It was here that they were issued with flat metal helmets, designed to protect them in the face of the 'Highland charge'. The helmets gave the soldiers more anxiety than protection. Much more welcome was the relatively new invention of a bayonet which could be fixed without blocking the musket barrel. In close combat, the troops were instructed to attack the man to their right, in the vulnerable area below his upraised sword arm.

In front of us now on the other side of the little square is the academy. The small building immediately to the left of the former school-turned-shopping and restaurant complex is James Dun's House, a comparatively grand residence built in 1769 for a former headmaster of the grammar school, which stood immediately opposite. There were several houses of this type all in a row. There is a very similar example with a shop pushed out into the garden at the Toy Bazaar, no. 53 Schoolhill.

We can now enter Aberdeen Art Gallery, one of the main attractions on our walk. This is one of the most pleasant and manageable picture and sculpture galleries in the country. It has a very fine collection of paintings, including the bequest of Alexander Macdonald of Kepplestone, a powerful granite quarrymaster and great patron of the arts. His long-time friend was the celebrated painter Sir George Reid who advised Macdonald on acquisitions. The two men were also near neighbours in Rubislaw, overlooking Aberdeen. Reid's house and studio is now the Gordon Highlanders Regimental Museum.

The gallery is open Monday to Saturday, 10 a.m.–5 p.m., and Sunday, 2 p.m.–5 p.m. It is one of the city's best loved buildings: a relatively small-scale art gallery with a superb collection. The building seems to continue Aberdeen's interest in internalised public spaces. There is a beautiful atrium with a fountain and its double-height space is lit from above with an arcade of gorgeous granite columns. The columns are an exhibit in themselves, representing granite from all over the world, but mainly Aberdeen examples. It is in this courtyard that the gallery's latest acquisitions are displayed.

Designed by Alexander Marshall Mackenzie, Aberdeen's Art Gallery, opened in 1885, was part of a seamless wall of civic design. With its impressive architecture, fine collections and excellent special exhibitions it attracts 300,000 visitors a year. There are new exhibitions on a regular basis, and there is always something different to see whether from travelling shows or curated from the gallery's permanent collections of paintings, sculpture, costume, silver and ceramics. Many of the visiting exhibitions have their only Scottish showing in Aberdeen.

The gallery's fine-art collections include paintings, sculpture and graphics from the fifteenth century to the present day. Two of the best-loved paintings are both by Glasgow Boys, Sir John Lavery's *The Tennis Party* and Sir James Guthrie's *To Pastures New*. Amongst the earliest portraits are those by the Aberdeen painter George Jamesone. The collection features works by Allan Ramsay, William Hogarth, Johanes Zoffany, Sir David Wilkie and Sir Henry Raeburn. From the mid-nineteenth century are Landseer's *Flood in the Highlands*, and a group of Pre-Raphaelite works by Millais, Burne-Jones, Holman Hunt and Rossetti.

The gallery is exceptionally rich in paintings of the earlier twentieth century, with works by Walter Richard Sickert and artists of the New English Art Club and the Camden Town Group such as Steer, Gilman, Bevan and Pisarro. The Scottish Colourists, Peploe, Cadell, Fergusson and Hunter, are each well represented. Vanessa Bell and Roger Fry from the Bloomsbury Group are represented, together with several canvases by Duncan Grant. Two of Paul Nash's best pieces are also here, *The Wood on the Downs* and *Northern Adventure*. There is a fine Ben Nicholson still-life from 1947 and three paintings by Winifred Nicholson. Some of the best of Stanley Spencer's work is in Aberdeen, including one of the *Resurrection* series. Both Gwen John and Augustus John are represented in the collection. More recently the gallery has added works by Francis Bacon, Frank Auerbach, Gilbert and George, and younger artists, Tim Ollivier, Clare Neasham, Emma Smith, Trevor Sutton and Ken Currie.

There are also works by the French Impressionists and Post-Impressionists such as Monet, Renoir, Sisley, Bonnard, Toulouse-Lautrec and Degas.

Aberdeen has bred several painters acclaimed both nationally and internationally. The foremost of these is William Dyce. The gallery owns the majority of his known oil paintings, including the early and Italianate *Lamentation over the Dead Christ*. John 'Spanish' Phillip, the favourite artist of Queen Victoria, is equally well represented, both by his earlier Scottish subjects and his later Spanish ones. The work of other important local artists including James Cowie, James McBey and Joan Eardley can be found here too. McBey (1883–1959) was born in Newburgh, Aberdeenshire, in 1883, and the gallery has the world's largest collection of his works. Like his contemporary George Walton in Glasgow, he worked firstly as a bank clerk. He eventually gave this up in 1910, 'to earn a livelihood as an artist'. In 1917 he became an Official War Artist with the British Expeditionary Force in Egypt. McBey met his wife Marguerite Loeb in New York in 1930, and the two travelled through Europe the following year, eventually settling in Morocco. In 1939 they were visiting the United States when war broke out; their passports were impounded and they were forced to remain in the US for the duration of the war. In 1946 they finally returned to Morocco. McBey died in 1959. Aberdeen Art Gallery and Museums has received many donations of the work of James McBey, most notably from Marguerite and from H.H. Kynett of Philadelphia.

On display can also be found highlights from the rich and diverse collection of applied art: craft and design including ceramics, glass, furniture, costumes, textiles and metalwork. Aspects of lifestyles, decorative techniques, skills and stylistic trends are represented. Enamelled plaques and jewels by James Cromar Watt, examples of the works of the eighteenth-century master silversmiths of Aberdeen as well as costumes and early Chinese ceramics are on display, together with contemporary work. Important recent acquisitions include the Peggy Walker Gift of Costume, the Cochrane Collections of continental and British porcelain, tapestry from the Scottish Arts Council Bequest of 1997 and an archive of drawings by the Aberdeen-born fashion designer Bill Gibb.

The gallery's sculpture collection dates from the nineteenth and twentieth centuries and includes important Scottish pieces by Alexander and William Brodie and James Pittendreigh MacGillivray as well as a number of works by English sculptors such as Papworth and Woolner. The twentieth-century collection is stronger, with important examples of the work of Jacob Epstein, Barbara Hepworth, Henry Moore, Eduardo Paolozzi, Richard Long, Anthony Caro and Gavin Scobie. A small holding of sculpture by French artists includes work by Degas, Rodin and Bourdelle.

On the left-hand side of the main atrium is the way through to Cowdray Hall. This is an extension to the museum, an unusual indoor war memorial erected under the terms of a bequest from the first Viscount Cowdray (see p.104).

You can end the walk here if you wish, or you can continue over the Denburn and through Rosemount, going from Cowdray Hall to **Byron's statue at Aberdeen Grammar School** and back on a circular route. There is a very gentle uphill walk on the way out.

A. Marshall Mackenzie & Son built Cowdray Hall between 1923 and 1925. The quadrant was to be embellished by a statue of Edward VII but this kind of monarchical tribute had lost popularity after the First World War, and a lion was instead installed, perhaps not quite successfully. A statue of Edward VII was placed on the corner of Union Street and Union Terrace, replacing Prince Albert. Weetman Dickinson Pearson, the first Viscount Cowdray of Midhurst, donated the hall. He was born in Yorkshire but was later based at the quite astonishing Dunecht House, just outside Aberdeen. Cowdray was an engineer who made a fortune as a contractor when he expanded the family firm into a worldwide enterprise. Among his projects were several railway tunnels under New York's East River. Cowdray also acquired land in Mexico and thereafter monopolised the fledgling Mexican oil industry. Baron Cowdray's widow, was interested in Scottish heritage. She bought the ruins of Dunnottar (p.259) and began its careful conservation. It is one of the few monuments of such importance still in private hands.

We should now start our walk over the **Denburn Bridge** past the partial ruin of the Triple Kirks (p.63). The Denburn was a little stream which was crossed further downstream by the Bow Brig. That bridge was demolished to make way for the Union Bridge in 1805. For centuries the Denburn Valley was on the edge of town, a little bit of 'green belt' between Aberdeen and Gilcomston. For a long time the Denburn was left to its own devices, with bleaching works and small-scale industry on its banks. With the coming of Union Street, everything was set to change as industrialisation began. The Denburn offered the line of least resistance for the railway when Kittybrewster station was linked with Guild Street. With Queen Victoria's interest in the Highlands and her extensive use of the train from which to view the scenery, the necessity of the railway for commerce and tourism became clear.

Nevertheless, the scene did not change radically. If you had stood in this spot prior to 1885 you would be looking over to the other side of the Denburn, which flowed down to the sea. So, instead of seeing Pizza Hut and the other shops, you would be looking at the rooftops of Guild Street and the Torry Hill in the distance. First the railway and then a road disrupted this. But it was really the coming of the railway, which allowed for the bridging of the Denburn at this point. The railway first arrived in Aberdeen in 1850. The station was just south of the centre at Ferryhill and connected the city with the south via Montrose and the east coast. In 1854 a more central location was found. A little later Aberdeen was connected with Inverness via the Kittybrewster and Waterloo stations. The line eastwards to Huntly had been opened by the Great North of

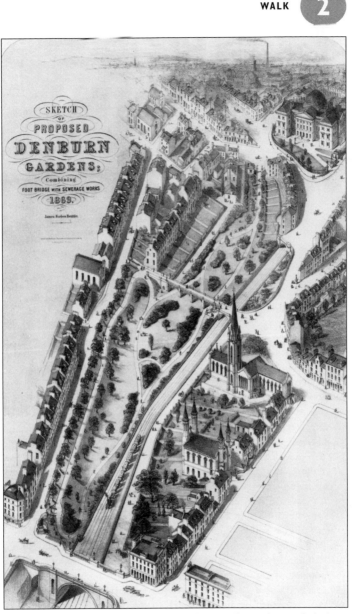

James Forbes Beattie's sketch of the proposed Denburn Gardens combining a footbridge and sewerage works, c.1869; the Triple Kirks is right of centre

Scotland Railway Co. in 1854. By 1866 the Deeside Railway Co. connected Aberdeen with Ballater, creating one of the country's most beautiful rail journeys – unfortunately savaged during Dr Beeching's infamous

The Lower Denburn prior to its demolition in the 1960s; the tenements of Roseburn Viaduct are visible on the upper right of the photograph

cuts of the system in the 1960s. In the unplanned way of the nineteenth-century railway scramble, many more lines were opened: Kintore to Alford; Peterhead to Dyce. During a period of compromise, the two railway systems to the north and south of Aberdeen were joined in 1867 via a link along the Denburn Valley and Berryden. Until this point, passengers had to walk a quarter of a mile between Waterloo Quay and Guild Street as part of their journey north or south. A 'joint station' of the Great North of Scotland Railway Co. and the Caledonian Railway Co. was built at this time, the predecessor of the present handsome building.

Aberdeen's population was growing fast and the railway station soon proved too small. A branch station was opened here at Schoolhill viaduct. To ease the congestion further and to provide more direct pedestrian access from the south, another entrance and bridge was built at Bridge Street. Kittybrewster and Waterloo passenger stations, which had been used for transferring from north to south, became largely redundant with the opening of the joint station. The station at Schoolhill was also soon closed along with many others even before Dr Beeching's report.

The present station and its related road-bridge at Guild Street were all rebuilt between 1913 and 1920 by the Caledonian and Great North of Scotland Railways. This was the last of the major Scottish stations to be built, with a 12-platform through station and a terminal station. There have been some alterations since the 1970s but the buildings are still essentially as they were. The station buildings are made of a colossal amount of iron and steelwork. You can see that many have the workplates of Alexander Findlay & Co., Parkneuk Works, Motherwell. The roof area is huge.

The station is approached from its long eastern flank. It is somewhat surprising that the railway station, which is a landmark building for any town or city, is not made entirely of granite. The main entrance is constructed of sandstone with a quite Parisian fan-shaped balcony. Perhaps the sandstone was intended to link the Caledonian Railway with its Glasgow headquarters and the granite of the other buildings were to represent the north-east. The station opens into a large open foyer covered by a shallow arched roof (like Glasgow's Queen Street). It was not intended to contain platforms. In this sense Aberdeen's station resembles continental examples. Immediately to the west of the station is the road-bridge which carries Guild Street over the new rail connections to the north. At the corner of Guild Street and College Street you can see another of the joint railway buildings.

Looking north from the Denburn you can see the infirmary, which owes its existence to the generosity of the Aberdonians. 'In order that those poor persons who have distemper upon their bodies . . . dislocations of broken bones might have medical assistance, the citizens of Aberdeen agreed in 1739 to build an Infirmary.' In the age of the Enlightenment, the idea of a scientific as opposed to the 'folk' remedy was a novelty. 'Hospital' meant something quite different in those days: it was a place for the ill to lie in with the expectation of death. The infirmary, on the other hand, was a new, dynamic place of treatment. Equally, it was a place where new ideas could be tried out on willing, and occasionally unwilling, patients. Demand for the services of Aberdeen's infirmary grew with the city, and the present building, which we see fronting the site at Woolmanhill, was designed by Archibald Simpson in 1832. The cost was £16,700 and the new facility had 230 beds. The new buildings at Foresterhill were put up in 1936 at the enormous cost of £525,000, an incredible sum for a pre-National Health Service voluntary hospital.

Having crossed the bridge, we now see the famous architectural trio of Aberdeen: Education, Salvation and Damnation. These are the Central Library (1891), St Mark's Church (1892) and His Majesty's Theatre. **St Mark's** was designed by Marshall Mackenzie as the 'Free South', or South United Free Presbyterian Church. This group is one of Aberdeen's most famous set-pieces and includes one of Frank Matcham's most celebrated designs. Matcham was a well-known and very busy Edwardian theatre and music-hall architect who perfected the art of creating sumptuous and comfortable auditorium buildings in the early twentieth century, from the Hackney Empire in London to the King's Theatre in Glasgow. His work epitomised Edwardian pomp. This building, His Majesty's, was constructed of Kemnay granite between 1904 and 1906. Inside, there is a very large auditorium which can seat up to 2,550 people, with three galleries and a dress circle. The private boxes are very elaborately treated and there is a frieze by the artist W.H. Buchan over the great proscenium arch. This is one of the most expertly executed surviving examples of Matcham's work in the entire country.

Just beside the theatre, until relatively recently, was a little branch line railway station called School Hill which was perfectly placed for those visiting Robert Gordon's, the theatre and the town centre. The station was shut down by Beeching in the 1960s. From 1933 a well-known local family, the Donalds, owned the theatre. They had many business interests in Aberdeen but are best known for their cinemas (including the former Picture House just opposite), their ice-cream and their involvement with Aberdeen Football Club. His Majesty's was bought over by the council after a threatened buy-out by Ladbrokes.

Opposite His Majesty's, and pre-dating the theatre, is the magnificent 16-foot-high **statue of William Wallace**, which was designed by W. Grant Stevenson in 1888. There are many Wallace statues and memorials all over the country, but this is surely one of the best. But what was the source of all this Wallace-mania?

> *'Wallace's heroic patriotism, as conspicuous in his death as in his life, so roused and inspired his country that within nine years of his betrayal the work of his life was crowned with victory and Scotland's independence gained on the field of Bannockburn.'*

These words were inscribed on the monument of 1900 at the scene of Wallace's betrayal near Glasgow. Sir William Wallace, 'Wallace', or 'The Wallace', is regarded by many as the father of the Scottish nation, like Arpad in Hungary or William Tell in Switzerland. His cult is rivalled only by that of Robert the Bruce or, in literature, Robert Burns, who set the modern Wallace and Bruce cult in train with his rousing hymn of praise to the two patriots, 'Scots wha hae'. The Bruce cult has its roots in Fordun and Barbour's late fourteenth-century biography, *Brus*, which was written in Aberdeen (p.134). The modern revival of the Bruce cult is as recent as the twentieth century. That of Wallace begins in the modern period with Burns and reaches its highest architectural point at Abbey Craig in Stirling where the astonishing 220-foot monument still commands the flat terrain below including the site of Bannockburn.

Literary interest in Wallace can be traced back at least as far as Blind Harry's fourteenth-century epic *The Wallace*. The cult of Wallace was taken up again later and he was made a national hero as a protest against James III's pro-English policy. Blind Harry celebrated Wallace's legendary exploits in Aberdeen, but the cult lay more or less dormant for centuries; it came to life again in an powerful nineteenth-century revival, during which a series of ever-more grandiose and ambitious monuments were

W. Grant Stevenson, sculptor of the Wallace Statue, in his studio

erected in honour of Wallace. There are more than twenty Wallace monuments throughout the Scotland, from Thomas Hamilton's tower at Ayr to the sculptured Iona Cross at Easterhouse in Glasgow. The first was at Dryburgh, at the instigation of the nationalist Earl of Buchan, who paid for the colossal statue himself. This was followed by the tower at Ayr, which introduced the idea of planning a monument set in an urban context, later logically developed at Edinburgh's Scott Monument. But the ultimate memorial to the hero is, of course, the National Wallace Monument at Abbey Craig in Stirling, designed by J.T. Rochead and built between 1861 and 1869. Funded entirely by public subscription, it is a massive tower, growing out of a thick forest on a hill, dominating the landscape for miles around. In a niche on the building is a massive bronze sculpture by D.W. Stevenson which is the model for the one here in Aberdeen.

The Aberdeen monument was opened by the Marquis of Lorne on 29 June 1888. It was a huge event for the people. Afterwards the Marquis received the freedom of the city. The burgess diploma bearing the city seal was tied round the Marquis's hat, as tradition demanded.

The original site for the statue was the 'mound' in Duthie Park (p.173) offered by the donor of the park, Miss Duthie. It had been chosen under the guidance of Her Majesty's Limner Sir Noel Paton and the architect Rowand Anderson. The council sent a deputation to visit the full-size plaster model of the statue in Stevenson's studio to check it met with their approval. The deputation was delighted with it and immediately began to make plans to find it a more prominent location in the city. A little precinct was created on the new municipal platform of Rosemount Viaduct. The idea was right, but the context changed when the neighbouring building was constructed. Today Wallace appears almost like a showman in a historical costume saying 'And, now, ladies and gentlemen, for your delectation!' as he appears to gesture towards His Majesty's Theatre. The statue was 'erected by funds bequeathed by John Steill of 38 Grange Road, Edinburgh'. On the statue is the whole story of Wallace's heroic life. Recently during conservation work it was discovered that the cast-iron armature inside the figure was completely eroded and that the statue itself was now hollow.

The Wallace Statue

Behind Wallace and grossly overshadowed by him is the boy-like figure of Prince Albert, seated in what appears to be an over-sized chair. This was the first statue to be raised to the deceased Prince Consort but it was moved from the corner of Union Street after a respectful period of mourning had passed and a statute of King Edward VII was put in its place. Albert was rather relegated to his current position. This statue was designed by the Glasgow-based Italian sculptor Baron Marochetti and was originally erected in Union Street in 1865. It was never a success, 'oppressed', as one critic claimed it was, 'by wardrobe and upholstery'. Further along Union Terrace is the occasionally garlanded monument to Scotland's national bard Robert Burns. This is a beautiful piece of work by H. Bain Smith (1892). In the poet's hand is (sometimes) a daisy, which is the occasional prize of trophy-hunters. The terrace on which the statue stands was part of the original Union Street plan and there is a group of houses of the period still there. However, the terrace was widened over arcades and embellished with balustrades by A. Marshall Mackenzie under the terms of the 1883 Extension and Improvement Act. The rebuilt arch of the Bow Brig of 1747 was incorporated into the structure. (The buildings of Union Terrace are discussed on p.64.)

Directly opposite Wallace is St Mark's Church, also designed by Marshall Mackenzie in 1892. The church was given a very solemn classical presence and monumentality because of its important position in the municipal townscape. Next is George Watt's Central Library, designed in 1891. All of this civic grandeur masked a rather forgotten area of the town, which can be reached by the steps called Donald's Way running down the side of the library. From old photographs this looks as though it would have been a fascinating if very run-down area, the Lower Denburn. The entire area was demolished in the 1960s. Recently an attempt has been made to give it back a sense of place. The Well of Spa has been restored and may be seen by going down the steps and back onto the walk via the rear of the library. The Well of Spa or 'Garden Nook Well' is dedicated to the Virgin Mary; it is an ancient one and was restored by the painter George Jamesone who acquired a lease of the 'playfield' near by where he hung his paintings.

The city's library has one of the best local-history collections in the country and a very friendly and knowledgeable staff. Carry on with the library on your right. On your left you will see the 'bookend' of Union Terrace. This is Arthur Mackinnon's clubhouse and hall for Aberdeen Union Club. Like the many Liberal clubs ostentatiously built during the early years of the twentieth century, the Union Club did not survive long. The building was converted to the Picturedrome Cinema in 1910 by a London-based businessman, Henry Phillips. Quite a small-scale operation, it was only the second permanent cinema in Aberdeen. Its auditorium was remodelled in Art Deco style in 1924 when it was renamed the Cinema House. From 1971 until 1991, like so many others, the building functioned as a bingo hall but it has now been nicely converted to a restaurant with a cinema theme and retains much of the detailing of the 1924 refit. The building seamlessly makes the connection between Union Terrace and Rosemount Viaduct. The change is marked by the use of smooth to rusticated (artfully rough) granite.

Aberdeen flattened out its inconvenient geography with a series of bold, magnificent bridges, viaducts and terraces, so for the visitor the city is built apparently on the flat, which makes for sudden views of buildings continuing four or five floors below ground level. The bridges are also treated as viewing platforms for the city. You can see this in the portrait of Archibald Simpson on p.28 where his wonderful cathedral-like Triple Kirks building is shown in the distant cityscape. It is a rationally laid out city with wide streets and sensible architecture but the backdrop is dramatic and artfully disordered.

Now we pass over Denburn and straight into a district fronted by suitably monumental tall tenements. We bear right over the magnificent Rosemount Viaduct. The Rosemount and Denburn viaducts were designed in 1886 by William Boulton after it was decided to link Rosemount and Schoolhill by a new 'bridge street' of the type begun as long ago as 1767 at Marischal Street (p.137). Under the terms of the Aberdeen Extension and Improvement Act of 1883 an 'iron-girder bridge' was 'to be erected across the Denburn'. The same logic had of course applied to Union Street and it has been part of an Aberdeen pattern of development ever since. The design of the bridge had to be modified in consultation with the Great North of Scotland Railway Company. The block facing us at nos. 1–27 Rosemount Viaduct on its sharp corner site is a huge curving complex of flats and shops designed in 1897 by the architects Brown & Watt for the Aberdeen Town and County Property Company.

Brown & Watt's design was for a massive group of six tenements, stylistically bonded into one huge composition. Almost opposite, at nos. 46–78, is a group of tenements of a more standard Aberdeen pattern. There are also six buildings, but they are kept apart by a pilaster defining each one. Further along is James Souttar's answer to the problem of creating a grandiose tenement. He uses rock-faced granite from top to bottom and makes a greater effort to present the building as a single composition by grouping the central windows in an advanced section. Sitting happily amongst all this is a typical Aberdeen tower block of the 1960s with the Denburn Health Centre at the base. The group seems to fit in well with the urban grain of Aberdeen in terms of colour and precision.

On our left is the Bon Accord Free Church of Scotland, opened in 1896 and designed by A. Marshall Mackenzie. This is a baroque-style church with a superb campanile that is best seen from Gilcomston Park. Gilcomston has its roots in a collection of weavers' houses built in the eighteenth century, but it became a full-scale suburb in the nineteenth when the word 'park' was added to lend prestige.

TENEMENTS

The tenement is a traditional Scottish building type whose function was to house the middle classes. It was not an inferior form of dwelling for 'artisans'. The first flatted blocks in the country were built in the late seventeenth century in Edinburgh at Mylne's Court. These were exclusive 'luxury flats' for lawyers with servants' quarters and all the offices of a town house on a slightly reduced scale. It is therefore a great misunderstanding to think of the Scottish tenement as historically inferior. The Aberdeen tenement is no different in this regard but it has been given a different architectural treatment, as we will see. It also has one crucial internal difference. The entrance passageway (the close) and its staircase are made of timber. This is unheard of elsewhere. In many Edinburgh tenements, even the private halls of the flats themselves and their kitchens have stone floors. Externally, the plainer Aberdeen tenements persisted with the 'nepus' gable, which takes accommodation past the roof line.

In Aberdeen tenements, generally of two or three storeys and an attic, bay windows never became very popular, but they were used widely on villas. Incised stonework in the manner of Alexander Thomson was translated into granite in some housing by the Aberdeen architects Pirie & Clyne, including a row of villas in Hamilton Place (1880s) and a highly ornate dwelling, with some Gothic detailing, at 50 Queens Road (1886). By the mid-eighteenth century, Edinburgh's New Town had more flatted dwellings than it did vertically stacked housing. So were these tenements fit for the new urban middle classes or not? Very often, tenements fronted main roads or formed the centre or end blocks of larger buildings, but there had been continuing worries over their status, even from the late eighteenth century when Edinburgh town council had rejected houses 'set in flates' for Charlotte Square. William Burn's Henderson Row of 1829 was a tenement masquerading, through its use of porticoed main-door flats, as a row of houses. Architecturally, indeed, there were many links with middle-class terraces of individual dwellings, but the overall aesthetic seemed to have remained closer to neo-classical uniformity and severity. Architectural embellishment tended to be graded on a scale with status. Scottish tenements are essentially European in character; in contrast with European tenements, however, the use of fine ashlar construction set Scottish tenements apart. Edinburgh in this period saw a vigorous redevelopment drive, based on a City Improvement Act (passed 1867), as in Glasgow or Dundee and Aberdeen. In the case of Edinburgh the romantic principles already established led to a Scotch Baronial street architecture. The linking of the tenement with national Romanticism through the use of the Baronial style was a crucial development and this was achieved largely through the example of Aberdeen. Billings had drawn attention to the 'peculiarities and merits' of old burghs using Aberdeen as an example and soon afterwards a Baronial improvement scheme was promoted privately in Edinburgh to build a curving street from the High Street down to Waverley Station. The resulting scheme, Cockburn Street (designed between 1859 and 1864 by Peddie & Kinnear), provided a new, romantic architectural gateway to the Old Town of Edinburgh. Typically, this Edinburgh street was very influential in Aberdeen.

Rosemount Viaduct from below

Beyond the tenements is a very pretty row of villas – or so they appear. The ones on our right are flatted houses formed in the likeness of villas to reflect the would-be suburban character of Gilcomston. When it was developed in the 1850s, Gilcomston was very much a suburb, set in the countryside with the Denburn flowing through. This was before the huge imposition of the Denburn and Rosemount viaducts with their ten- and eleven-storey buildings.

We now walk back up Gilcomston Park and turn right into **Rose-**

mount Viaduct. Stevenson Court, on the left, is part of a large redevelopment of the area which took place from the early 1970s. The new grey blocks fit in reasonably well with the tenements, keeping up a long-established continuity. Opposite, on the corner of Baker Street and South Mount Street, is a low tenement built of rubble ending in a typical Aberdeen corner. ('Rubble' is an architectural term for roughly finished stonework. The most basic form is 'random' rubble but it can also be laid in regular courses with its edges squared off.) And straight ahead is a tenement for the twentieth century, designed by Aberdeen city council after a visit to the much admired communal housing of turn-of-the-century 'red' Vienna, Karl Marx Hof. This is Rosemount Square, a pioneering housing block designed to reflect the city's housing tradition and to fit in, but to 'humanise' it with gardens and communal facilities for the residents. The idea of a curved building set within a flowing but geometric plan was a good one. As usual, Aberdeen took a good idea and

Rosemount Square

clothed it in native dress – granite. The city architect A.B. Gardiner with Leo Durnin drew up the scheme in 1938. It was completed ten years later. The structure is granite, of course, but with prefabricated details and concrete balconies to the courtyard elevations. At the entrance to Rosemount Square is a shallow relief sculpture above the archway by T.B. Huxley-Jones entitled *The Spirit of the Winds*.

On Leadside Road we are skirting the site of the Gilcomston Flour Mills. (The name 'Leadside' suggests the side of the 'lade' – the artificial channel taken off the Denburn to turn the mill.) There was a large amount of clearance in this area, including the mills themselves, which stood on the site of the unusual group of flats in front with their big mansard roofs.

Now we cross over Jack's Brae, named, like so many Scottish streets, after the feuar, in this case John Jack of Gilcomston. We find ourselves in **Northfield Place**, a tree-lined street of tenements, which brings us out into Esslemont Avenue, a great granite cliff of tenements with the characteristic 'nepus' gable taking the accommodation up beyond the roofline. It is easy to spoil this effect with the addition of box dormers. Peeping over into the back courts with their three storeys below pavement level is the Denburn flowing close to the tenements, under Esslemont Road.

To our right across Esslemont Avenue in its spacious park-like setting is the *alma mater* of one of Aberdeen's most famous sons, George Gordon, sixth Lord Byron (1788–1824) (see p.95). We know he has achieved superstar status by being known simply as 'Byron' on the **statue** which fronts the school. The statue is a late work of Pittendreigh MacGillivray, one of Scotland's greatest sculptors and an early Scottish

Northfield Place

The statue of Byron in front of Aberdeen Grammar School

Nationalist. He designed it in 1914 but it was not executed until after his death, by Alexander J. Leslie in 1920. The grammar school itself was rebuilt in a very suitable Romantic Scots-Baronial style by James Matthews between 1861 and 1863. Within the court of the building is the rebuilt centre feature from the old grammar school of 1758.

The relocated school was not without the controversy which often surrounds new buildings. There was a competition to find a designer for

Skene Terrace and the dome of St Mark's Church

the new building, which was won by George Smith of Edinburgh. Smith was no relation of the Aberdeen architect Smiths but he was an experienced architect who had built some of Glasgow's most beautiful terraces. James Matthews won the second prize, which was £50. Local architects felt that £150 first-prize money could have been saved by simply appointing a local designer. However, the council were obliged to pay up under the terms of the competition but they decided to ask the local man, James Matthews, to do the work even though he had not won the competition. Matthews offered an Italianate or a Baronial design. This was not unusual during the nineteenth-century battle of the styles. Another local architect, William Kerr, had published a successful architectural pattern book showing how a 'gentleman's house' could be adapted for any style without altering the plan. In the event, the romance of the Baronial, particularly with the Byron connection, was preferred.

Now we go down Skene Street. On the corner with Esslemont Avenue is the former Skene Street Congregational Church, designed by Marshall Mackenzie in 1887. The church's 'temple front' design perhaps shows the enduring influence of Glasgow's Alexander 'Greek' Thomson, an advocate of a powerful, monumental Greek Revival architecture whose work is closely associated with the growth of nineteenth-century Glasgow. Thomson's work had a presence which occasionally attracted notice from like-minded architects. Apart from the similarity with many of Aberdeen's churches, you will see the influence of Thomson in the domestic work of Pirie & Clyne at Hamilton Place (p.228) and Argyle Place. On the opposite corner is a more grandiose church design by Brown & Watt of 1901–3. This is the Melville Church, now converted to flats. Conversion is of course a good thing when a church becomes redundant, but here we have lost a good interior with a large 'horseshoe' auditorium. On the cast-iron lamps at the entrance you can faintly see the founder's mark, 'Walter Macfarlane of Glasgow'. Macfarlane's iron foundry at the Saracen Works in Possilpark, Glasgow, was one of the biggest in the world. They supplied everything from railings to bandstands and flat-packed palaces for export.

On Skene Street there are domestic buildings on the corner opposite the church and then a massive granite warehouse squeezed onto the neighbouring site, right up to the street line. This was a store holding grain from Gilcomston Mills. When the mills were lost it was converted to a furniture store. An American company took it over and turned it into the Huntly Hotel and it was thereafter refitted as the Copthorne Hotel.

Along Skene Street is one of Aberdeen's big 1960s interventions. This had been a run-down area of poor housing and industry and the council cleared it all away and redeveloped the area, keeping what they could. Most of these schemes seem to blend very well with the existing townscape. The big block is not oriented towards the street but towards the direction of the sun, in line with modernist thinking.

Now we can concentrate on more traditional ideas of heritage. The building opposite is Skene Place, which is quite an untypical piece of Aberdeen housing built about 1815. The houses are grouped in a 'palace block' format, as if one single composition. This is one of the city's few successful attempts at this. Even Union Street was in fact a succession of houses rather than groups, like Edinburgh's Charlotte Square which was the type of scheme to which many Aberdeen architects aspired. The building has all of its original glazing and delicate fanlights over the central doorway.

Mackie Place is just to the left of Skene Place. Here we have a picturesque enclave of very pretty houses grouped around the Denburn, which runs in the open at this point. The building at the end of the lane is a big Dutch gabled pair of houses of about 1810, but later overshadowed by the tenements of Northfield Place behind. The gables were an attempt to give interest to a standard plan and elevation. They were later much used in the city. The little haven was hemmed in by development as the city grew. We can walk by the burn a short distance and back up onto Skene Street via Skene Lane in front of us.

We should now go back up on to Skene Street, noticing in passing the little traditional buildings with their pantiles. Immediately on our left as we reach the main street is Gilcomston Primary School. This is where Aberdeen's Gaelic Unit is based. Children attending the unit are taught through the medium of Scots Gaelic. This is part of a national scheme, which is already reversing the long decline of the language. We should now cross the road and take the first right into Summer Street. The church on our right is Denburn Parish Church, which was built in 1771 by William Smith, the architect of Marischal Street and the father of the celebrated city architect John Smith, who added the vestry in 1845. Gilcomston was originally a 'chapel of ease', which meant that it was built for the convenience of Gilcomstonites who had had to travel all the way to St Machar's in Old Aberdeen since the area was in that parish. The church was made *quoad sacra* (full parish status) in 1834. Traces of the earlier building can be seen from the rear, but Duncan MacMillan added a new frontage to Summer Street in 1878.

Opposite the church is **Skene Terrace**. We should now continue our walk down this road. Here we have another row of houses, but this time all different and all feued and constructed in individual plots (although built at the same time). The first thing we notice is the different types of granite that have been used from building to building and the way these have been constructed. The range of treatments goes from rubble to squared and laid in courses at no. 40. We can also contrast the simplicity of the door at no. 46 with the comparatively grand arched entrance at no. 44. At the end of the block is an elegant screen wall, masking the rear of Brown & Watt's tenement on Rosemount Viaduct. Sir David Gill (1843–1914) lived at no. 50 Skene Terrace. He was the first person to photograph the moon, which he did as long ago as 1868. He was appointed His Majesty's Astronomer at the Cape of Good Hope in 1879. He was also a fellow of the Royal Society.

On our right now are two less grandiose survivors, both of about 1800. No. 35 is a single-storey house with a distinctive tea-caddy roof; its neighbour of 70 years later faces North Silver Street up the little steps. Continue the walk down Skene Terrace and we find ourselves back at Rosemount Viaduct where the walk ends.

Rennie's Wynd to Castlegate, Gallowgate, Mounthooly and the Lochlands

A walk through Aberdeen's oldest streets to the city's earliest industrial suburb

The Green

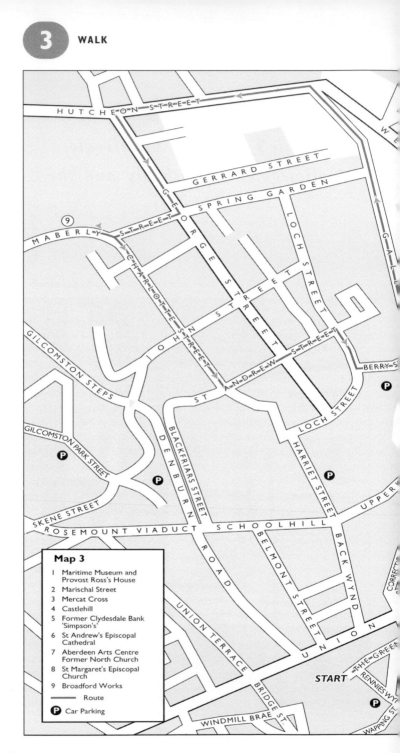

Map 3

1 Maritime Museum and Provost Ross's House
2 Marischal Street
3 Mercat Cross
4 Castlehill
5 Former Clydesdale Bank 'Simpson's'
6 St Andrew's Episcopal Cathedral
7 Aberdeen Arts Centre Former North Church
8 St Margaret's Episcopal Church
9 Broadford Works

— Route
🅿 Car Parking

START

Main Places of Interest	Maritime Museum, South Church, St Margaret's Convent, Broadford Works
Circular/linear	Linear, part circular
Starting point	Back Wynd Stairs
Finishing point	Marischal College
Distance	2 miles
Terrain	Pavements and (avoidable) steps
Public transport	n/a
Sections	Rennie's Wynd – Castlegate, Castlegate – Marischal College
Architects	Archibald Simpson, A.G.R. Mackenzie
Nearby walks	1, 2
Refreshments	Plenty of cafés, bars and restaurants
Notes	This is a fairly long tour which has a gentle incline along the side of St Katherine's Hill and continues through the two historic centres of Aberdeen.

'Be blythe and blissful, burgh of Aberdein'
WILLIAM DUNBAR

This walk starts at Rennie's Wynd where it meets the King's Highway, just at the foot of Back Wynd stairs. These stairs are a continuation of Back Wynd (see p.96) running along the rear wall of St Nicholas' Churchyard. It is perhaps an unlikely start to a historic walking tour. But we should press on. It may not seem like it, but here we are on the main road into Aberdeen from the south – the King's Highway – until its prestige was cancelled out by the building of Union Street high above. In a situation like this, history is often hidden in the most unexpected places and indeed this is probably Aberdeen's most historic area, where much archaeological excavation has been carried out.

Much of Aberdeen's past exists below the hurly-burly of the modern city. In this case we are beside a gigantic shopping centre straddling Aberdeen's medieval 'ring road' which had to find its way around St Katherine's Hill. There was a little bridge near here called Bow Brig, which took the traveller from the south over the Denburn. That stream is now underground. The new centre of the 1960s very controversially blocked out the view east from Union Bridge. It was a bold attempt finally to solve the problem of the railway station's link with Union Street, but the resulting staircase has the appearance of a compromise and has satisfied few. A low-tech, rather dingy concrete staircase begins in a rather intimidating area and places the intrepid climber in the back of a shopping mall.

The nineteenth century had provided an élitist elevator link for patrons of the Palace Hotel at a point near here. The Palace was a superb building designed in 1891 for the great North of Scotland Railway Co. The building's head was in Union Street and its feet were down here, near the station. The railway company would usher the rail-borne guests from the train to the hotel via a passenger lift provided, the company proudly advertised, by the American Elevator Co., lifts still being quite a novelty in 1891. Luggage was taken in a separate lift. It was a stunning building with a range of lavish interiors but the hotel was burnt out during the war and replaced with the C&A department store (now the Travel Lodge hotel in Union Street).

Rennie's Wynd was the location of a quite scandalous episode in Aberdeen's history, involving nothing less than slavery. The scheme involved selling workers for the colonies who had been kidnapped in Aberdeen, kept aboard ship or in a barn here at Rennie's Wynd and then forcibly sent to North America to work on the plantations. In the year 1743 alone, 69 young people 'disappeared' and were presumed 'stolen'. One of these youths was Peter Williamson who made something of a career out of his experiences. He published a book detailing his treat-

The Green Market

ment at the hands of Aberdeen's slavers. That was shameful enough for the good burgesses, but then Williamson created a kind of one-man show in which the adventure was graphically played out, complete with Native Americans. Taking the show on tour he arrived finally in Aberdeen and was promptly jailed for defamation. His book was ostentatiously 'burned by the common hangman' at the Market Cross. He was kept in prison until he signed a statement saying that his allegations were untrue. It seems that this confession was rather forced out of him. Undaunted, he raised an action in Edinburgh against the magistrates who had treated him so badly and was awarded £100. He used the money to set himself up in Edinburgh as a tavern-keeper, rather in the way that a retired footballer would hope to trade on his fame.

Walking away from the shopping centre and towards the open area in front of us we find ourselves in **the Green**. Historically, this was a market, a typical piece of widened road on the main entry into a burgh. It is traditionally also the very cradle of the modern city but most of the buildings belong to the late nineteenth century when the Green became an industrial quarter. At nos. 61–65 you can see a survivor of an earlier period. This is a pub, Old King's Highway, a building of the 1790s made of tooled Loanhead granite. It has arched openings to the ground floor suggesting its past commercial activity. We can also see the remains of a demolished house to the left, with a date of 1741 on the skewputt (the bracket at the bottom end of the flat piece of stone defining the wallhead, the skew). Recently the area around the Green has been beautifully restored with traditional paving and a sympathetic infill of flats and shops. There is a good deal of continental-style activity of bars

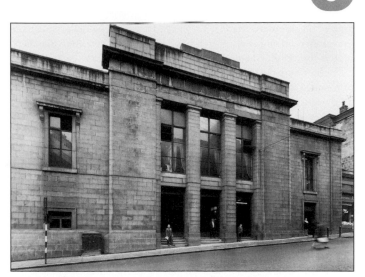

The former Aberdeen Market in Market Street, now demolished

and cafés: the best of these is Café 52 and Bistro Verde, opposite. Looking to end of the Green the great concrete drum of the **Aberdeen Market** makes its presence felt. The building is much maligned but in fact it has some of the power and monumentality of the building it replaced. This was Archibald Simpson's market of 1842, a very early covered shopping mall with a massive external frontage of great granite pilasters. Inside was a 'bazaar', a collection of stalls. This was really the forerunner of the modern department store. Simpson's great building was demolished in 1971 to the horror of the conservation lobby, including Sir John Betjeman. Aberdeen has rather specialised in shopping malls. The famous Edinburgh firm of Robert Matthew Johnson Marshall designed the replacement for the Aberdeen Market but since then the city has gone on to develop ever bigger and better examples. There was a plan to tear down this later building and to re-erect Simpson's original, but it failed on financial grounds. The cost of the granite alone would make the building ruinously expensive. If you look away up to your left you will see a death-defying oriel window jutting out over the Green. Just below this is the entrance to the East Green. For a real taste of underground Aberdeen, take a walk along the East Green to Carnegie's Brae. Look up at the huge structure carrying Union Street. If you're brave enough you can follow this road under Union Street where it pops up at Marks & Spencer's on Netherkirkgate. This was the place where John 'Spanish' Phillip (see p.36) served his apprenticeship as a house painter before becoming one of the most celebrated artists of nineteenth-century Britain.

We should now return to the Green and continue around the curved flank of the Aberdeen Market. Carmelite Lane and Carmelite Street are named after the monastery which stood on the site. There were members of this order in Aberdeen from the late thirteenth century. The Carmelites were the White Friars or the Friars of the Order of Our Lady of Mount Carmel in Palestine and were founded there in 1156. They were made a mendicant (begging) order in 1247, which is around the time they seem to have appeared in Aberdeen. The Carmelite Friars' habit was brown with a white cloak and scapular (the long strip of cloth worn about the shoulders). The complex of friary buildings appears to have spread all over the immediate area of the Green: over Rennie's Wynd, Martin's Lane and Carmelite Street. There was also a Trinitarian House near to the friary. Trinity Friars (an order founded in Rome in 1198 to redeem Christian captives from the Muslims during the Crusades). The existence of these buildings has been confirmed by recent archaeological investigations in the area. These excavations are carried out in the short period between demolition of an old building and the construction of a replacement. The opportunities for archaeologists in such a historic area are rare. The findings of the recent work have led to the suggestion that the Green was not at the very centre of Aberdeen but perhaps on the periphery. This is based on the knowledge that friaries were generally located on the edge of burghs.

The very skinny 'gushet' buildings of the area are packed onto the tiny sites defined by medieval ownership but with nineteenth-century patterns of dense urban development. The Grampian Hotel (formerly the Imperial Hotel) on Trinity Street and Carmelite Lane is an impressive design of 1869 by James Souttar with further additions by William Henderson in the 1880s. Unusually, the building has a Gothic style. It was very rare for a building in Scotland which was not a church or a religious institution of some type to be built in this manner. The second- and third-storey windows have pointed arches. There are also sculptured figures on a canopy over the entrance and a very handsome oriel window further to the north. The junction of Trinity Street and Carmelite Lane has a battlemented round tower to complete the effect, along with another three oriel windows in Carmelite Lane.

A hotel could possibly be built in the Gothic manner but it would be far more likely to be in a Scots-Baronial style, reminiscent of Abbotsford, Sir Walter Scott's home in the Borders. Scotland was associated in the minds of tourists with the historical adventures of Scott's characters and a hotel could not lose if it suggested that association through its architecture. The large building at no. 23 Stirling Street and nos. 20, 22, 24 Guild Street is another example of the big Baronial style of architecture applied to a hotel covering half a city block. Here the detailing is quite thin, almost superficial. Not surprisingly, hotels clustered around the city's main railway station and harbour. The biggest but not the best of these is the Station Hotel, which occupies the prime position directly opposite the railway terminus. Built in 1900, its eclectic design reflects the architecturally uncertain age.

In Hadden Street, The Market Arms pub is at nos. 11, 13 and has an excellent frontage with etched glass. At nos. 11, 13, 15 Exchange Street there is part of the original Aberdeen Corn Exchange built in about 1857 to provide a meeting place for corn merchants. At nos. 27, 29 Exchange Street is a fine example of a mid-nineteenth-century warehouse building very much in the manner of Archibald Simpson who had set the standard for this type of stately commercial building in the city. Simpson planned the nearby Market Street for the city authorities along with the New Market at the head of Exchange Street. The idea of commercial buildings forming part of a dignified urban group really caught on. The warehouse was built as the National Security Savings Bank in 1845. The big corner commercial block at 12 Exchange Street was built as a Masonic hall in 1870.

In front of us now on the opposite side of Market Street is the Hotel Metro, a typically suave, classical Aberdeen building. This used to be a Mechanics' Institute, a forerunner of the technical university. The building was designed by Archibald Simpson in 1846 and was one of the very last he produced. Both Simpson and John Smith were great patrons of this institution. Market Street was cut through along with many other civic improvements typical of the mid-nineteenth century when cities were taking their modern shape. The creation of Market Street also swept away a notorious slum called Putachieside. This early example of 'clearance' as usual involved the laying-out of subsidiary side streets, Hadden Street, Market Street and Exchange Street.

The tramways made much use of these improved streets. The converted electric tram depot of 1900–10 is on a prominent corner site at Market Street and North Esplanade West by the riverside. Aberdeen's tram network was one of the most progressive in the UK until 1955. Three companies shared the network: Aberdeen District Tramways Co. which established horse lines in 1874 which were extended and electrified between 1899 and 1902; Aberdeen Corporation Tramways with short lines in the congested streets of the suburbs (Duthie Park and Torry); and Aberdeen Suburban Tramways Co.

At no. 45 Market Street is another example of the work of James Souttar, who extended an earlier (1848) block for the former Douglas Hotel. This was itself given a new façade in an interesting Art Deco manner by Marshall Mackenzie & Son.

We now enter Aberdeen's famous **Shiprow**, which curved in its present line from the beginning, but which begins here a little inauspiciously, showing signs of wear and tear. Press on. Near here was Shiprow (or Trinity) Port which controlled access to the town from the harbour. There is now no sign of the structure. On the left as we enter there is an old Loanhead granite building with a typical Aberdeen arch.

Shiprow and the Maritime Museum

Beyond are the remains of an old and venerable structure at no. 64 Shiprow. This is an early fourteenth-century wall and doorway, possibly with other pieces brought from elsewhere. Tradition has it that these are the remains of the Friary of St Katherine. As Shiprow connects with the short section to the harbour via Shore Brae, you will see the off-centre tower of Marshall Mackenzie's harbour offices building (1883–85) right on the waterfront. This is part of a group of interesting buildings on Regent Quay, including a private house of 1771 converted to a customs house and several granite warehouses. You will also see more of the prolific work of Marshall Mackenzie at Regent House (1898) which, with its swelling centrepiece, is a dynamic composition.

Shiprow is an important street. It gave access to the harbour and therefore the city's maritime heart. It was the burgh's premier thoroughfare right up to the building of Marischal Street in 1767 (see below). The area became one of Aberdeen's great slums of the nineteenth and twentieth centuries but the jewel in its crown was saved. This is Provost Ross's House, onto which has been built the superb Maritime Museum. The church on the other side of the new building is the former Trinity Church.

The Aberdeen Maritime Museum is open Monday to Saturday, 10 a.m.– 5 p.m., and Sundays, noon–3 p.m. This is a marvellous museum which promises to give you some indication of what it's like to put on a survival suit, strap yourself into a helicopter and fly 150 miles to a North Sea platform. Hundreds of oil workers make this trip every week. And once you're there, what is it like to live and work on board an oil-rig, hundreds of miles out in the middle of the North Sea? The Maritime Museum's 8.5m-high model of an oil production platform dominates the stunning glazed wall of the entrance and is surrounded by three floors of computer displays, reconstructions and hands-on exhibits giving a very real account of life offshore. An actual accommodation cabin shows the living arrangements and the full-size replica oil platform control room shows how oil and gas are processed through the platform. The accounts of life on a trawler are also very well presented and really bring home the extreme conditions under which fishermen work.

Other major exhibits include the massive nineteenth-century lighthouse assembly from Rattray Head and an original (full-sized) teak deck-house of the kind used on the famous North Boats which sailed between Aberdeen and the Northern Isles. You can watch archive footage of ship launchings or see how previous generations of fisherfolk lived and worked. You can also view reconstructions of a 1925 ship's drawing office and a steam trawler deck.

The museum also takes in **Provost Ross's House** itself, which was designed in 1593 by George Johnstone. The house is the only survivor of a clean sweep that was made of the area in the 1950s and 1960s. It was decided by Aberdeen's quite conservation-minded planning authorities that this historic building had to be saved, even as its slum neighbours were destroyed. This indeed is the original basis for 'listing' historic buildings: to identify those that had to be saved as area demolition progressed. The handsome arcaded building on the left is an eighteenth-

Provost Ross's House, Shiprow

Provost Ross's House prior to rehabilitation; the cinema behind has since been demolished

century addition to Provost Ross's House. The towered building on the right is the original structure. The screen wall was restored in 1954 along with the rest of the building by one of Scotland's earliest exponents of the 'listing' of historic buildings, A.G.R. Mackenzie. Aberdeen now has more than 1,200 listed buildings. At first it was assumed that only the most ancient and venerated structures would be listed but the appreciation of architectural heritage has grown to the extent that a huge range of buildings, from the station to the Broadford Works (see p.154) are included. Some of the rooms in Provost Ross's House retain their original features such as simple fireplaces and windows. Until the late fifteenth century, glazed windows were a rarity in Scotland and elsewhere. Windows in buildings like this or Provost Skene's House (p.76) consisted of small shutters which had to be opened to let in the light – but they also let in the wind and rain. It was not until glass itself was improved sufficiently that windows, as we would recognise them today, were widely introduced. These windows took the form of 'casements', which opened simply and were hung on a hinge at the side. This system is still widely used throughout the world and in many buildings in this country.

On the other side of the street there is currently nothing but one of the best city views: right over the docks. There are plans to build here in order to re-establish the 'canyon' of Shiprow and its sense of being enclosed. We are now at the top of Shiprow and we should turn right into Exchequer Row. The street was formerly called 'Skakkarium' which comes from 'scaccarium', meaning 'the chequered cloth', from where we derive the word 'exchequer'. Go past Quinn's Bar in Exchequer Row and up into Castle Street. You should try to imagine that we've been confined in a close medieval street and now we break out into the great granite amphitheatre of the town market. This was a really ambitious 'double square' designed to underline Aberdeen's importance. But it was also quite necessary, given the amount of buying and selling that was taking place in the burgh. As the very centre of Aberdeen, from early times, the market square represented the inner sanctum of the burgh, the natural end point of the many royal visits which were made to the city. One such 'progress' was recorded by the poet William Dunbar in 1511. Dunbar was a Scots 'makar' or poet attached to the brilliant Renaissance court of King James IV. In 1511 he accompanied the Queen, Margaret Tudor, to Aberdeen on a state visit. The burgh made very lavish arrangements for the coming of 'so noble a lady', and Dunbar's poem 'Be Blyth and Blisfull, Burgh of Aberdeen' celebrates the event. One of the verses describes the scene:

> The Streitis war all hung with tapestrie,
> Gret was the pres of peopill, dwelt about,
> And pleasant padgeanes playit prattelie.
> The legeis all did to their lady loutt,
> Quha was convoyed with ane royall routt
> Off gryte barrounes and lustie ladyis schene.
> 'Welcum, our quein!', the commones gaif ane schout:
> Be blyth and blissfull, burcht of Aberdein.

The Queen was escorted by four burgesses 'in gounes of velout' to 'bear the paill of velues cramase [crimson velvet] abone hir heid'. As the procession passed by 'four and twenty madinis . . . all clad in greine, playand on timberallis [tambourines] and singand rycht sweitlie'. The 'royal routt' was a carefully planned journey from the harbour, up the Shiprow, as we have just walked, and through Exchequer Row to Castlegate where the Queen lodged.

We should now walk over towards Marischal Street. As we pass, notice the 'Mannie'. The Mannie, a lead figure of Eros, is sometimes also called the Green Fountain (on account of its former location) or the Castlegate well. It is a water cistern built in 1706 in the style of Sir William Bruce's Edinburgh wells. It was planned to be covered in gilt statues. This was later reduced to a single, rather diminutive figure when the cost was estimated at £1,571. This statue stands on the fountain to commemorate Aberdeen's first public water supply. It was originally at the east end of **Castle Street**, in what is popularly referred to as 'Castlegate', and it was moved to the Green in 1852, where it remained for over a hundred years. After much of the usual public outcry over the positioning of statues, the Mannie was re-erected at the west end of Castle Street in its present position in 1974. The well was fed by springs

Castle Street

from Cardensheugh (p.229) and brought by six lead pipes to Castlegate. The fountain stands on an area known historically as 'the plainstanes' where merchants met to do business.

As we continue along Castle Street, there is a pend (passageway) at no. 55. This takes us through to Aberdeen's first Assembly Rooms. These are two very grand rooms topped by a viewing platform where polite society could watch the comings and goings of the harbour from a safe distance. The building is to be converted to a pub. John Barbour (1320–95) lived on a site at 53 Castlegate, which is now a branch of the Bank of Scotland. Barbour was a chronicler or early historian who wrote a famous life of Robert the Bruce called simply *The Bruis*. An influential provost, Menzies of Pitfodels (see p.98), later had a house here which he abandoned for the 'new town' of Belmont Street.

The next building, on the corner with **Marischal Street**, is extremely important for the city. In the 1820s and 1830s the great 'discovery' of granite classicism was made but in the later period it was also brilliantly used in Romantic architectural compositions. The best of these is also here in Castle Street, namely Peddie & Kinnear's Town House (p.54). For the moment let us consider the first breakthrough in the invention of granite classicism.

Aberdeen granite was previously considered too hard to be used for decorative work, but the Greek revival offered the chance to bring out its hard-edged precision within a wide, modern frontage which cut across several feus (plots) for the Aberdeen Banking Company in

1801–2. This is the city's first fully dressed ashlar granite building. It was designed by James Burn of Haddington near Edinburgh. However, it was Aberdeen stonemasons who showed how the material could be used and this devotion to classical granite continued right up until the 1940s. In the 1830s the cutting of granite was revolutionised by the introduction of steam-powered technology. The north-east granite industry expanded and even began an export drive. To make way for the banks' showpiece new headquarters, several historic buildings had to go. The most important of these was the Earl Marischal's house, which had seen a great deal of history from its vantage-point overlooking the square.

Mary Queen of Scots had been in Aberdeen on a royal progress intended to bring the various feuding families of the north-east together under her sovereignty. Unfortunately, the Queen's presence in Aberdeen only seemed to make things worse. A long-standing quarrel between the Ogilvies of Deskford and the Huntly family ended with the famous Battle of Corrichie of 1562 between Ogilvie and Huntly. This was no trivial feud. It stemmed from the murder in an Edinburgh street of Lord Ogilvie by Sir John Gordon, one of Huntly's sons. This same John Gordon was widely rumoured to be Mary's lover and therefore a potential husband. Since the Huntly family were Catholics, it was feared, by Protestants of course, that a marriage of the two would lead to the re-establishment of Catholicism as the state religion in Scotland. Mary dealt with her supposed lover very harshly, throwing him in an Edinburgh jail. The young man escaped and made his way back to his native Aberdeenshire. Along with his father, he mounted an attack on Aberdeen with an army of a thousand men, rather playing into the hands of his enemies who collected a much superior force and routed his army at Corrichie,

Marischal Street

about 12 miles from the city. The Earl of Huntly died in the battle but his sons were taken prisoner. The younger of the two, 18-year-old Sir Adam Gordon, was pardoned on account of his youth, but his elder brother, Sir John, was held accountable, tried and sentenced to death. The execution took place here in Castle Street only two days after the young nobleman's defeat at Corrichie.

George Buchanan, the celebrated contemporary historian, says of Sir John Gordon that 'he was generally very pitied and lamented, for he was a noble youth, very handsome, and entering on the prime of his age'. At the time of the execution, Mary was staying in the house of the Earl Marischal, which stood just at the point where Marischal Street begins. From a window of the house she was able to look down on the scene. It is said that Mary was forced to witness the execution of her lover, which was carried out not in the usual way – by the hand of an axeman – but with a terrible machine called 'The Maiden', a very successful prototype for the guillotine. The blade of the actual instrument used in the execution is on display on the top floor of Provost's Skene's House.

Mary's father, James V, had earlier run into some trouble in the city. He had visited Aberdeen in 1537 immediately before his first French marriage, to Mary of Lorraine, the mother of Mary Stuart. During his visit a plot was discovered to assassinate him 'by shot of culvering', that is by sniper at one of his public engagements, possibly from one of the windows here in Castle Street. This was a particularly evil form of assassination, which Scotland seems to have given the world. The man behind the scheme was the superbly named Master of Forbes, who was accused by the Earl of Huntly. Lord Forbes and his son, the Master, were arrested and tried. The father was acquitted but the son was sentenced to be hanged. This was regarded as a gross insult – not the finding of the court but the sentence: hanging was for common criminals. Friends of the Master pleaded on his behalf for him to suffer beheading and quartering. With friends like that you might think that the poor young man didn't need enemies, but hanging in those days was a very undignified way to go – a very long drawn-out process involving slow strangulation rather than instant death at the hands of a good axeman. As we saw above, Mary Queen of Scots herself witnessed the much more scientific Huntly-inspired execution here 25 years later.

The Mercat Cross, which was placed exactly in front of the Tolbooth, was the traditional place for executions in Aberdeen from the seventeenth century. The last one to be held here was that of William Webster, who incriminated himself in time-honoured fashion in 1787. Among other crimes, including operating a loaded wheel-of-fortune, Webster had stolen a white linen gown from a young girl. Months passed before he was brought to trial and by this time the girl had grown. The gown was produced as evidence but Webster was confident that the case could not be proved. After all this time, surely the girl could not be certain the gown was hers. Webster wanted to press the point and demanded she try on the garment. Reluctantly she did so, but in pulling it over her head she noticed a tiny bloodstain which she had made on the gown after pricking her finger when sewing it. Webster was condemned to death and hanged on this spot. The traditional Aberdeen warning to a ne'er-do-well until quite recently was 'you'll die facing Marischal Street!'.

Marischal Street was the city's first attempt at radical improvement based on engineering. The houses were built from 1767 in a straight line from Castlegate on the site of the Earl Marischal's house down to the harbour. This is where the idea of cancelling out the city's uneven topography by building up on arches was first experimented with – very successfully. At the central point was Bannerman's Bridge, which was designed by William Law in 1767 and replaced in 1983 when Virginia Street became a dual carriageway. Two houses on the north side of the gap were also demolished as part of the road scheme. Marischal Street was above all to be regular and built of granite – still of the rougher Loanhead type at this date – its roofs made of slate. To see the contrast between the older and rougher Loanhead granite and the new polished granite of the bank on the corner, look closely at the junction of the two as you make your way down Marischal Street. Look up at the roofs of the buildings and notice how the chimney stacks are granite at the front but brick to the rear. This was grandeur on a budget. Anything you couldn't easily see was made of a cheaper material.

Many of the buildings of Marischal Street have been altered over time but at no. 30 there is a good 'survivor'. This was the home of Provost William Young of Sheddocksley. Below the level of the bridge the design changes slightly and varies to a greater extent from house to house. It is altogether more up-market, with columned doorpieces, fanlights, boot-scrapers and Edinburgh-style balconies. William Smith, father of the celebrated city architect John Smith, probably designed these buildings. Marischal Street was a flyover bridge street like Edinburgh's South Bridge and also, of course, the city's own later Union Street. In this enclosed street of 1760s houses, you suddenly hear the roar of traffic beneath you and you realise you are on a bridge, 'a very handsome arch which must attract the attention of the traveller', according to John Pennant, the celebrated early travel writer. The elegance of the bridge is reflected at no. 46, where there is a very tall house with columns and three bay windows. The artist William Dyce (1806–64) lived at 48 Marischal Street. He was one of Queen Victoria's favourite painters, a deeply religious artist who produced highly realistic large-scale pictures of biblical events, controversially set in Scottish landscapes. Just beyond, at nos. 50–54, was Aberdeen's first major permanent theatre, put up in 1795 'after a design by Mr Holland, architect'. It was later demolished. George Thompson, the owner of clipper ships, lived at no. 35.

Standing on the bridge, we can look down at the Aberdeen Shore

The harbour, photographed by George Washington Wilson, c.1880

Porters' Society warehouse complex to the east and west of the bridge. The Shore Porters is a very ancient institution, established (as the company never tire of announcing) in 1498. The Porters had a monopoly on the movement of goods on and off merchant ships, and they continue to this day as a private concern. The sweeping road beneath, which links the **harbour** with Castlehill, was named Virginia Street in honour of the New World trade, but Aberdeen lost out almost completely to Glasgow when the Clyde was dredged and a shorter link to the Americas was made, undercutting Aberdeen by days.

Looking down to the end of Marischal Street you may see a ship bound for the Baltic or, for a few days each year, the quite magnificent site of the Tall Ships Race which calls at Aberdeen and transforms the harbour into something truly magical. We should now retrace our steps and go back up to the Castlegate.

Such a historic area is full of stories, some of which may even be true. The tale is told that Rob Roy MacGregor once visited his uncle in Aberdeen, who was none other than the Professor of Medicine, James Gregory. (Many MacGregors dropped the 'Mac' in the aftermath of the clan's outlawing. Rob Roy himself was also known as Campbell.) The reason for Rob Roy's visit was to persuade his cousin, the professor's son, to join him in the Jacobite cause. The father was against the plan, of course, and Rob Roy left reluctantly, but he walked straight into a detachment of Redcoats, from whom he fled. The Redcoats gave chase all the way to the Leucher Burn at Culter where he had a choice: to jump or to die. Of course Rob Roy made the astonishing leap and a statue there commemorates his remarkable feat. This was a feat that Rob Roy apparently repeated all over the country if we are to judge the number of 'Rob Roy's Leaps' there are. Other stories are certainly true and were dutifully recorded in the Burgh Records. Witch-hunting broke out here in 1596. Investigators found that a grand 'witch dance' had taken place here on 'Allhallow-even'. An invisible Satan was the musician in chief but the dancers were 'transformit in other lykeness, sum in haris, sum in catts'. A confession that he was present in animal form was extracted from one Thomas Leys, who 'led the ring'. Leys and his fellow devil-worshippers were all burnt at the stake.

By now we should be back in **Castlegate** and ready to explore the second half of this huge urban space. The market cross is traditionally the ceremonial heart of the Scottish burgh. A great deal of importance was placed it, and this was often reflected in lavish designs. Aberdeen's Mercat Cross is one of the best in the country. The gloriously elaborate cross symbolised Aberdeen's high burgh status. It was designed by John Montgomery of Old Rayne in 1686 and came complete with proper dripping gargoyles, designed to keep rain water off the expensively carved stonework. The first stage is an elaborate arcade to suggest commerce and above this is a panel with armorial bearings of the crown and the city. This stresses the crucial relationship between the former, who grants burgh status, and the latter, who receives it. It was a mutually beneficial arrangement. The crown got an annual sum paid to it by the burgh. This was a sort of licence to charge tolls and taxes. The deference to the monarchy is underlined by 12 bas-relief panels of the Stewart monarchs from James I to our forgotten monarch James VII. Aberdeen had supported the Stewarts through thick and thin: James III in 1488 and Charles I in 1638. In spite of this, much is often made of the fact that the burgh accepted without a murmur the 'Revolution Settlement' which

Castle Street in an engraving of 1812

dethroned James VII in favour of William of Orange (1689–1702). We should remember that William was in fact Charles's grandson and that he was also married to Mary, James VII's eldest daughter. Bear in mind also that it was here in Aberdeen, at the very spot where we are now standing, that 'James VIII', the Old Pretender, was declared king on 20 September 1715. He had landed up the coast at Peterhead.

Although it would now be unthinkable today for a foreigner to serve at high level in a national army, the small professional armies of the eighteenth century employed military strategists from overseas the way we nowadays employ footballers. The Aberdonian James Francis Edward Keith (1698–1758) is a fine example. He was born at Inverugie near Peterhead, the younger brother of George Keith. He was educated at Aberdeen University and Edinburgh. Keith was 'out' in the Jacobite Rising of 1715 and was behind the failed invasion from Spain in 1719. He stayed on in Spain as a military leader and then moved to Russia and later Prussia, where he became the favoured field-marshal of Frederick the Great. He served Prussia during the Seven Years War and was killed at Hochkirk.

The Mercat Cross was moved from its position outside the Tolbooth as part of the Union Street–King Street improvements. Most of what we see on the south side of the square dates from the nineteenth century, some of it taken down and rebuilt in connection with a recent development at the rear of the site. The architect daringly covered the steep hill with flats, stepped all the way down to Virginia Street. Right in the corner of the square on the right-hand side is a neat way through to Castlehill. This is the site of Futtie's Port, which led down to the fishing village of Footdee (p.198) via Fittie Wynd. We can also walk a little way along in order to see Castlehill and all that Cromwell left behind him on his tour (see below). As we take the left turn along the side of the Salvation Army building, we can see the numbered stones of the old Futtie's Port.

At the end of the platform created by the barracks perimeter wall is a marvellous view of Fittie and the harbour. Immediately below, Virginia Street passes in the little excavated valley between Castlehill and the Heading Hill opposite. Castlehill Barracks were erected in 1794 and used right up until 1935. They were then converted to lodging-houses but, having become very dilapidated, were demolished in 1965. Now on the site is Castlehill Court and the lower Virginia Court municipal tower blocks. The juxtaposition of the two blocks seems to suggest the hall and tower of a castle on a huge scale.

The tradition of having barracks within the town faded and the soldiers were housed instead some distance away at the Gordon Highlanders' barracks at Bridge of Don, which were built in 1935. Soldiers were garrisoned in every major town and city until quite recently. The idea of their intervening in cases of riot was well established since the

Castle Street in the 1880s

eighteenth century, prior to the creation of a full-time professional police force. As can be imagined, relations between the soldiery and the townsfolk could be less than cordial. Sometimes they could be fatal.

On the evening of 4 June 1802 a rather riotous but good-humoured street party was well under way in Aberdeen, celebrating the birthday of George III. A Company of the Ross and Cromarty Rangers were garrisoned in the city and were among the revellers that night. They joined in the celebrations by firing volleys of musket shots into the air. Everything was fine until a party of officers of the regiment appeared. They had been dining very well as guests of the town council but on appearing on the street the crowd decided to give them what is known in Scotland as a 'shirricking' – basically a tirade of abuse, closely followed by pelters of mud and dead cats. The drunken officers were incensed at their rough treatment and ordered their men to fire on the crowd, which they did, killing four people and badly wounding another twelve. The soldiers immediately retreated to the barracks and were besieged by angry Aberdonians determined on revenge. The soldiers locked themselves away and later disappeared under cover of darkness. They were never again seen in the city. Months later, the officer commanding and two of his sergeants were brought to trial in Edinburgh for murder, but the case against them was not proven. The ensign of the regiment, fearing the worst, had skipped the country and was outlawed.

There is very little left now on Castlehill to attest to its centuries-old role as place of strength – there has been a castle on this site since the thirteenth century. However, there are remains of a construction of the Cromwellian period. Oliver Cromwell's occupation of Scotland began of course with a revolution against Charles I's rule in 1638. This was a

Castle Street, c.1875, showing the statue of the Duke of Gordon which was later removed to Golden Square; the tenement and Record Office behind the Mercat Cross were demolished to make way for the Salvation Army Citadel

revolution that was strenuously opposed by the city of Aberdeen. The end result of that episode was the signing of the National Covenant and the abolition of episcopacy (church government through bishops) by the Glasgow general assembly. The events which followed culminated in the Cromwellian military occupation of Scotland between 1651 and 1660. The consequences of the 1640s and 1650s in terms of architecture were dire in the extreme. Many people imagine that the iconoclasts were at work during the Reformation when 'idolatry' was outlawed, but it was during the second half of the seventeenth century that militant Presbyterians continued what they considered to be the 'unfinished business' of the Reformation. They even targeted churches built after 1560 to Episcopalian principles of design. This was the time when James VI's superb Holyrood chapel interior in Edinburgh was ripped out. Most tragically for Aberdeen, the north-east, which had been a stronghold of Episcopalianism and Catholicism after 1560, was now brought into conformity with the rest of the country. This meant that, among many other very regrettable acts, Bishop Elphinstone's tomb was smashed by Protestant militants and St Machar's interior was stripped (p.192). Architecturally, all that the Cromwellian forces left behind them were some forts, which are not without interest as examples of military architecture of the period. Here at Castlehill there was a pentagonal-shaped rubble-built fort, constructed with stone robbed from St Machar's.

Looking down on the harbour from our vantage-point here on Castlehill, you can see Girdleness Lighthouse in the distance (see p.213). In the middle distance is the tower of St Clement's Church, focal point of Footdee before it was removed to Sandness, just to the south (p.204). The large area of open ground enclosed by rubble walls to the right of St Clement's as we look down is the site of Waterloo railway station. The line itself still exists and could be converted to a walkway and cycleway. Originally, the railway to the north had its terminus here at Waterloo Quay. Before the opening of the 'Joint' station at Guild Street, travellers had to make their way along the quayside, past Regent Quay and Trinity Quay to make their connection south or north. These lines were run by different companies, the Great North of Scotland Railway and the Aberdeen (later the Caledonian) Railway. One would not wait on passengers from the other, so speed was of the essence in the frantic sprint along the quayside. Small boys would take delight in misinforming and annoying the hurrying passengers: 'Hurry up, the train's leaving early!' or, pointing to the ground, 'Hey, Mister, is that your five-pound note?' Aberdeen was one of the first cities to see sense and to create a single railway station to be shared between the competing railway companies. The link between the two stations had to be made by cutting through the Denburn (p.104) and as a consequence Waterloo became something of dead end for the majority of passengers who had used the station for transferring from north to south. Nowadays we take a national rail network for granted, but this was not the case in the mid-nineteenth century, when each company had their own gauge and platform heights.

Like many others throughout the country, the railway at Waterloo Quay was built on the site of a canal. The station was at Waterloo Basin, the terminus of the Aberdeen Inverurie Canal. The canal was first mooted in 1795 to bring produce from the Aberdeenshire hinterland straight to the harbour. It was opened in 1805 but constructing it had been a difficult and expensive project, particularly when it reached the city itself. Eleven locks were required between here and Kittybrewster, a short distance inland. The canal was eventually, and with some relief, sold to the Great North of Scotland Railway in 1853 for the sum of £36,000. It had cost £40,000 to build. There are some remnants of the canal by the railway near Dyce Old Parish Church.

On 6 September 1872 Queen Victoria received the keys to Aberdeen from Provost Leslie. As she herself recorded in her diary, she then went 'from Aberdeen by a line totally new to me – past Inverurie close past the hill of Benachie and got a good sight of the Buck of Cabrach and the surrounding hills, past Huntly to Keith. No British sovereign has ever been so far north. We passed Culloden and the moor where that bloody battle, the recollection of which I cannot bear, was fought.' Here we see the train in its new role as 'panorameter' of history: the stories, associations and historical landscape unfold before the traveller as the train journeys on.

We should now walk back down to the Castlegate. Make your way over to the Mercat Cross and look back at the large castellated building

BURGHS AND BURGESSES

Justice Port was one of the six city gates of Aberdeen. The other five were Futty, Shiprow (or Trinity), Netherkirkgate, Upperkirkgate and Gallowgate. The ports are at the heart of a definition of the burgh. The granting of burgh status by the monarch created a privileged community of burgesses. These individuals had a freedom to act and to arrange their community affairs and interest without the usual interference from the feudal overlord. The most severe punishment the burgh could mete out was exclusion from the burgh itself. The 'ports' were physical and judicial boundaries. To be shut out was to be cast into the feudal world at the mercy of the warring powers who struggled for supremacy beyond the burgh 'freedom' lands. The burgesses of Aberdeen recognised that their future economic well-being depended on trade and so they laid the basis for a free and unconstrained business community. The burgh also monopolised overseas trade by controlling the harbour.

So what did the crown get out of this arrangement? The burgh paid an annual sum to the monarch and in return was permitted to exact tolls and taxes on goods brought into or taken from the city. We should not confuse the people who lived in the burgh with the burgesses, who ran the burgh's affairs. This was not democracy as we would understand the idea today. Burgesses ran the affairs of the town. They paid an annual fee of thirteen and fourpence Scots and had to provide a banquet on admission. The early charters gave the guild members the monopoly of trade but the later charter transformed the town into a property-owning community, almost on an Athenian model. This was done by Robert the Bruce, who remained grateful to Aberdeen for their slaying of the English garrison. Further, the town clerk Thomas Isaac married Bruce's daughter Matilda.

The burgh hierarchy was unrelenting, but once a year in the 'daft days' of May a strange custom was permitted amongst the disenfranchised of the burgh. A so-called 'Abbot of Bonaccord', who was a kind of anti-provost, was put in charge of some chaos and wild revelry which could last for several days. The centrepiece was a playhouse, the beginning of the modern theatre tradition. The idea was to give the people a yearly outlet for any disaffection they might be harbouring against the burgh. The hope was that this would keep them happy for the remainder of the year. Of course these parties got out of hand. They were toned down by the officials of the burgh and eventually banned altogether.

which dominates the square. This is the **Salvation Army Citadel**, one of Aberdeen's most prominent buildings, and it is the largest, if perhaps not the best, work of James Souttar. He designed it in 1893–96. It replaced an eighteenth-century records office which was designed to keep a centralised births and deaths register. That function was later moved to Edinburgh, making the building redundant. The site at the end of Union Street was clearly an important one and Souttar designed a large-scale public building with a tower to finish the view. The Castlegate area had by the end of the nineteenth century become a slum of drinking bothies and brothels and the idea was to place Salvation at the heart of this urban squalor. It's easy to caricature the Salvation Army as spoilsports and do-gooders, but in the days before the welfare state they did a huge amount

Looking from Castlehill to Footdee and Girdleness

in the battle against poverty, disease and alcohol addiction. The Army was founded in London in 1877 and quickly spread through the UK.

The main front of the Citadel is clearly based on the palace block at Stirling Castle, with its crow-stepped gables above the parapet. This was a massive intervention in the area, which challenged even the mighty Town House. Rearing up behind the Salvation Army Citadel are the twin towers of Virginia and Marischal Courts designed by the City Architects' Department in 1969. You may not like tower blocks but Aberdonians seem to. The first of them was built in 1960 at the Ashgrove housing scheme and the last as recently as 1985 at Jasmine Place. They are very popular with occupiers and very well looked after. The blocks are faced with random shards of granite which help them to blend in with the local scene.

To the left of the Citadel is Justice Street. This is named after Justice Port (also called 'Thieves Port') which stood on the site, and many people have assumed that since this was the way through to the 'Heading Hill' – an outcrop of Castle Hill where decapitations took place in ancient times – that the 'Justice' referred to is that of the law. There are very few Scottish 'ports' or gates now left, most having been removed by the late eighteenth century when they were no longer required. The West Bow at St Andrews is a fine example still in existence, but the Justice Port here at Aberdeen was demolished as early as 1787, making it the last of the six ports of Aberdeen to be erected and the first to be pulled down.

The north side of the Castlegate dates mostly from the late eighteenth and early nineteenth century but is constructed on the plan of earlier buildings. No. 17 Castle Street is made of Loanhead granite, the

St Peter's Church, Chapel Court

material used before new technology permitted the quarrying of the much harder stone of which the greater part of the city is built. It has a rougher, more vernacular quality, which seems to belong to another age. Compare no. 17 with its much more precisely detailed neighbour.

In Justice Street, charmingly concealed by a tenement at nos. 7–13, is **St Peter's Church in Chapel Court**. It was designed by James Massie in 1803. From 1772 this was the very understated, almost secret, meeting place of Aberdeen's Catholics, who were associated in the public mind with the Rising of 1745. The tenement in front was rebuilt in 1843. Nearby was the home of Francis Peacock (1723–1807), dancing master and miniaturist: a well-known Aberdeen character in the middle years of the eighteenth century. He is, of all things, the 'father of Scottish country dancing'. His name is recorded at Peacock's Close and that is quite an honour for any Aberdonian. Walking down this close will take you along the side of St Peter's Church, but you can further explore the backlands here by walking down the close adjacent to no. 20 which is marked 'Peacock Printmakers'. Turn left at the John Skinner Centre and back onto Castlegate via Bremner's Court at no. 9 Castlegate. The large building in the heart of the backlands is the St Andrew's Schools of 1860.

We are now at the elbow of Union Street and King Street. These two streets were planned to offer a through route from north to south. The first building to mention is on the same side of the street as the Mercat Cross, at nos. 8–10 King Street, and was built on a scale and dignity that was wished for the whole street. James Burn and David Hamilton of Glasgow had both been asked for designs for the new street, for which a very ordered group of palace-fronted blocks was wanted. This model required the buyers of plots to conform exactly to the scheme. There was no great rush to buy the plots, however, so the Trustees decided that some leeway for individual proprietors might make the idea more attractive to purchasers. The Edinburgh model of, say, Moray Place, where wealthy individuals simply bought into a massive, pre-designed scheme, could not work in Aberdeen. The result here is a compromise between regularity and individuality, which is in fact very appealing. The tall corner block was finally designed as a gateway composition by John Smith in 1810.

On the opposite corner is the 'farmer's bank'. What is now Simpson's Bar was formerly the headquarters of the North of Scotland Bank. Appropriately enough, the building replaced the New Inn which had stood on the site for great many years. After Simpson had experimented with several schemes, the idea of a monumental corner entrance convinced the bank. The model seems to have been Sir John Soane's 'Tivoli corner' for the Bank of England in Threadneedle Street, London. However, Soane's corner was not an entrance. This was a daring and successful innovation by Simpson much taken up by later bank designers. The corner is conceived as the entrance portico with the conventional plain wings set back as if on a 'V' plan. Simpson's bank is therefore given dynamism, along with an image of strength, essential for a banking house. On top of the entrance is a statue, not of Queen Victoria as is often assumed, but of Ceres, Goddess of the Harvest. This shows where most of Aberdeen's money was coming from – the ever-improving farms of the rural hinterland.

The bank has been converted to a pub and this has been really well done. It is named in honour of the architect Archibald Simpson. It used to be you went to the bank to get drinking money. Now they have cut out the middleman. A returning emigrant would be mightily confused. The pub is well worth a visit and still has good interiors, including a gilded plaster-cast frieze of the Elgin Marbles, all the rage at the time of the building's construction.

Looking along King Street, on the same side as Simpson's at nos. 1–4 you will see another example of Archibald Simpson's work, this one built in 1839 for the North of Scotland Fire and Life Assurance Co., the two things being closely connected. The very successful and well-connected Edinburgh architect James Gillespie Graham designed its neighbour, nos. 7–9 King Street. Simpson seems to have disliked the out-of-towner and lambasted Graham's design, which seemed lazily to go its own way and not to respect the prevailing local style. Graham simply seems to have put up an offcut from his magnificent Moray Place scheme in Edinburgh. In the event, this was Graham's only design in Aberdeen. He was a very grand *arriviste* who had married an heiress and added her name to his (he'd been plain James Gillespie before). Simpson seems to have been a much more likeable man. For his part, although he was a very talented designer, he never entered Edinburgh competitions and strayed little from his home town after his early travels in Italy.

The two Aberdonians, Simpson and Smith, managed to share the architectural spoils quite evenly once Graham departed. We can contrast this Simpson–Graham contretemps with the amazing architectural harmony achieved in the group of buildings next door. The **Medico-Chirurgical Building** was designed by Archibald Simpson in 1818. The Medico-Chirurgical Society was founded by medical students of Aberdeen University, led by the surgeon-hero Sir James McGrigor (p.174). The story of the buildings construction rivals Edinburgh in its devotion to the creation of a monumental city. Simpson designed the massive Ionic portico, but that was as far as the landholding of the Medico-Chirurgical Society went. The terms of the feu (lease) were altered so that both would-be neighbours, to the south and to the north, were required to set their buildings back on the line of Simpson's block. The architect of the southern block (immediately on our left), Simpson's rival John Smith, went one better. In 1832–33 he designed a block for the County Record Offices which looks like no more than a wing of Simpson's building. If you look closely, you will see that Smith's building is in fact separate and has its own understated entrance. A further, respectful three-bay block which continues the composition was added in 1870, long after the deaths of Smith and Simpson.

Opposite the Medico-Chirurgical Society building is St Andrew's Episcopal Cathedral, also designed by Simpson in 1816. This little building is squeezed into a site between the houses of King Street and to make its presence felt is designed in a very spiky Gothic Revival style.

The necessary spikiness was aided by the controversial material, sandstone – for the front of the building only (the main structure of the church is granite). The sandstone was brought by boat from the Craigleith quarry in Edinburgh via the port of Leith. The design was made quite some time before a more academic interest in the Gothic style produced convincingly 'antiquarian' architecture. The chancel was added by the noted London designer G.E. Street, architect of the Law Courts in the Strand. The little porch was added by Sir Robert Lorimer in 1911 and the wonderful interior was redecorated by Sir Ninian Comper, complete with Stars and Stripes colours, so the little cathedral has had much attention lavished upon it by important architects. Indeed, we might have had a much grander Cathedral of Episcopalianism if some patrons from the USA had not lost their money in the Wall Street Crash.

The American Episcopal Church was founded as a result of an event that took place on a site near by at Longacre on 14 November 1784. The little converted chapel has since been swept away in the Marischal College extension. After the American War of Independence, the American Church was separated from its English counterpart. The US clergy elected Samuel Seabury as their bishop, but there was no one to consecrate him, since Seabury could hardly swear an oath of allegiance to George III. Also, Seabury had been elected, not appointed by the King. In the end the idea of consecration through the Scottish Episcopal Church was hit upon and Seabury was consecrated by Bishop John Skinner, Arthur Petrie, Bishop of Moray, and Robert Kilgour, Bishop of

Queen Street prior to its demolition in the 1960s; George Gordon, Lord Byron, lived at no. 10 Queen Street

Aberdeen and Primus of the Scottish Episcopal Church. In the 1920s the American Church planned to repay its debt of gratitude by funding the construction of a monumental church in Broad Street, the Bishop Seabury Memorial Cathedral, to be designed by Ninian Comper. In the end, the plans proved too ambitious but a scaled-down tribute was created in the form of the redecoration here at St Andrew's in 1936–43.

Aberdeen Arts Centre (formerly North Church) was designed by John Smith in 1829–30. The design is a brilliant mix of Greek Revival sources, culled from the pages of Stuart & Revett's *Antiquities of Athens*. The Greek Revival style, which started about 1810 and carried on in various forms for generations, was especially suited to Aberdeen. The style was particularly at home in its reduced, 'primitive' form and that of course suited Aberdeen very well with its massive granite blocks which were difficult to cut. Smith's church sits all on its own so it is seen in the round and therefore had to be dressed and composed on all faces. The crowning glory is of course the main entrance front which is set well back from the street for visual effect. Smith also built much of King Street itself in a very restrained classical style, which forms a backdrop to his 'signature' building, the North Church. The church was converted to an Arts Centre in the 1950s and little remains of the original interior scheme.

We have now reached the confusingly named West North Street. Turn left and walk a little way into **Queen Street**. At the end of the street on our right is the North Church of St Andrew, designed by W.E. Gauld in 1904 for the United Free Church of Scotland.

Just to our left now is Poultry Market Lane. In 1631 a fleshmarket was established here, an access lane joining Castle Street and Queen Street. An early shopping arcade was laid out here in 1809. In 1846 the meal-market was moved here. More recent uses of the site include a bleaching green and a drill hall. If we walk up Poultry Market Lane a little way, we can get a very good view of the rear of the Tolbooth's exotic, almost Russian-looking steeple. Interestingly, it has recently been discovered that the Kremlin was in fact designed by a Scottish clockmaker so there may be more in the similarity than coincidence. You can also see the crenellations (battlements) of the Tolbooth tower. You should now walk back to the waymarker post just outside the arts centre and look down West North Street and up to St Margaret's Episcopal Church.

Shoe Lane takes its name from the street's original 'developers' who laid out the street in 1785. This was the shoemaker craft of the Incorporated Trades who did charitable work funded by their property speculation as did all the other 'trades' once their original function of regulating their respective industries had disappeared. Shoe Lane was at the centre of a notorious slum area which was cleared in the 1960s.

Passing the Lemon Tree, a café-bar and arts venue, on our right and the huge thrusting bulk of the **Mitchell Hall** of Marischal College (p.79), we cross over Littlejohn Street (named after the architect-entrepreneur William Littlejohn whose house stood at the top of the hill). High above and in front of us now we can see the red-tiled roof of St Margaret's Church. From the 1950s there was quite a fashion for restoring buildings with these bright pantiled roofs. We now turn left up some steep stairs to Seamount Place. If you want to avoid the stairs you can take the gentler slope of Littlejohn Street and turn right into Gallowgate Street. At the top of the stairs turn right to St Margaret's Episcopal Church, named, like that at Edinburgh Castle, in honour of St Margaret of Scotland. This lovely little church was designed by Sir Ninian Comper in 1891. His beautiful chapel may be viewed at any time through a grille in the porch.

Gallowgate may not look it now, but this was Aberdeen's equivalent of the Royal Mile. The original houses were very grand and had gardens running down to the loch to the east. The name 'Gallowgate' referred simply to the road along which condemned prisoners were led to the gallows, just outside the town. These men and women would be offenders from the lowest class and their ritual parading through the town was intended as an elaborate display of the ultimate power of the rule of law – and, of course, as a warning to others. There were several places of execution apart from this: Castlegate (see p.135); the 'Heading Hill' just beyond Castlehill; or simply being drowned at the quay.

The area immediately to the west of Gallowgate was known as the Lochlands but by the eighteenth century this 'loch' had been reduced to a boggy strip in the centre. It was an obvious place to extend the city. In the *Aberdeen Journal* of 1790, the following report appeared:

> *The population and extent of this place [Aberdeen] seems to be going on with increasing speed. The well-known field called Lochlands, on the west side of the Gallowgate, is now partly feued out for building. It is to contain four principal streets – George Street, Charlotte Street, St Andrew Street and John Street. George Street is already begun, and from the spirit of improvement which so much prevails, there is little doubt but in a few years this will form a populous and elegant addition to Aberdeen. Indeed it is almost the only quarter where the town can be extended to any great extent.*

The writer's last sentence reveals a great deal. It was assumed that the valley of the Denburn represented a western boundary to development and the writer could not imagine that it could be bridged in such spectacular fashion as it has been.

To reach the Lochlands, continue down Gallowgate between the two modernist blocks of Seamount Court and Aberdeen College. Seamount Court is part of a huge 'megastructure' designed by the City Architects'

Mitchell Hall, Marischal College

Department in the 1960s. It was formerly a mixed area of engineering works, poor housing, an 'edible-fat factory', an ironworks and all the other small- and large-scale industries of a busy city. The idea of a dense 'megastructure' with everything packed into one site comes ultimately from the Swiss modernist architect Le Corbusier and his schemes for *unités d'habitations*. This type of high living really took off in Aberdeen. As mentioned above, a 'high rise' was built at Jasmine Place as recently as 1986, and with a shortage of space in the city centre the high rise could make a comeback. Already there are blocks of six and seven storeys being put up on the riverside overlooking the Wellington bridge (see p.171).

At the end of Gallowgate is Mounthooly and its famous, if not quite celebrated, gigantic roundabout. This roundabout started as a pretty standard affair of the 1960s but, together with the adjacent high flats at Hutcheon Court, soon came out at a suitably heroic scale. Many tenements were demolished in the creating of this wide open space. The name Mounthooly, which seems so appropriate for this heroic-scaled roundabout, has puzzled local historians for years. It has been variously spelt 'Mount Hooly', 'Mount Heillie' and 'Mount Hillie'. There are also plenty of other Mounthoolies around the country. One view is that it comes from the Gaelic *Monadh Chuile*, meaning 'corner hill'. Another source is convinced that it means 'Holy Mount' suggesting that it was church land.

On the other side of the roundabout is Spital, which is simply short for 'hospital' and, like all the other Scottish 'spitals', was the site of what we would now think of as a hospice.

In the middle distance on the right we can see the Balmoral Baronial of Causewayend Primary School which was designed by William Smith, the architect of Balmoral, in 1875–76. It was not Smith who gave the school its castle-like profile, however, but Dr William Kelly – he added the prominent tower in 1892. After the building of schools like Fettes College in Edinburgh, the Gordon Schools in Huntly or Aberdeen Grammar School (p.117), the revival of the Scots-Baronial style became strongly associated with education. It was a style particularly appropriate for the north-east, which was regarded as the true home of the exuberant seventeenth-century castle style. Now we should take a left into Hutcheon Street, which is overshadowed by slab blocks of flats from the 1960s. The huge shards of granite with which the Hutcheon Court building is faced was supposed to give local character, rather like the Gothic Revival churches of the nineteenth century.

The Aberdeen Combworks were at 38–40 Hutcheon Street. The main part of the building was put up between 1830 and 1840, with further buildings added in the 1880s as the comb business expanded. This was a big site, with a range of industrial and office buildings, all devoted to providing the world with combs. (It was all converted to offices in 1981, an early example of the reuse of industrial buildings.) Stewart & Rowell's combworks was for many years the world's largest. In the 1880s, as S.R. Stewart & Co., the works had been expanded with 'several large and commodious buildings of four storeys'. Nine hundred people worked on '100,000 horns per week, together with vast quantities of hoops, tortoiseshell and vulcanite'. In 1937 plastic injection moulding was introduced, spelling the end for tortoiseshell combs, shoehorns, horn-rimmed glasses and many other products made from natural materials. The process of comb-making seems to have been particularly flammable. There were a number of devastating fires at the complex over the years, and the blaze of 1969 was the biggest in the city's history.

As we arrive at George Street, look over to the continuation of Hutcheon Street and see the decorative ventilator shaft of the tunnel that led from the electricity board offices in Ferryhill. Take a left into George Street and cross Catherine Street. At no. 393 we can see an unusual conversion – from a bank to a church. This was designed as the Aberdeen Savings Bank by Dr William Kelly in 1927. Just beside the bank/church at no. 403 you can look over the shops and see that the street used to have villas set back from the road at this point.

Continue down George Street and take a right opposite Spring Garden into Maberly Street. We enter an industrial zone of the type that nineteenth-century cities used to have in the days before town-planning. We also get a flavour of what the cleared area of the Gallowgate must have looked liked in the not too distant past. We are now entering the huge industrial complex of the **Broadford Works** which was a textile mill producing linen from the early nineteenth century onwards, with many later additions creating a little town within a city. Fenton Murray & Woods of Leeds built the four-storey structures which are quite plain. Broadford contains the oldest iron-framed building in Scotland and the fourth oldest in the world. The mills were built for Scott Brown & Co., who went bankrupt in 1808 and thereafter sold the business to Sir John Maberly MP, a noted entrepreneur and speculator. It was he who introduced jute spinning to the UK, thereby setting up the conditions for the huge growth of manufacturing in nineteenth-century Dundee. Maberly developed the works here at Broadford, adopting the first gas lighting of an industrial complex in Scotland, by Boulton & Watt in 1814–15 and Scotland's second power-loom linen-weaving factory in 1824. Maberly himself went bankrupt in 1834 and the works became the property of Richards & Co. who had a bleachworks at Rubislaw and branches at Montrose, Richards made canvas tarpaulins and fire hoses. The tall beige-coloured tower on the site was for the making of hoses. Richards was once the largest employer in Aberdeen, with a workforce of over three thousand people.

Although such factories were described as 'mills', this was purely a figure of speech. Steam power allowed the textile factories to locate in the heart of cities. Power could now be brought in the form of coal to the factory instead of having to take the factory to the source of water, such as the River Don see (p.213). The Broadford Works was one of the few survivors of the slump in the textile industry of the 1840s and 1850s. The largest building in the complex is the huge flax warehouse on your left as you approach along Maberly Street. This is popularly called 'the Bastille'. Such a massive brick structure in the heart of the granite city was quite controversial. The whole building was wonderfully converted to flats in 1995. Included in the scheme were three new penthouses placed on the roof.

In this area you will become aware of the charm of the older style of tenement in its strictly regular layout and quite small scale. Turning left into Charlotte Street, we see a typical Aberdeen building with its gable swept down to meet the wallhead on the street. This is something of an Aberdeen trademark. This little district was laid out as an adjunct to

George Street, a trial run for the much grander Golden Square and Bon Accord Square developments off Union Street. There are also public buildings of a suitably lower status. The building at no. 46 Charlotte Street was built in 1887 as part of the Aberdeen Training College and later converted to a nursery in 1917 by the schools architect J. Ogg Allan. Its simple Gothic style was often associated with learning, even if it suggested Catholicism to certain of the more Presbyterian-minded architects. The nineteenth-century architect-polemicist A.W. Pugin had characterised Gothic as the 'true style' and Catholicism as the 'true religion'. The arched gateway is part of the design. Over the raised centrepiece is a sandstone statuette of John Knox.

Occupying an entire city block is the Robert Gordon University of 1920, again designed by the educational specialist J. Ogg Allan. The university's huge expansion into the area began on a small enough scale with the acquisition of a church in Blackfriars Street, which they converted into a gymnasium. In front of us is the rear of Robert Gordon's School (see p.100) on Crooked Lane and St Andrew Street. The gateway to the school is probably the work of the school's original architect, William Adam, but John Smith rebuilt the adjoining walls in 1828.

We should now turn left into St Andrew Street. There was a suspected 'Burking' shop here. This was the derogatory term applied to the very serious activities of the Anatomical School of the university. Advances in medical knowledge relied on researches into anatomy, but the activities of the researchers were viewed with great suspicion by most of the public. This was made much worse after the trial and punishment of the notorious Burke and Hare in Edinburgh. They had been stealing freshly buried corpses and supplying them for a price to the medical men; the introduction of mortsafes and nightwatchmen to counteract such activities was beginning to make their job more difficult, and the pair decided to take matters into their own hands. The evil duo murdered several poor souls to sell to the medics before being caught and convicted. The 'Black Kalendar' of Aberdeen records that in 1831 the people of the city feared that their dead relatives would get the same treatment as Burke and Hare's unfortunate victims in Edinburgh. Their suspicions centred on the anatomical school of Dr Andrew Moir, which stood here in St Andrew Street. Some boys playing in the yard had noticed a dog tugging at something buried just below the ground. When they investigated, they decided they had found the remains of one of Dr Moir's 'victims'. Word soon got around and a mob quickly laid siege to the house. Three cadavers found inside were taken away to St Nicholas' Church and the house was then completely destroyed minutes after Moir and several of his students had escaped via a rear window. Moir was the senior physician at Aberdeen Infirmary and was a founder member of the city's Medico-Chirurgical Society. He lived at Braehead Cottage before the house was bought by the Glover family (p.213). The Black

Kalendar is a good read. It contains 'brief accounts of the lives of the criminals who may truly be said to be distinguished – not for their good but for their bad deeds'. A watchman in the Gallowgate by the name of James Sangster is recorded as having sold his wife's body to the 'anatomists'. The Black Kalendar was first published in the eighteenth century, a kind of latter-day 'true-crime story' for the titillation of the book-reading classes.

Continuing down St Andrew Street, we soon rejoin George Street. As we cross George Street you can hardly fail to notice the John Lewis department store and the rear of the Bon Accord Centre at the end of George Street. The store was designed as Norco House (1966–70) by Covell, Matthews & Partners and built as the showpiece headquarters store of the Northern Co-operative Society as an image of progressive modernity. Just beyond the main store was a dramatically roofed food hall, which was demolished when John Lewis took over in 1987. Opposite, at nos. 119–127, is the Old Central Bakery designed for Hutchison's the Bakers by Brown & Watt in 1897. The building was fronted by a tenement but at the rear was the biggest bakery in the north. The principal designer of the firm, George Watt, had worked in Glasgow with the influential James Sellars. This is one of the best examples of his work in the 'free' style of architecture, which allowed mixing sources such as crow-steeped gables and turrets. The long vertical ends with their inset bay windows are derived from the staircase elevation of the Central Station Hotel in Glasgow, one of the key buildings of the free style.

We now cross over George Street and pass Jopp's Lane. This curious name comes from Provost James Jopp (1719–91). He was a wine merchant and landowner who was provost of Aberdeen for three terms between 1766 and 1777. During his time in office he sought to sweep away the medieval barriers to free trade and demolished the remaining ports of the burgh at Gallowgate and Justice Street.

Loch Street is, of course, named after the boggy loch that occupied the area until it was drained for improvement in the early nineteenth century. In front of us is Candlemakers' Lane and, right beside that, a part of a building rescued from demolitions in the Gallowgate. This is a gateway, which formerly led to St Paul's Chapel, an Episcopal church of 1720.

Back up on Gallowgate via the curving Berry Street, there is a good example of the re-use of granite in a new development. Historically, stone was never thrown away but was recycled as rubble or even dressed work for new buildings. The council today keeps a supply of the ubiquitous but precious granite from demolished buildings which can be incorporated in new developments. Here, the recycled stone is used as a conservation-inspired measure to fit in with the surrounding area. Crossing over the top of Littlejohn Street, we should now find ourselves outside Marischal College (see p.79) where this walk ends.

TIVOLI THEATRE, GUILD STREET

Also worth visiting on this walk is the Tivoli Theatre in Guild Street, near the railway station. It is occasionally open (and is usually open on 'Doors Open Day', a yearly event). It was built in 1872 by the celebrated theatre specialist C.J. Phipps of London with James Matthews of Aberdeen. It is an unusual design, which reflects the critic Ruskin's popularisation of Venetian Gothic in his publication The Stones of Venice. Inside, the auditorium is a magical space — even in its current state, with the remains of a conversion to a bingo hall. We may not all like bingo, but it has saved many such buildings from demolition. Now, of course, bingo is big business and is played mostly in out-of-town purpose-built halls leaving theatres and cinemas empty again. Much of the paraphernalia of the music-hall — the flies, the traps and the lighting rigs — are still inside the Tivoli, as is most of the set decoration. Behind the decoration was a concrete structure, the first use on any scale of the advanced construction material in theatre design. It is hoped that the building will once again become a theatre.

Main places of interest	Bon Accord Square, Duthie Park, Bridge of Dee
Circular/linear	Linear
Starting point	Junction of Crown Street and Union Street
Finishing point	Bridge of Dee
Distance	2½ miles
Terrain	Pavements, (avoidable) steps, sandy path or pavement
Public transport	Bus
Sections	Crown Street – Duthie Park, Duthie Park – Bridge of Dee
Architects	Archibald Simpson, Brown & Watt
Nearby walks	Walk 1
Refreshments	Pubs and cafés in the first part of the walk, including the Soho Bar and restaurant in Dee Street, Via Milano in Bon Accord Street and a tea-room and restaurant at Duthie Park
Notes	Possible return route via Deeside railway walk

Crown Street to Ferryhill and Duthie Park to the Bridge of Dee

A walk from the centre of the city through the early nineteenth-century suburbs and out along the riverbank to the historic Bridge of Dee

The former Head Post Office, Crown Street

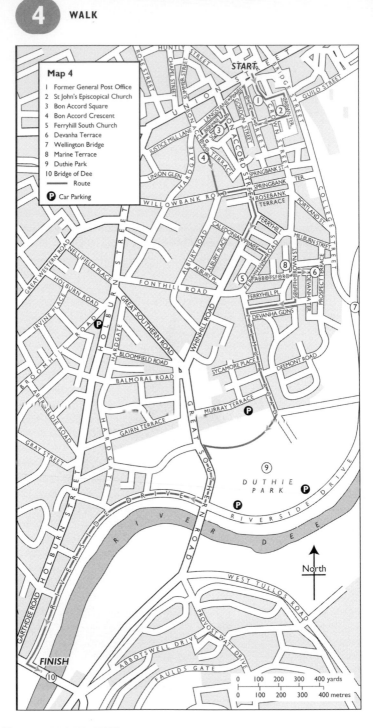

4 WALK

Map 4

1 Former General Post Office
2 St John's Episcopical Church
3 Bon Accord Square
4 Bon Accord Crescent
5 Ferryhill South Church
6 Devanha Terrace
7 Wellington Bridge
8 Marine Terrace
9 Duthie Park
10 Bridge of Dee

—— Route

Ⓟ Car Parking

START

North

0 100 200 300 400 yards

0 100 200 300 400 metres

FINISH

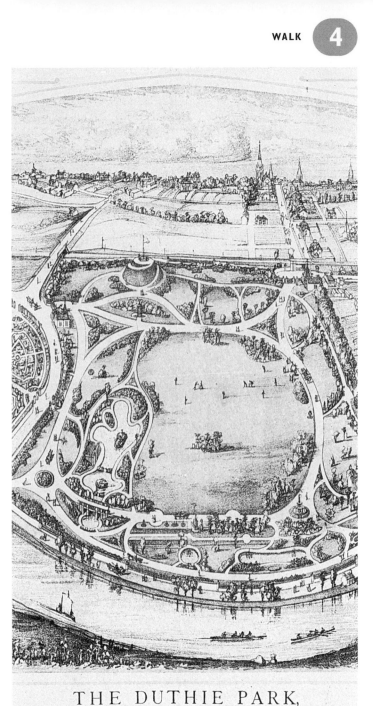

THE DUTHIE PARK,

PRESENTED BY MISS DUTHIE OF RUTHRIESTON TO THE CITY OF ABERDEEN

First Turf Out by Lord Aberdeen, Aug. 27, 1881; Opened by H.R.H. Princess Beatrice, Sept. 27, 1883.

'ae mile o' Don's worth twa o' Dee
Except for salmon, stane and tree.'

Crown Street, like Diamond Street, Silver Street and Golden Square, was laid out in 1806 by the Hammermen Corporation of the Incorporated Trades. The plan was to make an important street connecting with Union Street but to do so avoiding the huge expense of bridging Windmill Brae. (This was not achieved until the engineer John Willet devised a scheme in 1865 at the nearby Bridge Street.) If Crown Street had continued towards Union Street at the same angle, a bridge would have been necessary, so the feuars kinked the street near its junction onto the top of the brae. The result is the crooked street that we have today. This was not regarded as completely satisfactory, but it later allowed for the creation of the setpiece monument of the General Post Office to present itself as a great public building. Windmill Brae is the ancient route into Aberdeen prior to the construction of Union Street. The brae's name refers to the windmill that was once sited at its head. Provost George Skene noted in 1685 that 'There is a comely and strong windmill newly built, at the south entry to the town, which may be of eminent use to the town.' Windmills were once very common in Scotland but not one remains today. Most were converted to dovecots or stores when the more reliable watermills took over.

At the corner with Langstane Place and 10–16 Crown Street is a wonderfully typical Aberdeen tenement of the later type with four main large storeys and another two above the parapet. The building was composed in a turn-of-the-century 'free' style which allowed the architect, George Coutts, to express himself with a range of influences in the same building. These influences are chiefly Northern Renaissance, the other name for the style. Its trademark was the stone dormer window. The shaped gables define the rooftop accommodation. The pub on the ground floor, Macandrews, has some surviving Art Nouveau glass, all part of the same design. The point of the Northern Renaissance style was that it allowed for traditional Scottish restraint or canniness in architecture to be challenged as buildings became ever taller and more complicated. The style specialised in richly encrusted buildings, which heaped detail upon tiny detail. The key building for Scotland was the Caledonian Railway headquarters block at Central Station in Glasgow, where Robert Rowand Anderson balanced a busily gabled façade with a massive vertical punctuation, in the sheer, tall corner tower, crowned by gables.

As an essentially 'applied' style – as in the sixteenth- and seventeenth-century castles of the north-east of Scotland – the Northern Renaissance allowed the new office blocks and tenements to be masked with decoration. The most important architectural exponent of this was A.G. Sydney Mitchell, who used his Northern Renaissance as a 'house style' for a series of banks and commercial buildings, including large numbers of Commercial Bank branches built from 1883 onwards. In some higher-rent blocks, the tenement issue was spectacularly dealt with as here at George Coutts' building on Crown Street. The design's grandeur sought to differentiate between the 'ordinary' Aberdeen tenement and high-class 'flatted town houses'.

On our left now at nos. 23–25 Crown Street is the local office of the Prudential designed in 1910 by Paul Waterhouse, son of the Pru's more famous house architect, Alfred Waterhouse, who had died in 1905. Normally the company insisted not only on a house architect but also on a house style of red brick. As the Prudential expanded into Scotland from the north of England, a problem arose: although the material had a prestigious historical association in England, brick was regarded in Scotland as a low-class material suitable only for factories or warehouses. In Edinburgh there was no budging the Dean of Guild and the Prudential's St Andrew Square building went up in sandstone. In Glasgow a compromise of brick with stone dressings was reached. But in Aberdeen the council would not hear of anything but granite, so granite it is. The result is very good: a typical Edwardian composition with big, confident details.

Ahead of us now is the former **General Post Office**, which has been very well converted to residential use with new flats by the same company on the adjacent site. The sleek new block which fills a gap between here and Dee Street provides a thrilling contrast with the turn-of-the-century tenement. It was designed by Monaghan & MacLachlan of Glasgow and built of granite – brought from China! (There is no longer any suitable locally quarried material.) The Post Office is one of a number of public and commercial buildings which were put up in the eastern section of Crown Street at the start of the twentieth century in a kind of expansion of Union Street. The Post Office exploits the kink in the street by 'addressing' Union Street from a little distance away.

As a group these buildings represent a hectic episode in the history of style in architecture. There is the neo-classical simplicity of Union Street followed by the tentative development of classical and Gothic Revival styles; the creation of the exuberant 'free' style at the turn of the century and the calm after that storm represented by Edwardian Baroque. Finally, there is the Romantic Nationalism of the key building, the General Post Office. W.T. Oldrieve of the Ministry of Public Buildings and Works designed the Post Office in 1907. Oldrieve was the chief architect of the ministry and is often credited with every one of their buildings, but in such a large office each scheme had a 'job' architect. J. Cumming Wyness was the architect in charge here.

Turn left here into Crown Terrace, which continues as it turns the corner at the end. Look down Windmill Lane and again you'll appreciate the difficult land forms that the city builders were working with. Notice

in passing that even the rear of the Prudential has precise granite lettering. Continue around Crown Terrace. On our left is a Baptist church of
1870 by James Souttar. The great blank wall is the rear of the former
Palace Theatre. Follow the terrace around the corner. The Bridge Street
steps are on the left, giving all-important access to the railway, down
below. We should now turn right at the lovely little church on the corner
with St John's Place. St John's is an Episcopalian church designed
according to 'strict ecclesiastical rules' by Thomas Mackenzie in 1849.
Church building of the mid-century was dominated by the activity of
the three Presbyterian sects – the Established Church, the Free Church
and the United Presbyterians. The Episcopalians eventually challenged
that dominance. The Episcopal Church enjoyed something of a boom
from the 1840s, owing to the combined impact of an influx of English
migrant workers, an anglicising tendency among elements of the
wealthier classes and the continuity of Episcopalianism in Aberdeen. The
Camden Society, a religious pressure group in favour of more ritualistic
Anglican liturgy and architecture, was very influential. The Camden
Society and other fundamentalist groups required elements such as
east–west alignment and strict differentiation of parts such as nave,
chancel, vestry, porch and bellcote.

Going down St John's Place, we are soon back on Crown Street.
Diagonally opposite, looking back up Crown Street, is the former Trinity
United Free Church of 1891: another precision-built composition in
granite by A. Marshall Mackenzie, a test run for Marischal College. The
precision of the granite finish is quite remarkable although the style is
temple-orientated in the style of the Venetian architect Andrea Palladio
whose work was being revived at the time. Immediately on our right at
the corner with St John's Place and Crown Street at 85 Crown Street is
another temple, this time the Masonic temple designed by Harbourne
Maclennan of Jenkins & Marr in 1909–10. The rest of Crown Street after
the kink reverts to the low, simply detailed granite style of the earlier
new town. Most of the houses were built between the 1820s and the
1840s. The area has become a centre for bed-and-breakfast establishments, most of them offering good-value accommodation a short distance from the railway station. We should now cross Crown Street and
go over into Academy Street. The shallow castle-like bays of the rear of
the building at 57 Dee Street belong to Seabank House, a former YWCA
building. Dee Street is a very quiet little enclave with a typically Aberdonian mix of uses, from suburban-looking cottages to the huge warehouse on the right-hand side at the end of the street (no. 77) designed
in 1898 by William Kelly for the warehousemen Thomas Ogilvie & Son.
This street gives a strong flavour of what the original streets of Aberdeen's new town must have been like. The building with the pride of
place is a villa of about 1810, which finishes the view as we look down
the street to Dee Place. The architect George Watt of Brown & Watt lived

at 71 Dee Street and the celebrated opera singer Mary Garden (1874–1967) lived at no. 41. She trained in Paris where she joined the Opéra-Comique. She sang the lead role in Charpentier's opera *Louise* in 1900 but her greatest triumph was Debussy's *Extase*.

We should now walk up Dee Street towards Langstane Place. Here are the very stylish new blocks of flats near the top of the street, part of the development of the former Post Office fronting Crown Street. At nos. 11–11a Dee Street is one of Aberdeen's quite rare forays into the Art Nouveau style. In Glasgow, especially, the style was particularly associated with the city's tea-rooms, because of the work of Charles Rennie Mackintosh for Miss Cranston. In Aberdeen the link between tea and good taste was not quite so strong but here at least is a tentative attempt. There are stained-glass panels in the upper part of the shop front.

We have now reached Langstane Place and should turn left here. The 'long stone' that gives the place its name is thought to have been part of a stone circle of the Stonehenge or Callanish type. The old road to Aberdeen from the south would have passed by the stone on its way past Hardgate and then dropped sharply down Windmill Brae to the Green (see p.126). As we know, these stone circles were possibly places of worship. The Langstane itself is built into the wall at 10 Langstane Place, which is on the corner with Dee Street.

Langstane Place has on its north side the diminutive mews buildings at the back of Union Street with their heightened chimneys, trying to cope with their tall neighbours. In a few moments we reach Bon Accord Street. On our left as we have been nearing the junction is one of Aberdeen's more curious buildings, the huge livery stables and offices of Campbell's Ltd, Post Horse Masters. Campbell's monopolised the Aberdeen business in the late nineteenth century. They started here in 1889 but extended the building twice in the 1890s and again in 1908. An unusual feature on this dense urban site was the first-floor horse stalls accessed by a ramp. The stalls were constructed of cantilevered concrete. It is worth remembering how much not just the countryside but the city relied on horse power until relatively recently. Until the First World War, for example, horses also drew all wheeled road vehicles and canal boats. Scaremongers even predicted that the city would drown in horse manure!

The horses are long gone and this is now a great example of the city's urban renaissance, a conversion to flats and shops. There is hardly a gap site or redundant building in Aberdeen. It has provided a model for urban regeneration but it has never really suffered the neglect that our other cities have endured. Look around you and you will see no traditional inner-city problem areas, in spite of the fact that a large proportion of the city's working population lives outside the boundaries in rural Aberdeenshire.

Opposite the Galleria restaurant is a building or reconstruction of

Bon Accord Crescent

1937, pre-dating Aberdeen's other 1930s masterpieces, the Northern Hotel (now the well-restored Aberdeen Hotel) at Kittybrewster and Rosemount Square (see p.116). The civil engineer Gavin Williamson built Jackson's Garage with A.G.R. Mackenzie, the noted modernist from the Mackenzie architectural dynasty, as consultant. It was built as Jackson's Garage in a suitably modern but polite granite style. The doorpiece is typically Art Deco, with receding planes of granite, as is the rectangular clock and the winged torch motif above the door. Jackson's displayed the very first motor car in Aberdeen. I wonder if it was a four-wheel drive. Anyway, it's ironic that the horse's upstart rival, the motor car, had its premises right opposite the old livery stables. The east wall of the house that originally stood on the site of the garage has been sympathetically built into the new garage of 1937.

On the other side of Bon Accord Street, the large building with the arcaded ground floor is the telephone exchange, designed by the London architect Leonard Stokes around the turn of the century. Bon Accord Square was laid out by the architectural hero of Aberdeen, Archibald Simpson. He was 'a pioneer of civic design in this his native city', according to the monument in the centre of the square. This is a solid block of granite with the drill holes still visible: a fitting monument for

Simpson. The square was laid out by the Tailor Craft of the Incorporated Trades. It was not unusual for the Trades to speculate in property, for the benefits of their members. Their function as controllers of apprenticeships had long since passed and all over the country they were moving into a charitable role. The equivalent today would be a pension fund developing property. Simpson did not get on too well with this particular client. They seem to have been hard taskmasters. Nevertheless, the quarrel was not so bad that they could not patch it up and the architect ended up buying properties for himself and for his brother in the development, now nos. 13 and 15. Simpson later moved to no. 1 East Craibstone Street, where he died in 1847.

The idea of a whole square in a city put up to one design was still a novelty at the time of the Tailors' speculation. It was quite difficult to achieve because of the variation in land conditions and the amount of speculation required. This may explain the quarrel with Simpson. The square today is mostly converted to offices but it is still possible to imagine the sense of enclosure and exclusiveness that the residents must have enjoyed at a time when towns could still be quite rough and dangerous places. The square is rather neo-classical, with a very Roman circus type shape in the middle for the pleasure ground. There is a contrast between the layout of these houses and those in Golden Square. Here the entire first floor to the front is taken up by the elevated drawing-room. On the other side of the square, at its 'exit', is a delightful low cottagey terrace with big gardens in front. On the other side of these cottages is the Hardgate.

It was exactly at this point that one of the most infamous battles of the Covenanting Wars took place in 1644. Control of Aberdeen had changed hands between the Royalists and the Covenanters nine times during the conflict, the very last that the city had to endure, but Montrose's attack was the swiftest and bloodiest visitation that the town had ever suffered. Montrose brought his 1,500-strong army to a point near a small farm at North Garthdee not via the Bridge of Dee where he had met with difficulties before (see p.177), but crossing the River Dee at Mills of Drum and marching along the north bank. From there he sent a messenger to the town, offering terms of surrender. The town refused and therefore, under the agreed terms of war, laid Aberdeen open to pillage and murder should Montrose and his army fail to be repulsed. As the messenger was returning with the town's reply, a drummer from Montrose's detachment was shot and killed. Montrose immediately launched an attack. The head of the Aberdeen garrison, Lord Burleigh, rode out with his citizen army to meet Montrose and the two forces clashed on this spot at Justice Mill glen. Some 160 inhabitants of the city fell in the battle or in the three days of looting and pillaging which followed. The names of 118 of those who died have been preserved and include many of the most prominent people of mid-seventeenth-

Bon Accord Crescent; each house formerly owned a strip of land in the gardens

century Aberdeen: advocates, burgesses and tradesmen.

We can see granite at its most pristine here in the gentle curve of **Bon Accord Crescent.** Few details are worked into the composition, just the pure stone and the railings. Opposite no. 3 Bon Accord Terrace, walk over into Justice Glen, a piece of ground separating the Hardgate from Simpson's new development, raised up exclusively on its designed topographical platform. Justice Glen was named after Justice Port (see p.145), one of the six city gates of Aberdeen. The other five were Futty, Trinity, Netherkirkgate, Upperkirkgate and Gallowgate. There is an original viewing platform here, raised on brick vaults. From here we can see our destination, the new suburb of Ferryhill.

The scheme for Bon Accord Crescent is close in spirit to that of Princes Street Gardens in Edinburgh. The idea is to give amenity to the houses by preserving a green space opposite. This notion was taken right through the centuries in suburbs like Ferryhill, which we are about to enter. Even the North American idea of the 'City Beautiful' in its parkland setting is simply a continuation on an often huge scale of this simple idea. The suburbs represent a flight from the town, and the park was conceived as a way of sanitising the town, or forming a protective barrier for a middle-class area.

What caused the flight from the towns? The economic growth of the later eighteenth century had huge consequences for towns. The attitude of the landowning classes changed after the 1745 Rising and the abolition of heritable jurisdictions, which ended the last of their judicial powers. But as their ability to punish was taken away, their economic power increased, and the building of planned settlements accelerated dramatically, especially here in the north-east. Country houses and villas were built around the towns by the *nouveaux-riches*: lawyers, merchants, and soldiers enriched by their colonial adventures. The real growth area was inside the towns themselves, however. In Edinburgh, Glasgow and Aberdeen, new institutions, assembly rooms, chambers and hospitals were built. In all this, the crucial development was a notion that each building within a city could relate – on equal terms – to every other. The idea of the palace or the houses of the rich dominating the city disappeared completely. In its place was created a new conception of the entire city as a monument. By 1850 one Scot in five lived in the big cities. By 1900 it was one in every three. The idea of 'leaving' the city but staying on its outskirts was first experimented with by the rich and shortly thereafter by the middle classes, whose houses we see all around us now. The local council in turn wished to bring the benefits of suburban living to their tenants. The ground here at Justice Glen was completely open until 1930s when the granite tenemental housing was built to capitalise on the parkside setting.

On Springbank Terrace we have slightly less grandiose houses of one and a half storeys on the lower part of the hill, but they are still very uniform. They were probably designed by Alexander Ellis, who lived at no. 66. Ellis was born in Aberdeen and educated at Robert Gordon's Hospital (see p.100) and Aberdeen University. He trained with William Smith who designed Balmoral and was city architect of Aberdeen. He is best known for his churches in Aberdeen and the north-east. His masterpiece is St Mary's Church in Huntly Street.

Next on the left past Ellis's house is the typical granite rubble and harl (render) with some of the very summarised granite detailing over the doors in the next part of the block. This kind of detailing was the very least that the middle-class Aberdonian could aspire to.

When we get to the Bon Accord Street junction we should go right and over the bridge. This is another typical piece of Aberdeen's taming of topography with engineering, if on a very small scale. From the 1760s and the construction of Marischal Street, the city was always bridging, always levelling out with buildings placed above and below the bridges. This particular bridge was built to give access to Aberdeen's first suburb, Ferryhill, so it is a tiny version of the mighty Rosemount Viaduct (see p.112). Caledonian Place is a typical Scottish street of two sides. One side is four-square granite of two storeys, the centre expressed with two bay-windowed houses. But on the other side is a row of cottagey terraced houses. The unusual thing here is the introduction of sandstone detailing. Caledonian Place was built by James Matthews in 1859 and the idea was to introduce some variety into the miles and miles of new granite that were being put up as the city expanded.

Walk down Caledonian Place to Ferryhill Road, take a right and walk up the little hill to Abbotsford Place, again with its terraced cottages, but this time of the 1880s. Remember that these cottages were built for the rising middle classes, not for 'artisans'. Aberdonians seem to have a special affection for the single-storey house, an affection which carried right through to the twentieth century and can be seen in the incredible number of bungalows built from about 1900 in the suburbs around Anderson Drive.

We are now in the heart of the residential area of Ferryhill, which was Aberdeen's first true suburb of the nineteenth century. As with most cities, there had at first been individual 'villas' laid out in the area. As development pressure increased, these villas were bought up and their land developed in terraces. Among the original villas there were brick-works and small-scale industry as well as a group of workers' houses at Dee village in the low ground near the river. These have all gone, squeezed out by residential development.

The church in front of us at the top of the hill at the junction of Fonthill Road and Polmuir Road is the early Gothic style Ferryhill Church of Scotland. It was built for the United Free Church at the quite considerable cost of £5,500. The designer was the local architect Duncan MacMillan, a church member and session clerk. The church halls were added in 1885 and extended in 1894 with 'Aberdeen Bond' masonry detailing. This was a way of constructing in granite which involved placing little stones almost mathematically between the main stones. The effect is very pleasing. The enclosing wall and railings were built in 1942. The interior of the church is largely unaltered, except for the addition of side galleries to cater for the growing congregation. It is known that the original architect did not favour the use of such galleries because of the darkening effect he considered they had on the interior. Inside you can see a memorial plaque to the architect as well as stained glass and the unusually elaborate cast-iron columns on which the galleries rest.

In the very pleasant and spacious **Ferryhill Place** there is an interesting variety of house type. On the corner with Ferryhill Road at no. 34 is quite a grand 'double' villa: two houses composed as if they are one. It is complete with fish-scale slates and French roofs topped by a nice cast-iron weather-vane. The rest of the street is older. Nos. 20–30 are quite different, constructed of 'rag-rubbed' granite (rubble smeared with thin render leaving most of the stone exposed). Others, posher examples, have squared granite. You can see this contrast very clearly at nos. 17 and 19. These 'cottage' houses are actually two storeys high but the principal storey is raised up. This is a traditionally Scottish way of arranging things so that the public rooms are on the *piano nobile*. The street was laid out by Archibald Simpson from about 1831 but the east side is later, with a mixture of whole houses and original flatted blocks.

At Marine Place there is another Aberdeen triangle of pleasure ground, just like Abbotsford Place. The railings here have all been recently restored and how much more ordered and urban things look as

Ferryhill Place

a result. You should now cross over South Crown Street, and straight over to Devanha Terrace. During the neo-classical period from about 1750 to 1850 Aberdeen, like Bath, stressed its Roman origins. The Romans had been town-planners and this inspired the modern Aberdonians. *Devanha* of course was the Latin word for 'Dee'. On Devanha Terrace the gardens of the houses are separated from the buildings by a road and this perhaps explains their poor condition. This was another Scottish tradition, particularly in the planned towns but is more often seen in the fishing towns like Tobermory or the slate-quarry towns at Ellanabeich where the houses were rented to workers in the industries. Looking at the buildings of Devanha Gardens, we should be starting to recognise by now Archibald Simpson's trademark elongated consoles (brackets).

Go along to the end of the terrace and look down on the suspension bridge. We can see Aberdeen's first connection with the village of Torry on the other side of the River Dee. This bridge was designed by John Smith with Captain Samuel Brown in 1829. It was a division of labour typical of the time: the engineering dealt with by a military man who specialised in suspension bridges, and the aesthetic side – the 'pylons' at each end – dealt with by the architect. (The idea of separating the functions lasted right up to the 1930s with the designing of the Sydney harbour bridge pylons by the Scottish architect Thomas Tait.) To the left is the Queen Elizabeth Bridge, a satisfying work of pure engineering designed in 1983 by Grampian Regional Council Roads Department without the assistance of an architect. Further south on the heights of Torry is Craiginches Prison, which was opened in 1891 to replace the old East Prison in Lodge Walk. This was the scene of the last judicial execution in Scotland, which took place on 15 August 1963. Until relatively recently, if you had looked over the harbour and beyond Torry, you would have seen rolling hills jutting out into the North Sea. The entire area of Torry and Craiginches was densely covered with housing in the later nineteenth century by the Aberdeen Land Association (see p.224). The boom came largely as a result of the huge expansion of the trawling industry.

Back over on South Crown Street is Marine Terrace, which is by far the most pretentious of Archibald Simpson's residential projects. It is Aberdeen's version of Royal Crescent on Edinburgh's Calton Hill. Simpson originally proposed the name Belvidere Terrace because of the sweeping views over the harbour. 'Marine' was preferred, perhaps because it was also possible to see industry and slum dwellings – the opposite of what 'Belvidere' suggested. The terrace proposed in 1831 was of single-storey and basement height with two-storey end blocks. By 1837 only two of the single-story houses had been built. They were full town houses, though, with a service floor below and bedrooms above. The scheme was revised in 1877 by J. Russell Mackenzie and Duncan MacMillan, who used a granite cornice instead of the timber one proposed by Simpson. Timber details painted to look like stone were by no means uncommon. As you go along the terrace, if you get a chance look through through the houses right to the back and see the beautiful bay windows with gardens to the rear. Inside in some cases are big doors with parliament hinges (hinges which allow the large doors to fold right back on themselves) which were used so that the occupiers could have the flexibility of two rooms or one large one for entertaining. The block at the end was not completed until 1967, in a modern adaptation of the original scheme.

Among the quite ordinary twentieth-century housing of the area in Devanha Gardens is Devanha House, a remarkable villa redesigned by Archibald Simpson in 1840. This is one of Simpson's and Aberdeen's favoured low, lodge-like villas, which is a deceptively large house. Simpson added the unusual D-shaped ends, the smart portico and a trellised garden front to a pre-existing, much smaller and plainer house which had been built in 1796 for the brewer William Black. It had extensive grounds, a sort of mini-estate. The remodelling work was done for William Henderson, a partner in the ship-owners George Thompson & Co. and it was probably this connection which suggested the magnificent and unusual column screen of solid teak in the dining-room, which is to the right as we look at the house.

Amongst the later villas of the area, no. 2 Devanha Gardens West is the most interesting. This house was designed by J.R. Macmillan in a very reposeful English Arts and Crafts manner about 1900. Continue down Devanha Gardens to Polmuir Road and turn left. The entrance to Duthie Park is on the right at the foot of the hill.

To return instead to the city at this point, you can walk back down onto South Crown Street, until the junction with Millburn Street. On the opposite corner you will see the former headquarters of Aberdeen's municipal electricity-generating company, later taken over by the North of Scotland Hydro Electricity Board. Like the other big Scottish authorities Aberdeen Council began at the end of the nineteenth century to take over many of the functions such as transport and health that had been provided by private companies. The provision of electricity on a city-wide basis was an ambitious scheme. The company constructed a tunnel between their offices here and the industrial site at Broadford Works, where the ornamental head of a ventilation shaft can be seen at Hutcheon Street (see p.153). The building is on the site of Dee Village which was swept away for the new development.

You should now go back on to Bon Accord Street and recross the bridge over Springbank Terrace and walk up Bon Accord Street. At no. 64 you can see the home of the celebrated artist-architect James Giles (1801–70). Giles's work is to be found throughout Aberdeen and the north-east. He was elected RSA in 1829. Giles is best known for his paintings of animals and salmon but he also had a love of landscape, particularly with castles. Giles was also frequently employed as a consultant in Romantic architectural compositions such as Rubislaw Terrace and the design of the McGrigor Memorial (see p.174). He also acted as landscape consultant to Lord Aberdeen, the Prime Minister (see p.249), who is said to have been the first person to suggest Balmoral as a Highland estate to Queen Victoria.

Duthie Park to Bridge of Dee is a shortish walk or a continuation, which takes in Aberdeen's most celebrated and monument-studded park. The walk's terminating point is also one of its most famous monuments, the Bridge of Dee. Duthie Park is beautifully situated on the edge of the River Dee on its north bank but we can also approach it from Ferryhill. There are four entrances to the park but we start the walk at the entrance on Polmuir Road and walk down towards the river, cutting back along the park's edge to exit on the Great Southern Road. There is also an option for railway enthusiasts and others to take the line of the abandoned Deeside railway but it's better to pick this up after walking along the riverside with the Dee on your left all the way to the bridge. You will then have the option of retracing your steps or picking up the railway line again and taking that route as far as you wish – even all the way to Banchory by taking the bus from Peterculter to Crathes.

One of the big attractions of the park is the collection of modern glasshouses, designed in 1972 by the City Architects. These are replacements for the elegant buildings blown down in the fierce gale of 1969. The original building had been built between 1899 and 1900 using St Petersburg redwood. The first municipal Duthie Park was designed by

W.R. McElvie in 1881. Like so many suburban parks, it was originally the site of a villa, in this case 'Arthurseat' (a play on the owner's name and a reference to the famous Edinburgh hill). It was one of a number of small suburban 'estates' which were in the tradition of the renaissance villas around Rome designed for pleasure rather than any commercial purpose. The estate was left to the city of Aberdeen by Miss Charlotte Duthie for the purpose of creating a park. One of the things the visitor will immediately notice is how well used the park is. Aberdonians really know how to enjoy a park. In the centre is an excellent café offering full meals, not just ice-lollies. The whole place seems very continental in spirit.

On the other side of the glasshouses is the 'mound' which was to be the base for the Wallace Statue, now on Rosemount Viaduct (see p.112). The purpose of the mound was simply to allow a view of the villa and its Deeside setting. The summit of the mound gives a view of the whole park. The glasshouses, with their superb collection of cacti, look very interesting. Behind you, you will see the Deeside railway line where it skirted around the edge of the little estate behind a discreet granite wall.

In front of Duthie Park's mound, towards the river, is a little planted wilderness of trees. The idea was that one part of a designed landscape would be apparently left as nature intended. In fact it was carefully planted with attractive trees and shrubs with a walk through it. The Duthie Statue celebrates the gift of the park with a monument to Hygeia flanked by four lions. Hygeia was a goddess of health much invoked from the eighteenth century onwards as a kind of patron saint of fresh air and healthy living. Parks were increasingly regarded as an antidote to urban living with its confined spaces and disease. The statue was erected in 1883, not long after the showpiece park was opened. On the theme of clean water, we can also see a cistern house just on the edge of the park. It was designed in 1706 for Fountainhall but rebuilt here in 1903.

Parks can often be repositories for unwanted buildings. The great obelisk which forms the centrepiece here formerly stood in the quad-rangle of Marischal College (see p.79) but was removed here during the huge extension of the college in the late nineteenth century. The obelisk was originally put up by Alexander Ellis with the painter James Giles acting in his familiar role as artistic adviser. The obelisk was in honour of Sir James McGrigor (1771–1858), a distinguished army surgeon and one of a great many celebrated Aberdeen medics. He entered the medical department of the army in 1793 as surgeon of the Connaught Rangers and served in the Holland and Flanders campaigns of the two following years. In 1798 he was put in charge of the medical department of the Anglo-Indian army in Egypt, 'through the deserts of Thebes and Suez to Alexandria'. The Duke of Wellington considered him 'one of the most able, industrious and successful public servants I have ever met with'.

From the enormous size of the memorial, McGrigor was clearly well thought of at his *alma mater*. When the obelisk got in the way of expansion there was no great problem. Aberdonians have something of a can-do attitude to the removal of buildings. The best known example is the Wallace Tower, which was removed from Netherkirkgate to make way for Marks & Spencer's but there have been many others. The old pack bridge at Ruthrieston (see p.176) was moved a mere 30 metres east in 1923; and one of a pair of Duthie Park's lodges was removed as part of a road-widening scheme of 1901. That little house became a bijou residence at no. 72 Rubislaw Den South. Near the cistern house is a small building made up of architectural fragments that date from medieval times. These are seventeenth- and eighteenth-century fragments of the Old Burgh Courthouse, demolished to make way for the new Town Buildings (see p.53).

We leave the park at the Great Southern Road and, taking great care, cross the dual carriageway and walk over to the riverside along the front of Allanvale Cemetery. There are many good memorials here. One of the best is an example of the work of Pirie & Clyne, the monument to James Saint, 1892. According to Pirie's obituary, 'its execution relieved many an hour of illness, and not improbably the dying architect may have felt it to be his last work, and so made it his best'.

We now have the select suburb of Ruthrieston on our right on this side of the river. On the other side of the river, across the King George VI Bridge (1939, by Sir Frank Mears), is the little garden suburb of Kincorth. This estate was laid out on the hill along traditional lines by the city council in the late 1930s following a national competition. Granite and slate are used throughout. Even from this distance we can appreciate the Aberdonian's dedication to gardening. The scheme appears like a huge terraced garden, answering the exclusive private suburb on this side of the river. Ruthrieston's villas submerged an old hamlet whose ancient roots probably relate to its strategic position at the Bridge of Dee, for many centuries the most important crossing of the river. There is little remaining from those times except the old bridge of 1693 which was moved downriver in 1923.

We should now cross Riverside Drive and walk by the river on a lovely sandy path. You will see all sorts of bird life. This must be one of the most pleasant city strolls anywhere. Beyond the cemetery, notice the house on the corner of Ruthrieston Terrace and Riverside Drive. It was a villa converted to the Deeford Home for Working Lads, a place for youths from the country to stay while they got themselves established in the city. Over the top of this house, you will see the bellcote of Ruthrieston South Church in Holburn Street. A. Marshall Mackenzie designed the church in an Early English style in 1890.

The small rural hamlet of Ruthrieston had already been colonised by wealthier Aberdonians who built villas on the north side of the Dee from the 1840s. These were clustered around existing settlements, but the huge growth of the city in the later part of the century demanded the

Bridge of Dee

almost complete redevelopment of the area. Plans for laying out the whole district with more modest, but still large, suburban villas were produced from the 1870s. Since the area's great attraction was and is the proximity of the River Dee, the idea was to base the scheme around the creation of a wide riverside carriage drive, with grander houses to the river and more modest ones to Holborn Street. The new suburb was served by the Deeside railway. Commuting must have been a serene experience! Of this scheme, a few original houses are of interest, notably no. 74 which was designed in 1885 by Matthews & Mackenzie for Sir William Hall the shipbuilder (it has recently been converted to flats). The villa was originally known as Fordbank and is a 'survivor' of James Forbes Beattie's ambitious scheme to line the riverside with villas. Sir William Hall's firm, Hall Russell & Co. Ltd, was the last of a very fine tradition of shipbuilding in Aberdeen. The firm made iron and steel ships, ranging from cargo vessels to warships (see p.202).

We are now close to the bridge. Near the water's edge on the left is the 'plank' bridge or packhorse bridge over Ruthrieston Burn. The bridge was moved to the site and a coping added in 1923. It was solely for the use of packhorses, rather than motorised or wheeled transport.

The **Bridge of Dee** should be appearing now to your left. This is one of Aberdeen's best loved 'buildings', for a long time a trademark of the city even although it was, until the twentieth century, quite remote from the town itself. The Bridge of Dee was one of the pet cultural projects of the magnificent Bishop William Elphinstone (see p.183) but he did not live to see the work completed. In fact the bridge was barely begun on Elphinstone's death in 1514. (It is dated 1520 and 1525.) As at St Machar's, however, the project was enthusiastically taken up by Elphinstone's successor Gavin Dunbar, who ordered Alexander Galloway and Thomas Franche to carry out the work. Building river crossings was considered an important act of charity and any burgh which could afford a fine bridge was highly regarded.

The bridge is an early Renaissance design, rationally laid out with a flat deck and simple faceted cutwaters all decorated with coats-of-arms and inscriptions. A seven-arch design, each span measures 13.75 metres. The ends are marked with tall conical piers with ball finials. The design is as much about the beauty of solidity and construction values as architectural detailing. There was a chapel at the north side of the river which as well as being a gateway on the south side, was traditionally a place for giving thanks for a safe crossing. Both of these were removed in a widening scheme of 1840 overseen by John Smith who had gone so far as to recommend replacing the bridge. The council, whose conservatism saved many buildings in the past, decided against the bridge's destruction, and instead Smith was instructed to widen the existing structure. He did this by taking down the west side of the bridge, incorporating a broader base and then replacing the detailing.

After looking at the bridge, walk back towards the roundabout on the city side of the river. Where Riverside Drive meets Anderson Drive, you will see Bridge of Dee Court or Lorne Buildings. These were put up by the council last century to house employees of the City Waterworks. Aberdeen's water comes straight from the River Dee at Cairnton and is held in reservoirs at nearby St John's Terrace. There is a remnant of an earlier scheme at a fountain house at Garthdee, sited next to the B&Q store on the other side of Anderson Drive. This scheme of 1830 was the Water Commissioners' second attempt to provide the city with a clean supply. An earlier scheme tapped a spring near the mill of Gilcomston and brought the water via an aqueduct to a cistern in Broad Gate. The

BATTLE OF THE BRIDGE OF DEE

As with all river crossings, the Bridge was of major strategic importance and at least one major incident took place here. This was a key early skirmish in Montrose's campaign, which came about as a result of Lord Aboyne's ill-advised chase of Montrose into the lands of Mearns. Instead of fleeing, Montrose stood and fought Aboyne at Megray Hill. Montrose was equipped with an array of field artillery to which Aboyne's Highlanders were not accustomed and the advancing army was broken up in disarray. Montrose doubled back to Aberdeen and the townspeople decided to mount a guard on the Bridge of Dee. The defenders barricaded the south end of the bridge and placed large artillery at the north. Musketeers were stationed along the length of the bridge. The brilliant strategist Montrose feinted to the west as if to attempt a crossing of the river by a ford and the bridge's captain of defence sent a large number of his men to counter such an attempt. The result was that the weakened defence could not repel a sudden attack at the bridge and Montrose crossed with dry feet and entered the town.

later Garthdee project brought water to the city at the rate of 1,000 gallons a minute. The water was fed to a building at 478–484 Union Street which was a gigantic cistern masquerading as a tenement. This scheme was superseded by the Dee River project. Anderson Drive is named after one of the city's most celebrated lord provosts, Sir Alexander Anderson, who was in office from 1859 to 1866. Among many other achievements, Anderson devised the new water supply scheme for the city.

You can go along Anderson Drive until you meet the intersection with the disused Deeside railway walk, which is signposted as a walk back to the city just beyond Crathie Terrace.

Old Aberdeen

A short walk in the historic burgh of Old Aberdeen, including
King's College and St Machar's Cathedral

Our Lady of Aberdeen, from the fifteenth-century Church of Finistère, Brussels

Main places of interest	King's College, St Machar's Cathedral
Circular/linear	Linear, part circular
Starting point	King's College
Finishing point	St Machar Drive
Distance	1 mile
Terrain	Pavements
Public transport	Bus to King's College from Castle Gate
Sections	King's College to Old Aberdeen Town House
Architects	John Smith
Nearby walks	Walk 6
Refreshments	St Machar Bar
Notes	This is a relatively short and pleasant stroll. Care should be taken when crossing St Machar Drive

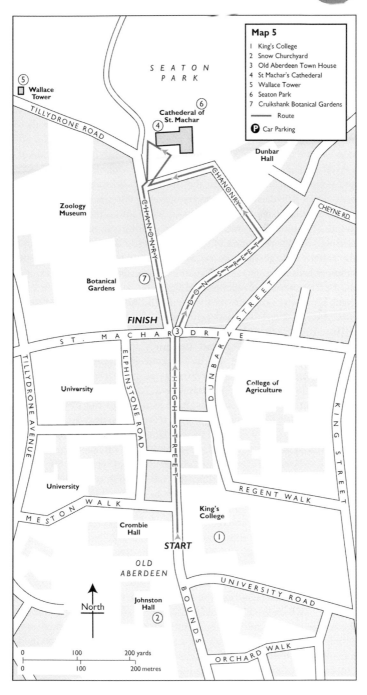

Map 5
1. King's College
2. Snow Churchyard
3. Old Aberdeen Town House
4. St Machar's Cathederal
5. Wallace Tower
6. Seaton Park
7. Cruikshank Botanical Gardens
— Route
Ⓟ Car Parking

'high strong walls and dikes'

This is a leisurely walk in the historic burgh of Old Aberdeen. I should remind readers right away that in fact there were two Aberdeens. This one is not the 'historic centre' of Aberdeen but a different place altogether. To distinguish the two burghs in the eighteenth century, one was simply referred to as 'old', the other 'new'. Neither was there any sense in which 'New' Aberdeen was particularly young – it was just that Old Aberdeen is even more ancient than its much bigger neighbour. Old Aberdeen was an entirely separate burgh, which retained its social and political identity long into the nineteenth century. But it was the port city of Aberdeen which was transformed into the industrial capital of the north, leaving Old Aberdeen to settle into a picturesque retirement. This retirement was only slightly disturbed in the twentieth century with the expansion of the universities in the 1960s. At that time the pattern of large villas set in generous grounds was disrupted by the influx of halls of residence and expanded university departments. For the most part these are only glimpsed as we make our way through. As with many apparently sleepy university towns, Old Aberdeen is an intellectual powerhouse behind its ivy-covered walls.

It so happens that Aberdeen has not one but two of Scotland's most important church buildings, and they are both here in Old Aberdeen. It was here that modern era in Scotland was ushered in with the establishment of a renaissance seat of learning to rival those of Paris and Orléans. During the medieval and Renaissance period of the fifteenth and sixteenth centuries, Aberdeen was in the forefront of a national revival. The leading figure of this movement was one of the country's greatest writers, Hector Boece (c.1465–1536). Boece (pronounced Boyce) led a full-scale intellectual onslaught against the English assumption of superiority over Scotland. He and his fellow men of religion, John of Fordun (c.1320–c.1384) and Walter Bower (c.1385–1449), contested English claims by tracing a line of rulers back to Scota, the daughter of an Egyptian pharaoh. Over these thousands of years, they argued, Scotland had never been conquered, and a range of invaders, including the Romans, had been repelled. Among other things, this allowed for a celebration of the 'golden age' of Scottish 'fredome' during the time of the MacMalcolm dynasty (1058–1286), an era followed by the 'dark ages' of war with England. All of this is important in understanding the design of St Machar's or Aberdeen Cathedral, which seems to recall an earlier period in Scottish history. We will see this magnificent building near the end of the walk. A new definition of national community and kingship gradually developed, moving away from its origins in chivalry and religious duty towards a broader idea of the 'state': much closer to what we now understand by that term. The psychology of this mind set is quite complex.

Like most emerging nations of the fifteenth century, Scotland needed a past as much as it needed a future: a history which could be shown to have been free of foreign domination. The medieval world was not conceived as a 'society' in our modern sense, but a strict hierarchy, with God at the top, and power cascading downwards through His worldly agent, the Pope. At the heart of Scotland's sense of insecurity, therefore, was the claim of England as superiors in a hierarchy. And we must remember that this was no mere technicality: the implications of overlordship were immense. In a 'devolved', feudal kingship, the final arbiter, indeed the 'owner' of the title to lands of Scotland, would have been the English crown. Of course, the Wars of Independence had been won, but the English claim continued, and had to be addressed. To understand a man like Bishop William Elphinstone we have to put him in the context of his times. He was the chancellor and Hector Boece was the first principal of the new college at Aberdeen. His salary was fixed at forty merks, or £2/4/5d.

To the left of the complex we see the earliest and most celebrated building of the group, **King's College Chapel** (1500–9). The college would not always have been so open, however. Formerly the complex was protected by a nine-foot-high stone wall, rather like the Chanonry, which we see later in the tour. The best view of the chapel can be had from the doorway in the wall at no. 51a (or 51½) College Bounds. Look up at the top of the tower. You'll see a rather unusual architectural feature. This is the crown spire, a kind of Scottish 'trademark' used all over the country from St Giles in Edinburgh to the Wallace Monument in Stirling as a symbol of royalty and therefore of Scottish patriotism. Right on the very top of the steeple is a little colonnade (a series of columns

John Slezer's view of Old Aberdeen, c.1693

King's College

linked by arches) wrapping round the spire telling us very clearly that the Renaissance had arrived in the city in 1500. Aberdeen was a centre of Renaissance humanism, the movement that began to study man and his environment. The amazing crown steeple should be seen in the context of experiments in stone construction which were taking place at the time all over Europe from Rouen to Glasgow. The idea was to create a structure which seemed to stretch engineering to its limits, almost to defy gravity. We know that the weight of the stone of the crown is transferred by means of the buttresses but to the early Renaissance mind this must have seemed like an almost magical proposition.

On the right of the chapel is a range of buildings put up by the City Architect John Smith in 1830. These replaced some of the earlier structures of Elphinstone's college, notably the south-west tower and the principal's apartments. Inside, Smith designed a new museum and a meeting room for the Senate, the governing body of the university. The style of Tudor Johnnie's building is suitably Gothic although it contained all the early nineteenth-century mod cons. The front of the building is sandstone, like Archibald Simpson's contemporary Episcopal Cathedral in King Street (see p.148). Technology was still not so far advanced as to be capable of producing intricately cut granite Gothic building. To the rear the building is plain granite, with sandstone dressings (decorative elements).

The beautiful memorial in front of the chapel is dedicated to Bishop Elphinstone. It was cast in bronze by Harry Wilson in 1911. The monument was too big to put inside the chapel. We enter the courtyard through a 'pend' (from the French *pendre*, 'to hang') or passageway. Inside the pend there is a notice listing a set of rules warning that 'the following offences are liable to fine as under: riding a bicycle within the gates of King's College, 2/6; injuring or defacing any part of the College buildings, 10/- [quite right]; and, for walking on the grass at the new buildings of King College, 2/6'.

Bishop Elphinstone's idea was to cure the 'almost barbarous' state of the region with learning and an understanding of its glorious history. As a result of looking backwards as well as forwards in late fifteenth-century church architecture as a whole, Romanesque architectural features began to appear in otherwise Gothic buildings. The clearest example of this phenomenon is the round columns of the nave of Stirling's Holy Rude Church (1450s–70s), which also included a detail dating possibly from James IV's marriage to Margaret Tudor in 1503, namely an archway, leading to the (later demolished) St Mary's Aisle, decorated with thistles and roses. The 'idea' of Scotland, having been expressed through the church here at Aberdeen, was now beginning to rest with the monarchy for its definition and development. James III, with 'ful jurisdictioune and fre impire within his realme', began the headlong drive to modernity and reconstruction based on the new power of a centralised 'state'.

Elphinstone was planning his college in 1497. The start of the building is inscribed on the west front of the building as 2 April 1500, although that may be have been idealised to coincide with a supposed anniversary of the building of Solomon's Temple. The date of 1504 can also be seen on one of the buttresses, but in the context of the early sixteenth century this is a cracking pace. A contract for the roofing of the structure with lead was signed in 1506 with an English plumber, John Burwel, and the chapel was ready for dedication in 1509.

We now enter **King's College Chapel** itself. (It is open most days.) Look up at the timber 'waggon' roof. The pattern of 'ribs' is purely decorative and meant to imitate vaulting. The roof is actually carried by great rough-hewn beams above the ceiling. Elphinstone had built a similar ceiling at St Nicholas' (see p.92). The source of these ceilings is a bit of a mystery. It may be that they were intended to recall earlier stone vaults in Scotland or that they were influenced by ribbed timber examples found in the Low Countries. Elphinstone had been on a diplomatic mission there in 1495 and may have been consciously or unconsciously impressed by what he saw. The tracery of the great west window at the chapel, with its heavy central mullion, may also have been influenced by what he saw in the Netherlands, but the very rounded shape of the window also suggests an interest in the Romanesque, the round arched style of architecture which was associated with patriotism in Scotland.

The finest surviving original feature inside the chapel is the magnificent carved wooden choir stalls and screen. Although they were restored in 1823 and moved to the west end of the chapel in the 1870s, this work remains the best example of its type in the country. It seems that Scot-

45–51 High Street, Old Aberdeen

land did not go in for elaborately carved timber as a rule in churches so the existence of so fine an example is all the more remarkable. Look at the detail of the mini 'buttresses' and the tiny carved arches between each one. The great pre-Reformation pulpit was originally designed for St Machar's and was moved here in 1844.

The next building on the way round the courtyard is in stark contrast to the chapel: a massive plain tower, which looks like a castle but was in fact an early hall of residence, built in 1658 for students by General Monck, Cromwell's lieutenant in Scotland. Monck had been ordered to reform King's College and he began by sacking the principal William Guild and installing the Hebrew scholar John Row in his place. Part of the reform meant attracting more students and they had to be accommodated. Each of the six floors originally had four rooms. The ubiquitous John Smith converted it to a four-storey building in the nineteenth century. The simple tower reminds me of the many student accommodation towers which were built in the 1960s. The heraldic panel above the door is marked 'VE'. These are the arms of William Elphinstone, the university's founder. The stone tablet in the west face commemorates the building of the tower, listing John Row and four of his regents. The brightly painted memorial is to Henry Scougal, son of Bishop Patrick Scougal.

On the south wall of Cromwell's Tower is a memorial, a replica of one in the Tower of London, commemorating Alexander John Forsyth. He was a country minister, a man of peace who carried out some very warlike studies, including experiments here at the tower into ordnance (guns and cannon) and who in 1807 developed the percussion system of firing on which the defence and expansion of the British Empire was based. The George McNicol visitor centre includes a permanent display on the history of the King's College and some of its illustrious students. It also has an excellent account of student life through the ages. (The University of Aberdeen is the third oldest in Scotland and the fifth oldest in the UK and the university celebrates its foundation in February each year with a special service in King's College Chapel.) This building, part of which has also been converted to a conference centre, was put up in 1870 by the government architect Robert Mathieson to provide a new library. The panel above the door represents the hand of God descending upon the open book of learning, with the coat-of-arms of Old Aberdeen and of William Elphinstone.

The building opposite King's College in College Bounds is Powis Lodge, its low eighteenth-century front masking quite a grandiose house behind. The house dates from 1697 and was remodelled in 1711 and again in 1829, probably by John Smith. It has a strange little tower, designed by Alexander Fraser in 1834. You will see this type of tower in an enlarged form as a double entrance to the grounds of the house. These towers are said to echo the demolished spires of King's College, which, like many historic buildings, was 'improved' in the 1820s by stripping away 'impure' later additions.

At 29 College Bounds is the Snow Churchyard. This is now a burial-ground occupying the site of the church of St Mary ad Nives (St Mary of the Snow) which was founded in 1497. The church was later called the Snow Kirk. In the eighteenth century this was known as the 'Papist's [Catholic] Burying Ground'. There is a notable monument of the slab type to Menzies of Pitfodels. Like many other older churches all over the country which have been abandoned, the churchyard has remained and cannot easily be deconsecrated.

Along College Bounds with King's College on the right you will see, set back politely from the street, some of the modern university buildings put up in the 1950s and '60s as part of the university's first big expansion of the post-war years. Very few of them are of great architectural interest, but the Fraser Building with its ultra-modern dome (as it was then) caused quite a stir. The arched building set back from the college is a connecting cloister built as late as 1927 by A. Marshall Mackenzie as part of a wider expansion plan. Directly ahead is the lovely portal for New King's which had already been put up by Mackenzie in 1912. The design has all the elements of the old King's. New King's was part of an ambitious plan to build a new quadrangle, one which was open to the street. The plan was only half realised and it was not until the 1950s, when the utility Taylor buildings were put up, that the square was completed in a respectful if bland style.

It's here that College Bounds becomes **High Street** and you will see the herring-bone pattern of the medieval street with its backlands and wynds leading off the main thoroughfare. It is a typical Scottish burgh

High Street, Old Aberdeen

high street. Some of the gables are to the street, reflecting an earlier 'burgage' (see p.84) pattern of development, and the more grandiose have a 'front'. These are interspersed with courts, wynds and ways. The long row of eighteenth-century houses with their gables to the street were put up according to the same site layout. The gabled building at Douglas Place has its first floor 'corbelled' out. This is a throwback to medieval 'jettying', when buildings might jut out into the street above first-floor level to colonise the air space.

At nos. 57–61 there is a charming building with the date of 1821 set into the skewputt at the end of the gable. This is an earlier building with a polished granite shopfront grafted on to it, topped by a nepus gable with its artfully 'Gothick' window. A little further on, at Thom's Court, the height of the traditional stone wall has been increased to give more privacy. The builder has done this using Seaton brick (see illustration below), a local material that is very characteristic of the area.

At no. 70 High Street we see the interface of the old and the new: a Georgian town house of 1820. At no. 81, well set back from the street behind grandiose gate piers, is the town house of the McLeans of Cott. What we are seeing here is a deliberate idealisation of Scottish burgh life: the big house, the medium-sized house and the little houses of the workers. This was a theme of Scottish architecture in the 1930s, which led directly to the preservation of the little burghs. It happened in the East Neuk of Fife first but then spread throughout the country as part of a broader 'heritage' preservation movement. The interest in the 'intimate' world of the Scottish burgh where 'big rubs shoulders with small' also influenced new development.

On our right as we go up the street we see together the two-storey

High Street, Old Aberdeen, and its characteristic mixture of granite and Seaton brick

Side elevation of the Town House, Old Aberdeen, showing architectural fragments and cells

houses of Wrights and Coopers Place, cheek by jowl with Grant's Place, a long row of single-storey eighteenth- and early nineteenth-century cottages with pantiled roofs. In the 1950s pantiles became associated with the 'vernacular', that is, the truly Scottish. A lot were used in Old Aberdeen when the whole place was restored in the 1960s by Robert Hurd, the leading conservation architect of the day. As Scottish cities prepared themselves for major rebuilding and renewal after the Second World War, Old Aberdeen was identified as a 'heritage' zone, to be carefully conserved but also enlarged with new university buildings.

We should now continue the walk up the High Street towards the building facing us at the end of the street. With its sleek but very plain frontage, the St Machar Bar on our left at no. 97 is a fine old pub converted from a house. The city does not seem to have gone in for exuberant timber bar fronts of the type that the Victorians liked so much. The interior has a good collection prints depicting Old Aberdeen. In passing, note that the ornithologist William MacGillivray lived at no. 110 High Street. He was a celebrated birdwatcher who in 1827 wrote the text to accompany to John James Aubodon's magnificently illustrated five-volume *Ornithological Dictionary*.

Now the street opens up to provide a market place and an apron of civic dignity for **Old Aberdeen Town House**. This was the town hall of the old burgh and the centre for civic justice. The Town House was a monument to the civic independence of Old Aberdeen, which was not subsumed into 'new' Aberdeen until 1891. The market cross stands in front of the Town House, the symbol of its burgh status. The cross has Bishop Gavin Dunbar's coat-of-arms on it, very faded. Above the door

20 Chanonry, Old Aberdeen

of the Town House is the Old Aberdeen coat-of-arms, with the Aulton (Old Town) Lily. On the north wall (Don Street) of the building there are features from an older structure which once existed on the site. You can also see a vent, the sole source of light and air into the two police cells behind. Behind the large timber doors beyond was kept the hand-cart used for picking up drunks from the streets and transporting them to the cells to sleep it off. At this point, unfortunately, the tarmac of the very busy St Machar Drive cuts through the Old Town. Beyond this road is the peaceful haven of Don Street where the causeys (cobbles) pick up again.

To cross St Machar Drive, we must walk a few yards to the right to reach a pedestrian crossing. After crossing, we go back towards the continuation of Don Street, past a nice little development of sheltered housing at Bedehouse Court, roofed with pantiles in order to fit in. Now we turn right into Don Street and immediately re-enter a really charming street lovingly restored with causeys and pantiles. Some of the houses here are very old indeed. No. 20, for example, is dated 1676. Its close has a moulded archway and the building itself is made of rubble with chamfered margins (angled stone window dressings) though originally it would probably have been harled (traditionally lime rendered). Many of the older buildings of the area were heavily restored in the 1960s. Opposite, at 43 Don Street, is a late seventeenth-century house of the type that had a strong influence on Charles Rennie Mackintosh around 1900. Opposite that, at no. 46, is Dun House, a typically Georgian house set back from the street with garden ground behind.

At this point we take a sharp left into the Chanonry, an ancient enclosure where the pre-Reformation élite, the canons of St Machar's, were housed. Behind these 'high strong walls and dikes' were their manses and gardens. Over the top of the walls you can see the spires of our destination building, **St Machar's Cathedral**. At **no. 20 Chanonry** is the seventeenth-century Chaplain's Court, which includes interesting relics from a building from the previous century such as a moulded passageway arch with the bishop's arms over it. All around Chanonry is a lovely, 'pinned' rubble wall, encircling the whole area. We pass the cathedral manse on our right and a very utilitarian box at no. 15 which is a much-altered early nineteenth-century reconstruction of an earlier building.

The interior of St Machar's Cathedral

The entrance to St Machar's is shouldered between two muscular gatehouses built in 1832 by John Smith. To the left of the entrance is the eighteenth-century wellhead of the Chanonry Well with its pyramid top. Continue into the churchyard but before entering the church itself walk over to the other side and look back at the west front of the cathedral. This is one of the glories of Scottish architecture and the only granite cathedral in Britain. The west front has fascinated scholars for centuries.

It has recently been argued by historians that Scotland's first architectural steps towards the Renaissance were taken, as in Italy, when buildings began to adopt the form of low, massive structures, prominently featuring round arches and columns and archaic 'dog-tooth mouldings'. Like the Tuscan revival preceding the Italian Renaissance, this may have been a conscious recalling of the Romanesque architecture of the Mac-Malcolm 'golden age' which John of Fordun, the Aberdeen historian, had researched. This revival of the architecture of the MacMalcolms took place in the recognised centres of patriotically inspired historical research: Dunkeld, St Andrews, Dunfermline and, most spectacularly, Aberdeen. In the third quarter of the fourteenth century, when Fordun was writing his chronicle here as a chantry priest, the first and most monumental setpiece of the style was begun: the nave of St Machar's Cathedral. Heavy, warlike towers with crow-stepped gabled cap houses flanked its stocky round columns and massive west façade, round-arched doorway and line of seven slender round-arched windows. Bishop Elphinstone built a central bell tower and spire very much like the one at St Nicholas' (see p.93) which was later destroyed in the fire of 1874. In the 1520s Bishop Gavin Dunbar altered the towers of the west front to their present form. So, at the height of the movement towards flamboyant Gothic in France and England, Scotland reintroduced a Romanesque style of architecture.

The cathedral must have presented an incredible sight to contemporary Aberdonians. Its construction had proceeded remarkably quickly but it was hardly finished before the Reformation was begun in earnest. Very unfortunately it was an immediate target for the iconoclasts and thieves. You get the feeling that the destructive work of the Reformers was only very half-heartedly undertaken in Aberdeen. Sometimes, though, an example had to be set. At St Machar's in 1560 the Barons of Mernes decided to show the locals how it should be done. They demolished the monasteries of the Black and Grey Friars and then set about St Machar's with equal force. The vandals took 'all the costly ornaments and Jewels, and demolished the chancell: they stripped the lead, bells and other utensils intending to expose them to sale in Holland, but all this ill-gotten wealth sank, by the just judgement of God, not far from the Girdleness'.

The church suffered again from vandalism in the 1680s. St Machar's length was reduced by half through the collapse of the central tower in

St Machar's Cathedral

1688. The collapse came about as a result of the earlier English occupation of Scotland by Cromwell's troops. Cromwell's men had removed much of the stone and used it for the fortification of Castlehill, thereby leading to the complete collapse of the central tower along with the transepts and the eastern end of the nave. Interest in the church as an antiquarian object steadily grew in the nineteenth century and from the 1830s the building was repaired by the City Architect John Smith.

The entrance to the church is through the beautiful little Gothic south porch, which was a later addition. This was traditionally the place where local betrothals were witnessed. Moving inside, there is excellent information available for visitors in the form of a 'bat' which you can carry with you around the church. It tells you that the church is dedicated to St Machar who was born in Ireland, the son of a king or chieftain. He was baptised by St Colman and was given the name Mochamann. He encountered St Columba who renamed him Machar and took him with him on his famous journey to Iona. Machar was commanded to go further north, to a place where he would find a river in the shape of a bishop's crook. The renowned artist Douglas Strachan tells the story of St Machar's pictorially in the stained-glass Crombie Memorial window. There is a full description below the window. If we also look at the stained-glass window to the left of the entrance celebrating the three builders of St Machar's, we can see what the west front of the church looked like prior to the installation of the spires between 1515 and 1530. Adjacent to these windows are three other very important signed examples of the work of Daniel Cottier. He was an artist-decorator from Glasgow who brought about a revolution in taste in late nineteenth-century Scotland by offering a complete design package from decoration to stained glass and even paintings. Cottier moved to London in 1869, and subsequently on to the United States; by 1873 his decorative-art and art-dealing business was disseminating 'artistic' taste across the anglophone world, with branches in New York, London and Sydney. His influence can be followed through to the work of John La Farge and other decorative artists, and examples such as Trinity Church, Boston. Of the other stained glass in the church, the best is the huge narrative piece incorporated within the seven slender windows of the west front. This tells the story of Christ and His Apostles. The windows in the north aisle were all designed after 1945 and are the work of Marjorie Kemp and Margaret Chilton. The font in the north aisle was designed in 1954 by A.G.R. Mackenzie. The sculptor was Hew Lorimer, son of Sir Robert Lorimer, the celebrated architect of the Scottish National War Memorial at Edinburgh Castle.

Going outside again, we should take some time to look at the churchyard monuments. The greatest of these is to Gavin Dunbar, who was bishop from 1519 until 1532. It is now covered by what was once a modern shelter to stop the steady erosion of the sandstone. Although there is a unique Scottish post-Reformation tradition of putting monuments in the graveyard, the irony here is that this memorial was originally built inside the church but is now outside. Only the walls of the transept surrounding it remain, leaving the monuments exposed to the elements. To the rear of the churchyard is a lovely view over Seaton Park. If you look over at the church from the back of the churchyard you'll see the remains of the demolished building and the scar where it was repaired. Notice the beautiful carving of the columns.

If you're feeling energetic as you leave St Machar's you can continue your walk into Seaton Park. Otherwise, take the southern section of the Chanonry.

In **Seaton Park** can be found the reconstructed Benholm's Lodging or **Wallace Tower** which in 1962 was removed stone by stone from the site in Netherkirkgate now occupied by Marks & Spencer's. The tower, which has nothing to do with William Wallace, was built originally in about 1610. It is a good reminder that what we refer to as 'tower houses' were also built in towns and cities. When it was originally put up, by Sir Robert Keith of Benholm, however, it was located just outside the city wall. The tower was carefully taken down, rebuilt and restored in its present position under the supervision of the late Dr Douglas Simpson, one of the country's leading architectural historians. From this point it is a short walk to the historic Brig o' Balgownie (see p.214).

Directly opposite St Machar's is no. 12, Tillydrone House, built in 1820 by John Smith. This is one of these cottage villas that the early nineteenth century and Aberdeen particularly so much enjoyed. The idea was to present the image of a cottage but at the same time to have the

The Wallace Tower, Seaton Park

space and comfort of a substantial villa. The house was originally named St Machar's Cottage but later owners clearly thought this would send out the wrong signal.

As you walk past the gate lodges of St Machar's directly opposite, notice a nice little post box built into the wall. This is a small thing, but it gives character to the area. The box has the initials 'GR' (for 'George Rex' – King George). There are no 'QE II' post boxes in Scotland. Nationalists attacked them in the 1950s, arguing that since Scotland had never had a Queen Elizabeth I, there couldn't be a Queen Elizabeth II! The government took a pragmatic view and withdrew the new boxes. No. 9 is the former Mitchell Hospital, a single-storey courtyard block of alms-houses, latterly a home for 'aged ladies' which was converted to cottages by A.H.L. MacKinnon in the 1920s. The next few houses are more predictable early nineteenth-century villas. If we look at no. 7 Chanonry, however, we see a huge version of the very simple houses of the High Street, pumped up to provide a very grand house. The house is on a basic three-bay plan but it has basements and attics and shows how the simple classical model could be extended or contracted according to the wealth and status of the owner.

Next door is the Cruikshank Botanical Garden which is open to the public, Monday to Friday, 9 a.m.–4.30 p.m.; Saturday and Sunday (May to September), 2–5 p.m.

We should now continue our walk back up to St Machar Drive. At the corner with it is Cluny's Port. This was formerly the gatehouse to Cluny's Garden, now the Cruikshank Botanical Garden. The land around the cathedral was a kind of Holy See, administered by the bishopric. Some of these ecclesiastical rights were retained until the incorporation of Old Aberdeen within the modern city in 1891. The cathedral and the buildings associated with it were surrounded by high walls, some of which we have seen on our walk. Cluny's Port was the main entrance to these lands and represented the boundary of the bishop's jurisdiction.

This is where the walk ends.

Main places of interest	Fish Town, Aberdeen Harbour, Brig o' Balgownie
Circular/linear	Linear
Starting point	St Clement's Church, Footdee
Finishing point	Brig o' Balgownie
Distance	3½ miles
Terrain	Pavements in first section. Rough track on Donside, which can be avoided
Public transport	Bus from Castlegate to Footdee and from Beach to Brig o' Balgownie
Sections	Footdee to Beach, Beach to Brig o' Balgownie
Architects	John Smith
Nearby walks	Walk 5
Refreshments	Cafés and bars of the Beach. Silver Darling restaurant
Notes	This is a long walk, which begins among the docks and quays of Aberdeen and ends at the thirteenth-century Brig o' Balgownie, beyond Old Aberdeen. Please bear in mind that the walk begins in an industrial area with trucks and ships coming and going. The immediate area around St Clement's Church is also something of a red-light district (on a very small scale) from the early evening. Footdee is a very old and interesting area and the thriving commerce and industry only adds to its charm. Afterwards, the walk opens out into a bracing walk on the beach and from there to the famous Brig o' Balgownie.

WALK 6

Footdee and the Harbour, Aberdeen
Beach to the Brig o' Balgownie

*A walk through Aberdeen's bustling harbour, past the charming 'Fish Town' of
Footdee and along the Beach promenade to Balgownie*

Girdleness Lighthouse

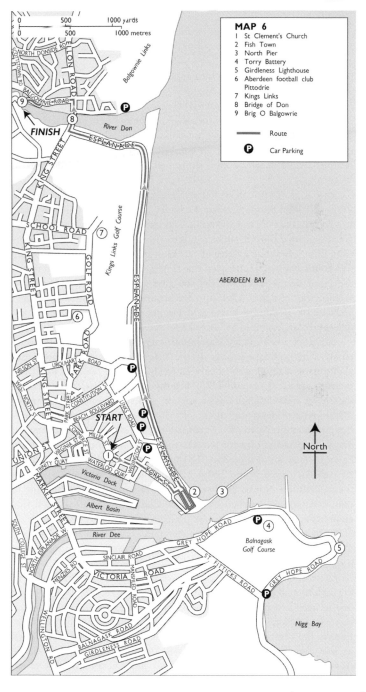

MAP 6
1 St Clement's Church
2 Fish Town
3 North Pier
4 Torry Battery
5 Girdleness Lighthouse
6 Aberdeen football club
  Pittodrie
7 Kings Links
8 Bridge of Don
9 Brig O Balgownie

━━━ Route

🅿 Car Parking

6 WALK

'Here likeways, they walk for their health.'
GORDON OF ROTHIEMAY, 1661

Footdee is really the Sunday name of a settlement which even the most upwardly mobile Aberdonian will pronounce 'Fittie'. The place was always separate from Aberdeen, yet this was not, like Old Aberdeen, a separate burgh. Fittie was Aberdeen's Leith, the business end of town, and it has seen many industries come and go, including, very sadly, shipbuilding. The 'Fittie' in question most probably referred to the nearby Chapel of St Fotinus, shortened as usual by Aberdonians to 'Foty'.

The original settlement of Fittie grew up around the church of St Clement's. John Smith, the City Architect, designed the church in 1828. It is no longer in use today but it has an interesting graveyard which will get us in a maritime, if rather sombre, mood. St Clement's dates originally from 1498 when a chapel was built for the devotional use of the fishers of Fittie. Each fisher paid one shilling a year per line and in return the priest was required to celebrate two masses each week. After the Reformation the church became derelict and was eventually replaced in 1828 by the present structure when it became a parish church by the division of the parish of St Nicholas.

There are a few granite warehouses to be seen in the vicinity of the church but nothing remains of the original settlement. John Smith planned a new town in the area with St Clement's as the focal point, but industry soon took over. If you look at the Edinburgh style-tenement on the corner of Wellington Street, with its arcaded ground floor, you will see the type of development the city had in mind. Walk along towards this tenement up Wellington Street to York Street with the long range of granite warehouses on your left. On the left now is York Street Nursery School which was designed in 1881 by the celebrated Aberdeen masters John Bridgeford Pirie and Arthur Clyne. It has a very church-like street frontage, almost Nordic in character with its stumpy tower. It is one of only two schools designed by Pirie & Clyne, who normally designed churches and houses. The 'primitive' aspect of the design clearly leads on from their earlier work but here the influence of Alexander 'Greek' Thomson is even more apparent, particularly in the bold massing and the battered (sloping) base.

As we continue down York Street we are now seeing all that is left of the famous Hall Russell shipbuilding yard. Hall Russell & Co. was founded in 1864 as a partnership between James and William Hall; Thomas Russell, a Glasgow engineer; and John Cardno Couper of Sussex. Initially the company built engines and boilers but in 1868 it produced its first ship, the iron steamer *Kwang Tung*. As trawling took off in Aberdeen in the 1890s, the company built many of the specialist vessels for this industry including *Strathdon*, *Strathtay* and *Strathspey* for the Aberdeen Steam Trawling and Fishing Co.

During the First World War, Hall Russell made minesweeping trawlers but after the Second World War the company returned to fishing and cargo vessels. *Star of Scotland*, produced in 1947, was regarded as the most advanced fishing trawler ever built and became a symbol of Scotland's progress in harvesting the seas. In 1971 Hall Russell built the largest ship ever constructed in Aberdeen, the 10,500-ton cargo vessel *Thameshaven*. The company became part of the state-owned British Shipbuilders in 1977 and was one of its most successful yards, producing a number of offshore patrol vessels and torpedo-recovery vessels for the Ministry of Defence. As worldwide competition increased, the launching in 1990 of the *St Helena*, a cargo and passenger vessel, marked the end of Aberdeen shipbuilding. The last yard here closed in 1992. At its peak in 1907 the yard had employed 1,200 people. All that is now left of the shipyard is the junior football club which continues to use the Hall Russell name. The father of Eurythmics singer Annie Lennox spent most of his working life as a boilermaker at Hall Russell.

James and William Hall were the sons of Alexander Hall, who had established his own company in 1790. He took over the business of Cochar & Gibbon, where he had been an apprentice and then a partner. Alexander Hall & Co. were Aberdeen shipbuilders from 1790 to 1957. The earliest ships built by the firm were wooden sailing vessels. The *Scottish Maid*, a schooner of 1839, was the first to have the famous forward curving Aberdeen bow for which the firm is now best remembered and which improved speed and sailing performance. When Alexander died in

Aberdeen harbour, c.1919 – sail gives way to steam

1849 he left James and William to run the business. The brothers were responsible for many famous clippers such as *Torrington* and *Stornoway* for the opium and tea trades – speed was everything in this highly competitive trade. William took charge of ship design while James managed the business. The brothers were among the first to pay attention to employee welfare in the often dangerous business of building ships. The Hall's Dockyard Sick and Medical Fund was started in 1846 and workers would receive sick pay, medical attendance and medicine. If the worst happened, the fund also provided funeral expenses.

One of Hall's best known ships was *Jho Sho Maru*, a barque-rigged steamer, which was built for the Japanese Navy in 1868. This wooden corvette had a belt of iron armour-plating and carried eight 64-pounder guns and two 100-pounder guns. *Jho Sho Maru* was nearly finished when a fire broke out near by. James Hall was worried that the corvette would catch fire. He ordered that *Jho Sho Maru* be pulled into the middle of the dock, away from the flames. Sadly, while helping to fight the blaze, he suffered a fatal heart attack.

Although best known for its sailing ships, Hall also constructed steamers. The company built its first marine engine in 1887, for the launch *Petrel*, and its first trawler, *Maggie Walker*, in 1888. During the Second World War, the company specialised in steam tugs, most of them for the Admiralty. The company was taken over by Hall Russell in 1957.

John Duthie (1817-72) established Duthie's ropeworks on the far side of York Street in 1869. Duthie took over the firm of Catto Thomson and changed the name. This was a branch of the family business, which was shipbuilding. The aim was to produce everything that went with the ships, from the sails to the ropes. The Footdee works employed over 100 people in 1889. The ropeworks were long low buildings for stretching out the material. These would be almost impossible to convert to another use and have been demolished. The buildings were roughly on the site of the 16th century Blockhouse, which defended the harbour. James' son Alexander (1870-1929) ran the rope works until his retirement in 1920. In addition to rope and sailmaking, the family were also involved in whaling and fish processing. The Duthie family were important Aberdeen shipowners and builders. They built the full range of vessels: from wool clippers (sailing ships) to steam trawlers. The Duthie shipyard was established in 1816 by William Duthie (1789-1861), who had been an apprentice at the Alexander Hall yard. At first Duthies specialised in small vessels but soon they were in competition with Hall's for clippers. These were often named after members of the family. William Duthie was a shipowner as well as a shipbuilder and, under the name William Duthie Bros. he established a range of products and services related to shipbuilding. By 1835 the vessels *Circassian* and *Ann* were taking emigrants to North America, *Hercules* and *Brilliant* carried timber.

In 1841, the Duthie vessel *Undaunted* brought the first guano back

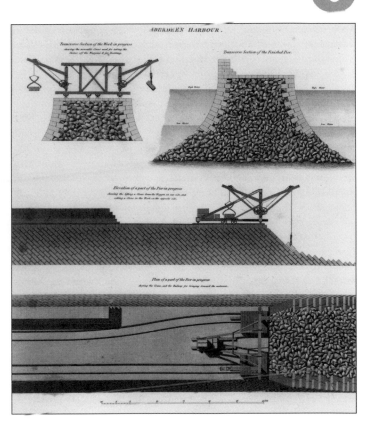

Details of the pier construction at Aberdeen harbour from Atlas to the Life of Thomas Telford, *1838*

from South America and William also set up the first regular service between London and Australia. The shipyard was taken over by his brothers, John (1792-1880) and Alexander (1799-1863). On Alexander's death in 1863, the firm was renamed John Duthie Sons & Co. Now the company began to build larger vessels such as the *British Merchant* which was built in 1857 and twice as big as any vessel yet built by the company. The Duthies were seafarers as well as shipbuilders. Every new ship owned by the family was skippered by one of sons, James, William and Alexander. The Duthie vessels voyaged regularly to Australia with emigrants and returning with wool. When James retired from the sea, he took over the Duthie Ropeworks. The yard also carried out repair work. One of their specialist skills was the lengthening of steel ships, which was done by cutting the ship in two and adding an extra section in the middle, a bit like a stretch limousine today. In the late nineteenth century, the company built steamships, mostly fishing vessels. They produced the first Aberdeen screw trawler, *North Star*, in 1883. The Duthies were at a disadvantage in this market as they did not build engines, and so business went instead to neighbouring yards: Alexander Hall and Hall Russell. John Duthie, Sons & Co. closed in 1907 and the yard was taken over by Hall Russell.

At the bottom of York Street you will see the sign 'Pocra Quay'. Take a left here and then a right immediately into New Pier Road. The 'new pier' referred to here was the Pocra Pier, built to accommodate the whaling industry. We are now on the public side of the tiny and charming new town of Footdee, which was moved from the area around St Clement's to this place, an area referred to as Sandilands or Sandness. This was really land reclaimed from the sea beach. John Smith laid out Footdee's squares in 1808–9. The first to be built were North and South Square. Pilot Square was added later. All the houses were originally only one storey high, but the council sold them to the occupiers in 1880 and the results are there to see. Space was maximised in a series of San Giminiano-like towers.

We should now continue down New Pier Road to the quayside towards the Royal Navy monument at the end of the street. The work is by the sculptors Gaie and Rett and commemorates the dead of the two world wars. We are now on the edge of Pocra Quay, which gets its name from a by-product of whaling. The whaling industry in Aberdeen thrived in the late eighteenth and early nineteenth century but dried up by the 1830s. The most profitable by-product of the industry was whale oil. The terrible stench pervaded the whole area. There was no whaling after 1850, by which time gas lighting had been pioneered by none other than Walter Scott at Abbotsford, his home in the Borders.

The safe navigation channel into the harbour was called the 'Raich'. Before the construction of any piers at Aberdeen ships sheltered in the lee of the Girdleness promontory on the south and on the Sandness dune to the north (where the North Pier was later built). Development of the harbour was achieved by reclaiming the land of the Dee estuary and by building upon it whilst protecting it from tidal encroachment with piers. The first attempts at this type of development were made as long ago as 1658 when a small pier at Shore Brae was extended over to Footdee, thereby enclosing the tidal sands and creating the 'shore lands' on which Virginia Street, James Street and Commerce Street now stand. The English engineer John Smeaton built two much larger piers – Smeaton's Pier and Abercromby Jetty – in the eighteenth century. Both of these large structures helped to keep the tide at bay. The celebrated engineer Thomas Telford recommended further expansion of Smeaton's Pier and the building of an 800-foot breakwater. The North Pier was later extended seaward by 900 feet, again on Telford's advice, along with 600 feet of breakwater. This gave an increased draft of 21 feet. The last extension of the North Pier brought the total length of the jetty to 1,050 feet.

In 1829 the River Dee burst its banks and flooded the quay, sweeping away great chunks of its walls. Afterwards, to counter this, it was decided to deepen the channel of the river, with the result that ground was reclaimed on either side. On this ground Trinity and Blaikie's quays were built. A wet dock was constructed between 1844 and 1848. Finally, the very course of the Dee was altered in 1879 to facilitate the construction of the Albert Basin.

It is possible to walk right out along the gigantic North Pier. In its day this was a marvel of engineering and sea taming, much visited by visitors to Aberdeen. As early as 1836 Lord Teignmouth noted that: 'The pier would form an agreeable promenade to the natives of Aberdeen, if the road to it did not pervade the dirty lanes or fetid store yards of the maritime part of the town.'

The oddly shaped building in front of us is the Harbour Master's Station. There is a nice use of strips of granite and harling (render) on this late eighteenth-century building. Just past the Harbour Master's Station is the well-known Silver Darling restaurant, considered by many to be one of the best in the country. The 'silver darlings' were the herring which, for a brief period, brought a Klondike-style rush to sea.

The 1880s herring boom brought sudden wealth but, as one old historian noted, 'the herring is an ambulatory fish', and the shoals moved on. Neil Gunn's book *The Silver Darlings* gives an account of the herring fishers' lives. The herring swam in great shoals near the surface and could be caught in huge numbers by swift little boats using drift nets. Herring was cheap and became a staple of the diet, usually cooked in oatmeal or smoked as a kipper. With the flight of the herring, Aberdeen was forced to develop a new speciality: the steam trawler. This was a fast new boat with a sunken net that caught the deeper-swimming fish. The original fish market was at the foot of the Shiprow. Many of the distinctively shaped smokeries can still be seen between Market Street and the railway.

Nearer to us here on the quayside we can also see what appear to be tiny lighthouses. These are the leading lights, used to guide ships through the safe channel to harbour. One light is red, the other green. The tall brick structure is an earlier form of navigational device. Over on the other side of the channel can be seen the fortified wall of the nineteenth-century Torry Battery, built to protect the harbour in case of invasion by the French. The Battery can be visited as part of a walk around Girdleness, taking in the lighthouse (see p.211) and the ruins of St Fytock's Church. There is a marvellous view back to the city from that point.

We now commence a brisk and sometimes blustery walk along the Esplanade via the shelter of the settlement of Fittie. Walk over in the direction of the beach via the pedestrian way to the left of the white-painted stone shed and take a left just before the play park into a lovely neat row of cottages in Pilot Square, which is a later addition to the 'Fish

Town'. You can saunter through here, just enjoying the regularity and neatness of the scene and the vibrant colours of the 'sheddies', no two of which are the same. There is a really nice balance of conformity and individualism. This is the legendary Aberdeen neatness at its most attractive. Notice also the many Gaelic house names: *Mo Dhachaidh* ('my home'), *Tigh na Mara* ('house by the sea'). Although it is often thought of as being just the language of the Western Isles, Gaelic penetrated as far east as Aberdeen and beyond. Local place-names such as Cammachmore attest to this. Linguists among rival football supporters have pointed out that the Gaelic derivation of the local football team's ground Pittodrie is 'midden' (a rubbish tip).

Walk right through and out the other side, passing the church in the centre of the little town, the Footdee Mission. You will find yourself near the beach and can easily reach the raised walk of the Esplanade from this point. From this point you will often see brave windsurfers speeding over the rough seas. Further out are the fishing-boats, trawlers, oil-supply vessels and, every day, the ferry bound for Shetland. We should now walk straight along the Esplanade to begin our tour of Aberdeen Beach. On our left is the Queen's Links. The word 'links' is of Old English derivation but has become a peculiarly Scots expression describing gently undulating ground beside a seashore. This has by association become the word for a seaside golf course, because this is where the game was originally played. The idea of a sand bunker comes from the naturally occurring sandy outcrops found in these areas.

Now on the left are the strangely canopied blank walls of the cinema backs. After these, we pass a row of seaside cafés and restaurants, including Harry Ramsden's famous fish restaurant. Here is also the Inversnecky Café with the Pavilion next door. 'Inversnecky' is in fact a mythical place popularised by the 'Laird o' Inversnecky', Harry Gordon (1893–1957). Gordon was one of the great comedians to have come out of Aberdeen during the variety years. He began his career at the age of 15 at the Old Empire in George Street as Aberdeen's very cheeky answer to Sir Harry Lauder. He was a clever broadcaster who worked with the BBC in the 1920s and '30s and made many records. The Pavilion was the seaside theatre home of Harry Gordon's Entertainers.

Further on is the wonderful Codona Fun Park. The Codona family have been expertly providing this type of entertainment for generations. In a world of Disneyland and Alton Towers, this is perhaps on a smaller scale but, to my mind, it is much better. If you like fairs and amusement arcades, you will love this. It's tremendous, well-run fun. Aberdeen was a thriving beach-based holiday resort until cheap package tours lured the holidaymakers abroad but this fun beach has, thankfully, survived as a permanent attraction, albeit now augmented by TGI Friday, Burger King, Pizza Hut and the rest. Traditional seaside resorts all over Scotland such as Rothesay, Portobello (which is Edinburgh's beach) and Montrose

Aberdeen Beach, King's Links

all suffered. However, Aberdeen did not, of course, rely on summer tourism. Nevertheless, the fun beach tradition has continued here and shows signs of further development.

There was another, rather strange, tradition which was apparently practised down here at the beach. This was the place for one of Scotland's long-standing, inexplicable social customs. This was the rather forcible 'washing' of the bridegroom's feet prior to his wedding. One event is recorded in Margaret Bennett's fascinating book *Scottish Customs from the Cradle to the Grave* (1992). The man who tells the story is Norman Kennedy:

'Well, this was more than 25 years ago, but the lad, a friend o mine – he wis a piper, and his father wis a piper – and this was aboot two nights before the weddin, an we went oot for a drink, whole bunch of us. So we got real happy, an we decided – well, we'd arranged, to tell you the truth, we'd the stuff with us to do it – tae gie him a feet washing, ye see. And we went doon tae the beach, doon on the sands in Aberdeen, an a bunch o us grabbed him an held him doon, an pulled off his troosers. An we had brown boot polish and black boot polish. An we took one leg and it was a' black and the left one got brown!'

The 'feet washing' thereafter extended to a much more sensitive part of the lad's anatomy, again with the dual colour treatment. Anyway the story has a happy ending as was usual.

'We took him home an they had sanwiches an tea, an whisky, an we'd a good night eftir that.'

We now cross over the wonderfully named Beach Boulevard. Boy (and a few girl) racers tour the area at high speed late at night. This wide dual carriageway was cut through like the commercially orientated Market Street in the 1840s. The idea here was to give 'direct access to the sea beach' in the days when there was a dramatic increase in holiday-making. The plan were drawn up in 1930 but the road was not constructed until 1959, when it was opened by the Queen Mother. It is interesting that the Parisian boulevard remained the model for these setpiece roads right up until the 1960s. At the time of its opening, one councillor objected to the name 'boulevard' which he thought suggested a tree-lined avenue. He offered 'Sea Gate' as an alternative, with no success. The council invested a lot of money in this area. Look at the amount of engineering work it has taken to create this huge beach. The far-sighted Provost James Rust (1873–1945) conceived much of it.

Looking back inland is a great view of the city skyline: the Town House, the North Church and Marischal College's Mitchell Hall. Behind the very good Patio Hotel is one of Aberdeen's neat medical complexes, the City Hospital, formerly the Epidemic Hospital intentionally set in a blowy, out-of-town location. Aberdeen's advances in medicine are known throughout the world, but in the summer of 1964 the city gained unwanted worldwide attention as the centre of an outbreak of typhoid. Children had to be kept in isolation wards away from their parents and friends as the city found itself in the grip of a panic. For several weeks the public health authorities searched for what had caused this dreadful disease. The breakthrough came when the source of the infection was identified: a batch of tinned corn beef. For years afterwards schoolchildren referred to anything even remotely resembling corned beef as 'typhoid' and refused to eat it.

We are near the site here of the much-lamented Beach Bathing Station, which was designed by the architect John Rust. Opened in 1885, the Beach Bathing Station was the centrepiece of huge municipal improvements that were made to the beach from the 1880s onwards. Oddly enough, the building was constructed of brick, even if it had the municipal trademark of twin towers. You can see traces of it in the viewing platforms at this point. The beach had been at the industrial end of Aberdeen and there is still an interesting tension between the two uses, with large new clean and modern industrial sheds sitting alongside the various leisure facilities and barely distinguishable from them.

In front of us now is the Beach Ballroom, a rather sedate design, won in competition by Thomas Roberts & Hume of Bathgate. It has a large octagonal ballroom roof with three thermal windows (windows based on Roman Baths). The ballroom of course conjures up many happy or heartbreaking memories for generations of Aberdonians and holiday-makers. The interior has a domed ceiling and is surrounded by galleries. Beyond the ballroom is the Leisure Centre and further on is the Linx (get it?) Ice Arena. Near by, and on a very large scale, is the Queen's Links

Leisure Park with cinemas and restaurants.

At this point we should look back again and take in a distant view of the stupendous Girdleness Lighthouse. Robert Stevenson built this magnificent structure in 1833. It was considered to be the best lighthouse seen by the Royal Commission during the compiling of their report in 1860. At the foot of the great tower are the flat-roofed dwellings of the lighthouse-keepers. Alongside, on the other side of the road, is the 'Torry Coo' – the gigantic fog signal added to the complex in 1880 to warn ships off the treacherous rocks when visibility was poor. The signal was powered by compressed air from an engine house to the north of the main road. The idea of a foghorn was relatively new in 1880; until that time lighthouses had used great clanging bells.

The next significant building that you will see is Aberdeen Football Club's stadium, Pittodrie. Aberdeen FC was founded in 1903 and has gained an international reputation. The club has always been a strong contender in the Scottish league, latterly as the main rival of the big Glasgow clubs, Celtic and Rangers. Among many other honours, the team has won the Scottish league four times and the Scottish Cup seven times. The club enjoyed a great period of success at home and abroad during the reign of Alex Ferguson, in 1983 famously beating the mighty Real Madrid 2–1 in Gothenburg to win the European Cup-Winners' Cup. For many this event has eclipsed Bannockburn in the league table of famous Scottish victories. Pittodrie was the first all-seater stadium to be built in the UK and has played host to international as well as club games. Guided tours are available.

Pittodrie stadium sits just on the other side of the Old Town or King's Links. Golf has been played here since the sixteenth century. The Aber-

Aberdeen Beach, 1907

deen Golf Club was founded in 1815 and members originally played over seven holes here on the King's Links. There is no particular reason why we play 18 holes. It was the number first adopted at St Andrews. In 1866 the Aberdeen Golf Club moved to a site near the end of our walk, at Balgownie on the other side of the River Don, where the club has two fine 18-hole courses. As well as being a municipal course, various clubs share the King's Links, including the Northern Golf Club and the Caledonian. It is most likely that the founding of the club here at the King's Links simply formalised an activity that has been going on for centuries both in Scotland and the Low Countries where the two very similar games of 'gouff' and 'kolf' were played.

The King's Links are formed over the former course of the River Don. Rob Roy MacGregor's uncle, Professor James Gregory, altered the course of the river, the work of building a 'bulwark' being carried out by the citizens of Aberdeen 'to direct the current more easterly for better fish'. It was this same James Gregory who was visited by Rob Roy MacGregor in 1715 (see p.138). After heavy rain it is still possible to see the old course of the river. The pools which form in the links are called the 'Canny Sweet Pots'.

Aberdeen's beach is worth seeing in the morning light with the sun breaking up the famous 'haar', the fog that rolls in from the North Sea. Outsiders often complain about it but the haar is an essential part of the city. You can see the mist hanging around the base of the towers of Aberdeen's links, as high-rise fingers of concrete seem to grow straight out of the rough grass. The towers represent an experiment in Modernist high living that really works. Think of the alternative: individual houses with their own gardens, 'privatising' this great open space. Instead we have dense buildings set in a free-flowing open landscape.

The Esplanade now turns inland towards Bridge of Don. Just before it does there is a witty modern sculpture entitled *Windows to the Sea* on our right. We now walk up towards Bridge of Don, which is the name of an area as well as that of a bridge. Down on the right is a signboard explaining the background to the Donmouth Nature Reserve and the bird hide there. The hide is open during daylight hours.

John Smith with Thomas Telford designed the original structure of the bridge in 1827, which gave rise to the suburb. Smith's role as city architect was to make sure that good taste would prevail over economic considerations. The bridge is carried on five arches but it was widened in 1958 to take the heavy traffic which still thunders across to Ellon and Peterhead. Looking from the bridge out to sea we can see the huts of the salmon anglers on the north side near the beach.

We can now take a riverside path up to the Brig o' Balgownie. Alternatively, if you wish, you can carry on further up Balgownie Road (which is next on the left) to see the boyhood home of the 'Scottish Samurai', Thomas Blake Glover (1838–1911), one of the most interesting and colourful individuals that Aberdeen has ever produced. He was born in Fraserburgh and brought up near here at Braehead House in Balgownie Road. This typically enterprising Scot is credited with nothing less than helping to mastermind the modern Japanese economic miracle whilst overthrowing the Shogun and restoring the Emperor. Glover travelled to Japan in 1859 and was largely responsible for opening up that country to the phenomenal capitalist expansion that it experienced in the later nineteenth century. He imported the first steam locomotive and was a key adviser to the Mitsubishi company. Instead of importing ships from Aberdeen, though, the Japanese began to build them themselves. Glover was a key economic adviser to the Japanese government and was awarded the Order of the Rising Sun from the Emperor in 1908. His life and marriage to a beautiful Japanese woman was dramatised in Puccini's opera *Madame Butterfly*. The Glover Garden in his adopted city of Nagasaki attracts 1.8 million visitors every year.

Braehead House is open to the public, Tuesday to Saturday, 10.30 a.m.–4.30 p.m., and Sunday, 1.30–4.30 p.m. (closed Mondays) but you must first make an appointment (telephone 01224 709303; fax 01224 709301; e-mail: info@glover-house.freeserve.co.uk). It is a very pleasant cottage on the banks of the Don which has been extended several times to make a picturesque villa. There is a curious piece of recycling at the entrance, where the gate piers are clearly marked 'Cranford'. The attempt to disguise this has only made it more obvious.

For a time Braehead was the home of the celebrated Dr Andrew Moir, senior physician to Aberdeen Infirmary and a founder member of Aberdeen Medico-Chirurgical Society. He lived at Braehead Cottage before the Glover family bought the house. Dr Moir narrowly escaped violence when his Anatomy Department in St Andrew's Street was attacked by an 'anti-Burking' mob (see p.155).

On our right above us as we approach along the riverside path is the Cottown of Balgownie, terraced cottages built for industrial workers in the eighteenth century. The River Don was sufficiently strong at a point just above here to power the various mills which sprung up in the area. There are paper and woollen mills but the most impressive is slightly further upriver at Grandholm (pronounced 'Granom') Works. This was the home of the famous Crombie cloth. These mills no longer operate and the complex is set for conversion to an urban village: a complex of houses, a few local shops and some offices. The textile industry here and in the centre of Aberdeen was huge and employed some 12,000 people at its height in the 1840s.

We now approach the Brig o' Balgownie. The balladeer and prophesier Thomas the Rhymer issued a prediction concerning the celebrated bridge.

Brig o' Balgownie

> *Brig o' Balgownie*
> *Wight is thy wa*
> *Wi a wife's ae son*
> *And a mare's ae foal*
> *Down shalt thou fa.*

The sensitive Lord Byron recalled the verse just as he was crossing the bridge, 'a wife's ae [only] son', mounted on 'a mare's ae foal'. Of course the 'childe of passion' thought the words applied to him.

The bridge is an ancient structure, built originally by Richard Cementarius between 1314 and 1318. Cementarius was the first provost of Aberdeen; he also built the keep at Drum Castle (see p.239), the first in a line of architect-politicians. (This was a tradition which carried right through to the twentieth century and included men like James Matthews.) Until the building of the new bridge just down river, the Brig o' Balgownie was the only route north from Aberdeen. When the Bridge of Don was built near by, our bridge was bypassed, indirectly helping it to be preserved. It was long ago reduced to the status of a pedestrian bridge and this too has helped its cause as a heritage object like Robert Burns' famous Brig o' Doon at Alloway. Nevertheless, the bridge has had its fair share of alterations. It was extensively repaired in 1444 and was largely rebuilt in the seventeenth century. It was repaired again in 1861 by William Smith, assistant to the City Architect John Smith and executant architect (with Prince Albert) of Balmoral. Smith repeated the exercise in 1877 and the bridge was finally widened in 1912, with the addition of further buttresses and approach walls.

Below on the left is the former salmon-fishing station. On the other side of the bridge is a very picturesque collection of late eighteenth- and early nineteenth-century houses. The grandest of these is the Chapter House of 1653, which was reconstructed in 1975 with a Parisian-style screen wall. The house was built for George Cruikshank, Dean of Guild in Aberdeen between 1653 and 1655. The coat-of-arms is his, along with those of his wife, Barbara Hervie of Elrick. This was a feature of Scottish houses up until the end of the seventeenth century. The most famous example is Argyll's Lodging near Stirling Castle. The device was also adopted for public buildings well into the eighteenth century. Edinburgh's Municipal Chambers (the former Exchange of 1751) is the best example.

We have now reached our destination. As we are on Don Street, we have the option of carrying straight along this street or cutting through Seaton Park and picking up the Old Aberdeen Walk at St Machar's Cathedral (see p.192). You will see the entrance to Seaton Park just on the right a few yards from the Chapter House.

Main places of interest	Queen's Cross Church, Hamilton Place
Circular/linear	Circular
Starting point	Former Free Church College, Alford Place
Finishing point	As above
Distance	1½ miles
Terrain	Pavements
Public transport	Bus to Alford Place (Holburn Junction)
Sections	Free Church College to Queen's Cross Church, Queen's Cross Church and back through West End
Architects	Pirie & Clyne
Nearby walks	Walk 1
Refreshments	Cafés and pubs and the Courtyard restaurant at the beginning of the tour. The Olive Tree restaurant is midway at Queen's Gate
Notes	This is a tour which includes social history but concentrates on the architecture of churches, villas and terraces

A Sunday Stroll in the West End

A stroll among the villas and terraces of the city's nineteenth-century suburbs

Queen's Cross Church

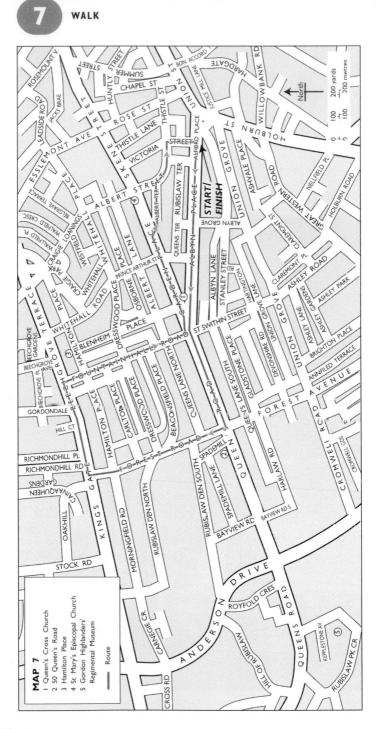

MAP 7

1 Queen's Cross Church
2 50 Queen's Road
3 Hamilton Place
4 St Mary's Episcopal Church
5 Gordon Highlanders'
  Regimental Museum

—— Route

'the granite age'

For many years it was popular throughout Scotland to 'promenade' after church in your Sunday best: men in top-hats and morning-coats, bustled ladies and girls, and boys in kilts and Tam o' Shanter hats. The fashions changed over the years but the tradition of strolling continued until surprisingly recently. This walk takes us along some of the streets which witnessed these changing fashions. They are the avenues and terraces of the second phase of Aberdeen's expansion from about 1820 until 1900. You can take this walk at any time, of course, but it is perhaps more pleasant for a Sunday stroll, when the traffic is light and the buildings of the first new developments are largely empty (this first part of the walk takes us through a former residential area that is now almost entirely given over to offices and banks). Like many other suburban expansion schemes, this was the idea of a landowner, James Skene of Rubislaw. Skene's plan was to 'improve' his land, in the sense of capitalising on Aberdeen's growth. He planned his estate as a wide and spacious mixture of villas and terraces.

We can begin our walk at Alford Place (pronounced 'Ah-ford'), com-memorating the village and the battle of the Covenanting Wars where Montrose defeated Baillie on 2 July 1645. Alford is almost 30 miles from Aberdeen. We start at Christ's College, the Free Church seminary designed in 1850 by Thomas Mackenzie. This was the college where Free Church ministers were trained. The main Free Church college in Edin-burgh did not particularly want what it considered to be an 'outstation' here in Aberdeen, but the city's Free Church adherents insisted.

Opposite, at no. 2 Alford Place is the library of Christ's College designed by A. Marshall Mackenzie. The college and its library were created as a result of a quite cataclysmic, but now largely forgotten episode in Scottish history, referred to as the 'Disruption'. In 1843 some 451 of the Church of Scotland's 1,203 ministers walked out of their annual assembly in Edinburgh in protest at the Church's continued 'establishment' (its connection with the state) and with the rights of the 'inheritors' (the landlords) to appoint ministers. The dissenting ministers created the Free Church of Scotland, inadvertently unleashing one of the largest single building campaigns of that century. It resulted in exhila-rating architectural monuments like the Free Church Colleges of Edin-burgh and Glasgow or the Triple Kirks here in Aberdeen (see p.63). The Free Church was a child of the nineteenth-century version of 'improve-ment' — dominated by the new middle classes and the rich, and by artisans and farmers. From 1847 the merger of the various Secession Churches created another wealthy, modernising denomination, the United Presbyterians, who gave us some of the most advanced church designs in the country. The UP congregations were mostly influential in

Glasgow, where they built sumptuous churches on a huge scale. In Aberdeen the main rivalry was between the Established Church and the Free Church. We can see the architectural results of that rivalry as we walk.

The protesting ministers wished to be free to decide for themselves how to organise the Church's affairs. Many adherents of the newly set-up 'Free Church' were enterprising city dwellers who were part of a general breakaway from landed to urban interests in Scottish society. Of course, as well as building new churches like the Triple Kirks, the new Church had to set up a parallel organisation for training and administration. Soon the Free Church, with its wealth and free thinking, began to produce world-famous ecclesiastical scholars, at a time when the separation of science into the practical and the theoretical was not taken quite so much for granted as they are today. Here in Aberdeen William Robertson Smith, the famous Semitic scholar, taught at the Free Church College between 1870 and 1881. It's difficult now to appreciate quite how important religion was in Scottish society. It used to be until quite recently that arguments raged in households throughout the land on theological issues. Smith himself went a bit too far in his assertions, which were published in the *Encyclopaedia Britannica*. He was sued for heresies and falsehoods and then sacked. Undaunted, he continued his successful career with *Britannica*.

Aberdeen is still something of a last redoubt of religious observance in our materialistic age. It has proportionately more churches in use than any other city (even if, as you will see in front of you rather bizarrely, the Free Church College is converted to bars and restaurants). The Church of Scotland and the Free Church were reunified in 1929, though a minority remained who still referred to themselves as the Free Church. They were concentrated in the north and the Highlands and Islands. There is now no state religion in Scotland.

The main developments in the new church architecture of the later nineteenth century were in Glasgow but while these developments were under way in that city, a very powerful school of neo-Gothic church design was also established here in the north-east, emphasising soaring steeples and the power of granite monumentality. As a result Aberdeen has a superb collection of churches. Much of the dynamism of its wonderful church design probably stems from a competition between the Established Church and the rich and powerful Free Church. The former built Rubislaw parish church (1875, by J. Russell Mackenzie) with a tall, spiky tower, so the latter went one step further by commissioning one of the most exciting Gothic Revival designs of the century, Pirie & Clyne's Queen's Cross Church, opened in 1881 and famous as the first charge of the charismatic preacher George Adam Smith. Pirie & Clyne's main rivals in the 1890s were Brown & Watt, who worked for the Free Church and also for the United Free Church (a union of

Presbyterian sects). These churches included the neo-Gothic Holburn (1894) and Beechgrove (1898, with a tall steeple and gabled nave and transept plan), as well as the classical Melville (1901–3), with its campanile and horseshoe auditorium (see p.119).

We will see the two main players in this ecclesiastical contest in a little while. As we pass Alford Lane, one of the city's nicely restored passages, you'll see the Courtyard Restaurant (one of Aberdeen's best, without being either pricey or stuffy). Albyn Place was laid out in the early nineteenth century with very smart villas, carefully arranged in identical feus (lots). A scheme was prepared in 1819 by Archibald Elliot (1760–1823), a successful Edinburgh architect, in partnership with his brother James. Elliot was one of the chief architects of 'Modern Athens' and was commissioned to do the same for Aberdeen. Elliot prepared a scheme which extended as far as the Rubislaw Burn, but only Albyn Place itself was built as intended. Archibald Simpson designed the rest of the scheme but his plan too was also amended to allow for greater density.

At no. 19 Albyn Place is Archibald Simpson's Aberdeen granite classicism at its most effective. The low architectural look was very appropriate for schools and academies with their Greek associations. Harlaw Academy is one such. It was designed in 1837 for Mrs Elmslie's Institution, a school where orphan girls were trained for domestic service. The institution was bought over by the School Board in 1892 and became the Girls' High School. The poet and author Rachel Annand Taylor (1876–1960) taught here. Just in front of no. 24 Albyn Place is one of Aberdeen's many public wells, St John's Well. As has happened in the suburbs of many cities, a lot of these very large houses have been converted to offices and banks. The loss of the setting – the garden walls, railings and gardens themselves – is quite severe. Look at no. 9 and you will get an idea of how the whole street would have looked prior to the commercial invasion. Further on, at no. 38, is the home of the medical pioneer Sir Dugald Baird (1899–1986) and his wife Lady Mary Baird (1901–83), the social improver. They must have been amongst the last residents of the area.

There is architectural variety here of a very limited sort. Variety was not considered a particular virtue in the 1820s, although as the century went on this attitude changed, as we will see. The main architectural theme is a low, brooding neo-classicism of a type found throughout northern Europe, especially in Germany, and enthusiastically taken up in Aberdeen. These were really quite large houses masquerading as simple villas in the fashion of the day. If you stand outside no. 28 Albyn Place, you will see what I mean. Aberdeen's greatest architect, Archibald Simpson, designed it in 1838. Looking at the main entrance of the building, it appears low and not very imposing. But look above the first roof and you'll see a higher roof at the back where the building is of three storeys. There are about 25 rooms in this house, and it, like its

Albyn Terrace

neighbours, had a very large back garden. Most of these have been built over as the demand for office space has increased.

Directly opposite us on the other side of the road, with its sweeping carriage drives, is the superb Romantic setpiece of Rubislaw Terrace. This is a very grandiose piece of work which is of a later date and belongs to a phase when the city was spreading out but could not really afford the luxury of very large villas set in huge gardens. It is a Romanticised version of the first terrace on Albyn Place. Money and power were cascading down through society and the newly affluent demanded suitable accommodation. A newspaper report of the day was ecstatic about this 'exceedingly beautiful . . . splendid project, the merits of which cannot be sufficiently unfolded in a written description'. This was perhaps going a bit too far and straying into the area of what used to be called an 'advertising feature'. Nevertheless, the houses were models of efficiency, with an 'upstairs-downstairs' arrangement whereby servants and masters could enter the building and live there separately. There is also the interestingly subtle hierarchy of glass. Large sheets of plate glass were manufactured from the 1850s, but they were very expensive and not for everyone in the household. There is a variety here. The plate glass is most likely to be on at the public rooms, the divided panes with astragals (glazing bars) on the basement or the second floor. At Rubislaw Terrace, which was built by Mackenzie & Matthews in 1852, we see the new fashion for Romanticism in architecture appear in the towns. The 'consultant' on the project was the celebrated Aberdeen artist

James Giles. Peddie & Kinnear, the architects for Aberdeen's Town House (see p.54), had just built their new curving street in Edinburgh, Cockburn Street, which linked Waverley Station with the High Street. Both Peddie & Kinnear and Mackenzie & Matthews had as their source book *The Baronial Antiquities of Scotland*, which was published by Robert Billings between 1845 and 1852. This included examples of Aberdeen's 'street architecture' of crow-stepped gables, turrets and dormers (see p.84). It is perhaps ironic that just as these ancient examples were being swept away in the historic centre of the city they were being built again in up-to-the-minute form on the new outskirts.

Prior to the publication of Billings' series, much of Scotland's architecture, like much of its culture, was determinedly 'North British'. When architects wished to be 'historical' they would build in a Tudor or a Jacobean style. The architect W.H. Playfair explicitly stated, in his design for Donaldson's Hospital in Edinburgh, that he wanted to create a building where 'Henry VIII might have met Anne Boleyn'. The introduction of Scottish forms into new Scottish buildings had been begun by Sir Walter Scott at his country retreat, Abbotsford, but the movement was taken forward by reference to real examples in the north-east, the great castles of Fyvie, Huntly and Castle Fraser (see Chapter 8). The crow-stepped gables of Rubislaw Terrace represent a hallmark of the Baronial Revival in architecture, but here each step has its own diminutive triangular pediment.

The terrace is set back with an expensive stone balustrade in front of a large pleasure ground. The ground was designed to be shared with the villa owners opposite but it is now in council ownership and open to the public. The council has restored the railings to the pleasure-ground, improving the site enormously. Most of Aberdeen's railings were cast in the iron foundries of the city, such as McKinnon's at Spring Garden, Henderson's at King Street and Barry Henry & Cook Ltd, West North Street. Other cast-iron manufacturers such as the huge Glasgow firm of Walter Macfarlane & Co. (see p.119) also supplied the necessary extra pieces such as lamps and cresting. It was a large industry, which rose and fell according to the health of the building industry. Architects would generally specify railings which were suitable for the scheme, but unlike in other parts of Scotland, they might differentiate between the staircase and the boundary-wall railings. You'll see this at Rubislaw Terrace. Beyond the terrace there is a much simpler range, but it has very fancy railings. You can appreciate that railings are an essential feature of Aberdeen buildings but the city lost most of its cast-iron examples during the Second World War. This happened almost everywhere else too, apart from outlying places like Stornoway in the Western Isles. The plan was to use the melted-down iron to make battleships and Spitfires but the project was a failure and most of the material was dumped in the sea. Railings were only removed where it was safe to do so (on enclosing walls but not on stairs or in front of a drop) and because of the peculiarities of Aberdeen streetscaping with its very low 'dwarf' walls surrounding gardens and parks, it happened a lot here. The loss of character was considerable but the city authorities are now very keen to put the railings back, as they have done around the communal garden on Albyn Place.

Beyond Rubislaw Terrace and set forward on the main drive is the plainer but very powerful **Albyn Terrace**. J. Russell Mackenzie designed the terrace in the *château* style favoured by some upmarket New York apartment builders on the Upper East Side. It has some of their power, particularly in the huge projecting turret bays at the ends. It is built from top to bottom in 'bull-faced' rusticated granite. Just look at the size of these blocks and try to imagine their weight. The whole terrace is beautifully assembled and symmetrically composed over the whole of its length: a superb piece of work.

On the right near the major crossroads ahead is one of Aberdeen's best and most unusual Gothic Revival churches: **Queen's Cross Church** by Pirie & Clyne. It was designed for the Free Church in 1881 as a wonderful landmark in the smartest part of the town, cocking a snook at its rather tame Established Church neighbour diagonally opposite (built in 1875 by J. Russell Mackenzie). J.B. Pirie was one of Aberdeen's most original designers. He was determined to break out of a formulaic approach to architecture. His churches and terraces are always a delight. The last stage of the tower with its base of stumpy columns might remind you a bit of King's College Chapel but the design is really inspired by French examples and the 'primitive' element of the Gothic Revival in England. Furthermore, the idea of a pinnacle sitting on a colonnade had already been popularised by Alexander 'Greek' Thomson in Glasgow, an architect who had also influenced Pirie & Clyne's domestic work. The dramatic 'gateway' setting on the corner site also reminds us of Thomson, even if the Gothic style of the building was totally alien to the Glasgow architect.

The new popularity of instrumental music was at first reflected in Presbyterian architecture in the 1860s, when the prohibition on music in churches was lifted. This was quickly followed by a spate of organ building. Sometimes organs were tucked away in an 'organ loft' above the entrance, but just as often great play was made of the new instrument by placing it theatrically facing the congregation. The interest in organ music was only part of a wider desire for a 'renascence of worship' in Presbyterianism. The Church Service Society of the Established Church was founded in 1865 to investigate old ceremonies and liturgies, which would give credence to their 'revival'.

Having reached Queen's Cross 'we enter on the neighbourhood that has had its appearance completely transformed in recent times by the operations of the Aberdeen Land Association'. This was written in 1911

2 Fountainhall Road

in appreciation of the main 'developers' of this large area. The Association was formed in 1875 with the idea of buying large pieces of ground and selling it off in smaller lots according to a comprehensive plan. In order for this to work there had to be careful preparation, so that the individual lots would effectively form a whole district. The result is a minutely planned neighbourhood of villas and terraces. The Association's first purchase was from the Skene family and took in the districts of Rubislaw, Fountainhall and Morningfield, the area which we are now entering. Later the Association bought into Torry and Craiginches on the other side of the Dee where they laid out a large district of working-class housing. The Association is still in existence and is better known as CALA.

In front of Queen's Cross Church and now operating as a traffic island is an unusual but appropriate pedestrian bronze statue of Queen Victoria by G.B. Birch (1893). Her Majesty appears to welcome people to the city, but she has her back to us. The statue was moved from the corner of Union Street and St Nicholas Street (see p.57). It had replaced a marble statue of the Queen as a young woman, which was placed for safe-keeping in the Town House (see p.54). When they were formed originally in the 1890s, the streets in the West End were beautifully laid with 'causeys' (cobbles). Around the statue of Queen Victoria they were laid in a radiating pattern. Later, in a spirit of 'improvement', the city began to tarmac its roads and the practice of concrete or 'granolithic' paving was also adopted. These things certainly changed the look of the city but there has been an attempt to restore the original stones with the help of the Heritage Lottery Fund. You can see the results at Shiprow (see p.130) and elsewhere throughout the city centre.

On the other side of Carden Place at 12 Queen's Cross and 2 **Fountainhall Road** is an unusually planned double villa on a very prominent corner site The 'double villa' was the forerunner of the ubiquitous 'semi'. In Scotland the word 'villa' has clung on surprisingly well in the face of change, so that we can have a villa, a semi-villa or even a quarter villa, which is actually one of a four-in-a-block flat, just more picturesquely described. This lovely double villa was designed in 1875 by J. Russell Mackenzie. It is asymmetrical, a feature which adds to the presentational trick of a single house. Some of the timber decoration has been removed but look at its decorative bargeboards, its dormer windows and steeply sloping slate roof with iron brattishing (cresting). Mackenzie also built Rubislaw Church, opposite, in 1875. He had a tremendous site, which he handled well enough, even if sandstone was a poor choice of material. The tower was added later but the whole thing was spectacularly overshadowed by Pirie & Clyne's church across the road.

We now cross Fountainhall Road and continue along Queen's Road in the direction Queen Victoria faces – west towards Balmoral. We are on our way from Queen's Cross to the pretentiously named Queen's Gate, which is at the next roundabout. This was obviously laid out as a high-class district. The best houses still fronted the street in the days before motor traffic compromised things. All the main Aberdeen architects were involved here. They seemed to have shared out the work

1 Rubislaw Den North

reasonably equitably. No. 9 Queen's Road, on the south side of the road (the house next door has a marvellous monkey-puzzle tree, *Araucaria imbricata*), is now the International Casino. It was designed in 1878 probably by Arthur Clyne with a very high quality later interior, including a superb Art Nouveau painted frieze.

Continue along Queen's Road and cross over the next roundabout. We are now in Queen's Gate. The low building with the curved end on the right – the Olive Tree restaurant – which very cheekily juts out into the street is an eighteenth-century tollhouse at Spademill Road. This was the site for a spade handle factory which was then converted to a studio for George Washington Wilson, the photographer. At this point Queen's Road follows the line of the 'turnpike' west to Ballater and beyond. The traveller would stop at the tollhouse and pay the fee for entering or leaving Aberdeen. The little tollhouse survived the regularising activities of the Land Association but the owner of a house just beyond was not so fortunate. At no. 50 Queen's Drive, just beyond Spademill Lane, is probably the best house of Aberdeen's nineteenth-century expansion. But it nearly did not get built.

This is the house of John Morgan, one of Aberdeen's great builders. Morgan left a fascinating account of his life and times in his *Memoirs* of 1899. His close associate, the architect John Pirie of Pirie & Clyne, designed his house in 1886. It is a most bizarre masterpiece of Baronial forms, crushed together in one composition. The whole thing is beautifully detailed and executed by the master builder himself, Morgan. Morgan was an antiquarian and had a famous collection of books, for which the architect specially designed a library. Morgan had at first wanted to convert the existing building on the site, Old Rubislaw House, a seventeenth-century mansion, rather than having a completely new house built, but the city and the feuar, the City of Aberdeen Land Association, wanted a straight line for their new road and that house was in the way. Morgan records that the only thing he was allowed to keep were the front stairs, which he recycled as the steps to his new conservatory.

We should now walk the few steps back towards the city and take a left into Forest Road. The 'forest' in question is the Old Stocket Forest, which has historic associations with the city. The lands were given to the burgh of Aberdeen by Robert the Bruce in return for their loyalty and the income from this formed the basis of the Common Good Fund, which is still in existence today. As we go along, take a look over to Queen's Lane North and see the almost endless straight lines of the district. This can be contrasted with the sweeping curves of the later suburb on the hill to our left. Here, we are among the later and often very grand houses of wealthy Aberdonians. First we pass by the entry to **Rubislaw Den South**. At no. 2 is a typical granite mansion of 1899 by Arthur Clyne. The twin chimney stacks and central crow-stepped gable subtly invokes St Machar's (see p.192) but with two types of granite to enliven the composition. The pink stone is striking. By this time granite had become the preferred material for rough-hewn Arts and Crafts architecture. It had been rediscovered as an 'everlasting' material. In the early nineteenth century Aberdonians had amazed the world by modelling granite into the precise geometry of neo-classical architecture. By the end of that century the material's quality of 'eternal grandeur' was preferred. The great advocate of granite was the critic John Ruskin. In his *Seven Lamps of Architecture* he admired the 'rocky walls of the mountain cottages of Wales, Cumberland and Scotland'. Elsewhere harling (rendering) was being used as an alternative to the 'machine-made' regularity of stone. In Aberdeen the perfect antidote was rough-hewn granite. Ironically, this type of building finish recalled the earlier use of the material but it was now being achieved with the new technology, for example in the gigantic quarry at Rubislaw just up the hill from here. The Aberdeen architect James Souttar may have introduced granite to Sweden when he lived there in the 1860s, for it soon became the preferred building material in that country too. The geologist Hjalmar Lundbohm popularised the use of rough granite in his publications, citing Aberdeen as the best source of the material after visiting and inspecting the local quarries.

We now continue along Forest Road and past the end of Rubislaw Den North. There is a superb Arts and Crafts house by George Coutts at no. 1 with an unlikely combination of granite and half-timbering superbly brought together. You see this gigantic composition later crushed into the unlikely form of bungalows in the 1920s and '30s.

We should now walk along Forest Road until we reach King's Gate. The remarkable-looking building 'finishing' the street is the Atholl Hotel. This is a villa of 1860 with substantial additions by Pirie & Clyne in a thin manner which is not typical of the firm's robust detailing. We are now in the heart of 'Pirie & Clyne country'.

The need for variety in architecture, particularly villa and terrace architecture, was felt throughout Europe, but some of the responses in Aberdeen were quite astonishing. The best of these is here at Pirie & Clyne's **Hamilton Place**, named after local worthy and civic improver Professor Hamilton whose monument is in St Nicholas' Kirkyard (see p.90). Hamilton lived in Fountainhall Road. The overall conception is undoubtedly 'Greek', certainly influenced by Alexander Thomson, but there is really nothing else quite like this in the country. The design is bound up with an almost inexplicable Egyptomania which swept the country from the 1840s. This was an interest in the primitive and the mysteries of the ancient world, which were being investigated by religious scholars and scientists alike. The design is probably also connected with Masonic philosophy which we can see in the use of the 'omega' entrance doors. The bowling club opposite gives a little apron of

Hamilton Place

space to the houses. The railings here with their circular heads are of a type that you see all over Aberdeen but nowhere else.

Just beyond Hamilton Place are two more terraces, Argyle Place and Argyll Crescent. Also by Pirie & Clyne, they are on a lesser scale but share a similar design. For the moment, we should retrace our steps to Fountainhall Road, named after Fountain Haugh; a 'haugh' being a hollow. As we walk down Fountainhall Road, look at the almost completely glazed bay windows of nos. 28–34. George Coutts designed these houses in 1884 in reply to Pirie & Clyne's unusual houses near by. Here in the suburbs competition between architects was intense but the controls as to height, materials and building line were very strict, making such areas seem extremely well ordered.

Just before Queen's Cross are the headquarters of Grampian Television on the right. This was formerly a tram terminus. Aberdeen had one of the most progressive tram systems in the UK and it expanded with the city (see p.129). When we reach Queen's Cross go along the opposite flank of Queen's Cross Church and into Carden Place. This unlikely street name is, in fact, one of the city's most exotic. Aberdeen's famous university attracted scholars from all over Europe, and in 1552 the world-famous scientist Jerome Cardan of Pavia was brought to Scotland to treat the asthma of Archbishop Hamilton. Cardan journeyed north to Aberdeen to witness the intellectual progress of the relatively new university. It was clearly an important day to have such a 'superstar' visitor and Aberdonians were not going to let it pass. The importance of

WINDOWS

The sash-and-case window such as we see here was a revolutionary new invention, which was brought from the Low Countries and first used in Scotland around the 1670s. Original examples, such as at Balcaskie House, still exist. A window of this date has many 'astragals', the timber pieces dividing the windows into panes. As glass technology improved in the 1850s, larger pieces of glass could be used and the astragals became fewer and thinner. This meant that very large panes of could be used along with 'horns' (moulded timber blocks supporting the upper sash on either side). But plate glass was extremely expensive and was only used on show fronts. Just to confuse things, later architects revived the use of thick astragals to suggest the architecture of the seventeenth century. You will see many examples of this type of Arts and Craft house in the late nineteenth-century suburb of Rubislaw Den.

The sash-and-case window, with its clever use of pulleys and ropes, allowed the window to be opened easily to the desired level without letting in the driving wind and rain which is an occasional feature of Scotland's weather, but which is quite rare in Aberdeen. In general, windows were made by a craftsman to suit each house individually, so they are unique: they belong to the house for which they were constructed. From 1700 to 1840, highly refined 'Crown' glass was used in prestige buildings. Many examples can still be seen. The glass is distinguished by its delicate traces of 'spinning' marks. The techniques for producing large pieces of glass known as 'plate glass' were developed in France in the seventeenth century but the manufacture of the material did not begin in this country until the 1830s. Relatively expensive at first, plate glass was reserved for use in the principal rooms. Astragalled windows, making use of smaller, cheaper panes of crown glass, will often be found at this period in service areas and to the rear of the same building. By the 1860s a single sheet of plate glass in each sash was the norm on principal elevations but you can still see astragalled sashes on rear elevation in early twentieth-century buildings. In late Victorian and Edwardian buildings it was common for windows to incorporate a single-pane lower sash and an astragalled upper sash.

water for the burgh was, of course, huge. The idea of water as having curative powers was moving from a 'magical' to a scientific basis and during his visit Cardan cast a critical eye over a well near this site. He pronounced it very satisfactory and it was immediately christened 'Cardan's Well'.

The buildings of Carden Place are typical of Aberdeen: straight and well ordered, low and made of granite, with the simplest details around the entrances and windows. To cut the stone into anything more elaborate would have added very significantly to the expense. The architect James Henderson built these houses in 1867, but probably to Archibald Simpson's design. As a result they could be thirty years earlier. At Carden Place we see the contrast between the earlier suburb and the powerful desire to create uniformity with the later scheme on the other side of the street. We are looking here at two different phases of develop–

ment. With the later phases variety was not only possible, it was demanded and this is clear when looking at the buildings.

Now we go past Prince Arthur Street, which was named after Queen Victoria's son. We see **Albert Terrace** going off at an angle in a very similar vein to the houses of Carden Terrace. Albert Terrace was begun in 1839 and finished in an unvarying style in 1867. The houses are bigger than they look, especially at the end of the street where they go to two storeys without breaking the roofline. This is achieved by using raised basements. You can tell the number of rooms in any house by counting the chimney pots. And amongst all this grey solemnity and conformity is another moment of amazing lightness on our left at the so-called Tartan Kirkie. The church's proper name is St Mary's Episcopal Church. The design was an unusual collaboration between client and architect, although quite how much say the latter, Alexander Ellis, had in the final composition is doubtful. Over-ambitious, like many would-be builders, the Reverend Lee, the client, overstretched the parish budget and was forced to flee his creditors, leaving behind a rather strange piece of architecture and some very dissatisfied contractors. The unfinished sculpture is 'blocked out' on the chapter house. Pieces of stone have been set in position, waiting for the sculptor to come along. This unfinished business is not untypical of church architecture where expensive items, such as (very often) the steeple, were left until last and never completed. Contrast this with the elaborate slate patterning on the roof of the main church. This was done in imitation of ancient timber shingles (tiles) which were cut into fancy shapes. The Tartan Kirkie was badly damaged on 21 April 1942 during the most serious air-raid of Aberdeen's war.

Now walk down Albert Terrace. Here we're turning right but stop a moment to look left towards the lofty spire of Carden Place United Presbyterian Church (Ellis & Wilson, 1880–82). This was an attempt to beat Pirie & Clyne at their own game. The church is equally unusual but perhaps not equally good. It has the same elements of attached spire and nave but the very Scottish south tower on the main entrance front is less successful. The interior is good, however, and has many original fittings. It is worth a look. Behind us now at nos. 47–49 Waverley Place is a little pair of semi-detached houses with shaped gables. This motif was very popular in Aberdeen, as you have probably noticed. The city's connection with the Low Countries remained strong, and these 'Dutch' gables struck an appropriate note.

Victoria Place was originally feued in 1835 but, unusually, the people taking up the plots were allowed considerable latitude at first. There is therefore quite a variety in some of the details, which is quite uncharacteristic of Aberdeen. In 1849 the east side of Victoria Street had been built as far as no. 41 but the west side only to no. 22. The idea of two-storey houses on one side and single-storey on the other was fine and quite typical of Aberdeen. It was the variety of details which made the

GEORGE REID'S STUDIO AND
THE GORDON HIGHLANDERS MUSEUM

The house of Sir George Reid, the eminent Aberdeen painter, can be visited as **an outpost of Walk 7** when that walk reaches its furthest point west at Queen's Gate (see p.227). Continue along Queen's Road to Viewfield Road. Take a left turn and you will see the house is clearly signposted a few yards down the hill as the Gordon Highlanders Museum. On the way, there are many spectacular villas dating from the start of the twentieth century laid out along the slope of the hill. As you turn into Viewfield Road, tucked away on the left is Kepplestone Mansion, the house of Alexander MacDonald, Sir George Reid's friend, confidant and neighbour. MacDonald amassed huge wealth after inheriting his father's granite-quarrying business. MacDonald senior had invented machinery for polishing granite so that it took on the appearance of marble. It was an instant success. The remains of the immense operation at Rubislaw are still visible, just on the other side of Queen's Road. MacDonald junior's house was designed by J. Russell Mackenzie in about 1875 and it is important as a piece of architecture, not least because it is designed in an informal cottagey style with a remarkable interior. Incredibly, too, with all that granite at his disposal, the house is rendered in an Arts and Crafts manner. The real surprise was inside, however. MacDonald was the most important patron of the arts in Aberdeen and the collection which he built now forms the basis of Aberdeen Art Gallery's collection (see p.101). We are lucky to have a collection of contemporary photographs of the interior, which show exactly where each of MacDonald's paintings was placed. We can also see the important scheme of decoration, which was carried out by the Glasgow artist Daniel Cottier. The trick here was to present a homely external image and to surprise guests with the wonderful interior. The Art Gallery currently displays the contemporary photographs of the house along with the paintings themselves.

Just across the road from Kepplestone Mansion is Sir George Reid's house, which was built about 1800 as a relatively small, single-storey villa in the country. Like Alexander MacDonald's house opposite, this is not a country 'cottage' but a very smart country house. Before going in, walk around to the entrance front of the house and see the elegant bay windows with their original 'lying' panes with their sash-and-case windows.

Sir George Reid's house was extended and a studio added about 1900 by Dr William Kelly (see p.30). The whole house is now the Gordon Highlanders Museum. The regiment first paraded on 24 June 1794. The historic association of the regiment with Aberdeen was recognised in 1949 when the Freedom and Entry into the City was conferred on the regiment. This honour gave the Gordon Highlanders the right to march into Aberdeen on ceremonial occasions with bayonets fixed, drums beating and colours flying. The museum brings the illustrious history of the regiment to life, along with the more humdrum aspects of the soldiers' daily lives. The collection includes 19 of the 25 Victoria Crosses won by Gordon Highlanders and the flag which flew over Montgomery's headquarters when he accepted the German surrender in 1945.

Albert Terrace

scheme stand out. This is not quite a riot of individualism but in the context of Aberdeen's architectural conformity it was a serious departure from the norm. The feu superiors (those letting out the land for building) didn't like what they saw and introduced much tighter controls after 1849 when the scheme was put in the hands of the architects Mackenzie and Matthews.

Walking down Victoria Place to the right we are soon back where we started at Alford Place.

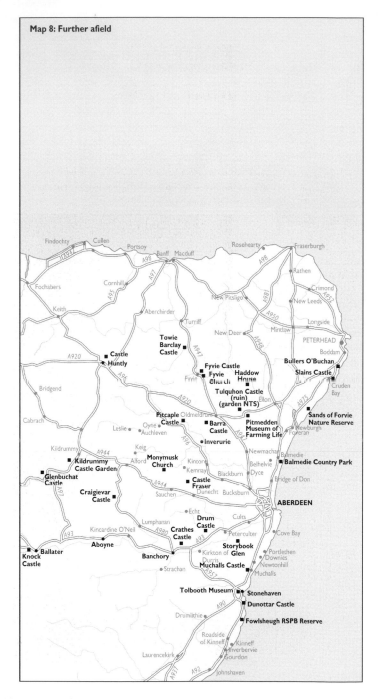

Map 8: Further afield

CHAPTER 8

Further Afield

There is a huge amount to see in Aberdeen's vast hinterland. I have chosen three 'days out' which cover history, sport and a traditional seaside, but there is much else besides

Huntly Castle

The Castles of the North-east

The north-east of Scotland is rightly famous for its castles. During the seventeenth century the area enjoyed an Indian Summer of castle building which has left us with a collection of the most beautiful houses in the country. We should say 'houses' because these buildings, with their gardens and their beautiful interiors, are far from being mere strongholds. If we look at the great garden of Pitmedden or the stunning oriel windows of Huntly, we will see that these were first and foremost places of culture. This trail takes us by a circular route to the best of these castles. The sites are all run either by the National Trust for Scotland or Historic Scotland. NTS tend to have houses which are presented with their contents, such as Drum and Fyvie, where Historic Scotland usually look after historic ruins like Huntly. The sites all have an admission charge but season tickets can be bought at the monuments.

The official trail is marked by blue-and-white Castle Trail signs. I have also included some sites of interest that are not 'castles' as such. Individual monuments can be visited by public transport, but of course the easiest way to do the trail is by car. I have also included a short description of the town of Huntly.

Throughout the seventeenth century the aristocracy took the place of the monarch at the head of Scottish society. The Scottish court had gone south in 1603 at the union of the crowns, and to a large extent the aristocracy had a free hand, especially in matters of taste such as architecture. The nobles also began to lead Scotland on a more commercially orientated path to 'improvement' and industrial development. As the old world faded from view and commerce began to displace kinship, there was a renewed interest in dynastic architecture, the romance of castle building. This was especially true in the north-east, which produced the greatest monuments to family heritage. These families began a process of 'packaging' the past and presenting it in a particular way, usually with themselves and their forebears portrayed in a heroic light. The aristocracy were poised between the presentation of a 'natural' order of things and their own wish to exploit and, therefore, to change that order by becoming commercial landowners.

The hundred years from the Reformation to the Restoration of the

Stuart monarchy in 1660 was a time of great architectural complexity. Up until the Reformation, the monarchy continued to dominate the production of architecture, but increasingly, the power of the nobility was evident – all too evident. At Huntly Castle, for example, in 1556, the French ambassador, on seeing the grandeur of the work, remarked to Mary of Guise, Queen Regent, that the earl's 'wings will need to be clipped'. And, as large as it was at that time, Huntly's magnificence was only a prelude to what would follow. The aristocracy avidly took up the licence to castellate, and the results were astonishing in their variety and complexity.

Scotland's devotion to its own brand of castle-like architecture throughout the seventeenth century was almost unique in Europe. This devotion went very far beyond an unwillingness to cast aside traditional forms because of conservatism or through a fear of aggressive neighbours, however. We would be doing the builders of these castles a great disservice if we thought of their creations as machines of war. The use of castle-like forms represented both a survival and a conscious continuation or revival of 'traditional' Scottish architecture, as represented by the Stewart 'house style' of round turrets and crow-stepped gables. Internally, however, things were changing. A lot of the prestige of the new architecture was expressed through a rigid segregation of living accommodation and especially through grandiose staircases. The best example in the country of this type is to be found at **Fyvie Castle** (see p.247).

Even though the grandees now had new luxurious interiors, this is not to say that the exteriors were no longer important. The noble families wanted to promote the right 'image' for their new dwellings. This was particularly so in the north-east, where family and tradition were so important. In rebuilding schemes, there were constant echoes of the grand Stewart residences of the previous centuries. Linlithgow Palace's courtyard and James V's gatehouse were also evoked in the 'new wark' built at Tolquhon by William Forbes in 1584 in the form of four ranges round a courtyard, with a gallery on two sides, entered by a twin-towered gatehouse (see p.250).

Many castle complexes were dominated by an earlier tower and here the aim of expansion was obviously severely restricted. One answer was to create a hall-and-tower composition but the most popular way of creating more space was by adding wings; this is where the castle builders, particularly the famous Bel family of architect-masons, really excelled. They added one or two side wings to a main block, or extended it with two diagonally placed towers at Huntly (see p.244), Castle Fraser (see p.240) and elsewhere. The most stunning examples of the diagonal-towered pattern of castles were in the north-east. At Castle Fraser there were three main stages of development: first, a square tower at the core; second, the addition of diagonal wings (one square, one round) by c.1592; and third, in 1617–18, the elaboration and heightening of this group into a monumental composition by John Bel. He heightened the round tower by all of four storeys, finishing it with a balustrade. He also raised the remainder of the building to match. A broad symmetry was achieved by the building of turreted wings. The Castle Fraser tower was much referred to in the nineteenth-century Baronial revival.

The greatest of the north-east castles was Huntly, a house which followed the same three-stage building process as Castle Fraser, but culminated in a later phase (c.1600–10) of massive additions by George Gordon, first Marquis. This created a new palace of immense refinement, recalling palatial French precedents. Gordon created suites of apartments on two upper floors (above the Great Hall), with inner chambers in the huge round corner tower and a line of oriels, spiky dormers and a tall frieze inscribed with his name and that of his wife, Henrietta Stewart. There was a particular emphasis on heraldic carving, including a vertical panel above the main entrance (with lavish Catholic imagery, smashed by a Covenanting army in 1640), and decorated chimneypieces inside.

In both royal and landed building, the most popular way of signifying sophistication was through the application of classical detail, including columns, pilasters, pediments and balustrades, no matter how 'Scottish' the building type. There was no inherent contradiction in a Scottish stair tower topped by a Renaissance balustrade as, for example, at Castle Fraser. The spread of printed French or Italian pattern books, by authors such as Serlio (from 1566) or du Cerceau (1576–79), gave patrons and designers throughout Europe access for the first time to an international standard of detailing. Now it became necessary to dress up sheer walls with details, often taken from pattern books. Within the northern Renaissance, different countries developed their own variants of applied 'classical' ornament. The huge, vertical overdoor panel of Huntly Castle (1602) is a case in point. In the north-east of Scotland, the spectacular castles built by the Bel family of masons concentrated their pediments, turrets and other decorative features above a heavy, stepped corbel course, giving the characteristic burst of architectural flourish above the wallhead.

Many more castles were built by the Bel family and others in the north-east to the Huntly pattern. These castles used a similar formula of corbel table and exuberantly castellated skyline, included Crathes and Craigievar built between 1553 and 1596. Craigievar is one of the Bel's most impressive architectural feats. It was a six-storey tower bought partly completed in 1610 by 'Danzig Willie', William Forbes, a wealthy Baltic trader, and finished (1626) with the help of John Bel. The castle, like many others, was originally enclosed by a small courtyard. Inside, Craigievar still followed long-established principles of tower-house design, stacking vertically no fewer than 18 rooms and a great hall, but its exterior was brought right up to date with a typical rush of Renaissance detailing at the wallhead and incorporating the new device of viewing platform.

Drum Castle

DRUM CASTLE

National Trust for Scotland

Drum Castle is 10 miles (16km) from Aberdeen off the A93 Aberdeen–Banchory road.

We begin appropriately at Drum, with its strong Aberdeen connection. Just ten miles from the centre of the city, Drum Castle is the historic home of the Irvine family but it has been extended many times from its original stark keep with a large Jacobean house and a Victorian wing. The massive keep is one of the oldest tower-houses in Scotland, built by Richard Cementarius who was the first provost (mayor) of Aberdeen. The keep is a simple but beautifully constructed building with exceptionally thick walls tapering to the top. The window is a later addition, made to light the library which was inserted in the 1840s. The next tower was added to improve the accommodation. The keep is linked to a mansion house of 1619 by a short wing. Later a wing was slipped in behind this house by David Bryce, the noted nineteenth-century Baronial-revival architect. Bryce's wing allowed for a new entrance via an enhanced courtyard setting with Castle Fraser-style 'biggins' (low courtyard buildings). The former main entrance became a kind of garden front.

Drum has a marvellous interior full of excellent furniture and paintings, which are expertly displayed and interpreted by the NTS. In the library formed in the 1840s in the old tower, the painting of the Archangel Gabriel above the fireplace is by Hugh Irvine (a self-portrait!), a member of the family and friend of Byron. Notice also the painting of Tolquhon by the Aberdeen artist and architectural consultant James Giles.

CRATHES CASTLE

National Trust for Scotland

Crathes is 2 miles (3km) east of Banchory off the A93

Crathes Castle is the work of the Bel family of masons who designed Craigievar and Castle Fraser. Notice that each wall face is different and the variety of profile achieved as you walk around the building is quite astonishing. This is one of the best preserved sixteenth-century tower-houses in the country. It can be contrasted with Craigievar, which is a simpler house, and with Huntly, which is much grander. The main reason why Crathes managed to stay in a well-kept and ordered condition over many hundreds of years is because of its continuous occupation by the Burnett family. Unlike Huntly whose star rose and fell with royal favour or Craigievar which was a rich merchant's country retreat, Crathes was home to the middling sort of lairdly family, producing steady individuals always in demand in an expanding country: these were admirals, bishops, generals and a governor of New York. The Burnetts gained the rights to the country hereabout through Robert the Bruce, who proclaimed the area a royal forest and one Alexander Burnard as its forester. For the next 250 years the Burnetts lived in a fortified wooden house on an artificial island on the nearby Loch of Leys, rather like the 'motte' at Huntly (see p.245). The Burnett fortunes increased through a fortunate marriage in 1543 between Alexander Burnett of Leys and the daughter of Canon Hamilton, a wealthy churchman. The money brought by Janet Hamilton paid for the new house, which took 40 years to build. Alexander Burnett of Leys fought with Mary Queen of Scots' army at the battle of Corrichie (1562) on the nearby Hill o' Fare. On the opposing side was the 'aged and corpulent Huntly' who died of heart failure at the battle. His son Sir John Gordon was executed for his part in the affair (see p.135). The next influential Burnett was the great-grandson of Alexander, and was also called Alexander. It was he who added the final architectural flourish to Crathes, the magnificent top storey and the famous painted ceilings. Crathes contains a notable scheme of ceiling paintings (dating from 1599 to 1602) of classical figures and warrior kings, with accompanying inscriptions including verses in praise of the 'Auld Alliance' with France. A later Burnett, Sir Thomas (1658–1714), fathered 21 children and added a new wing to the castle to house them.

As we approach the castle, notice the two ice-houses on either side of the drive. These were eighteenth-century 'fridges', sunk into the earth and covered with turf to insulate them.

CASTLE FRASER

National Trust for Scotland

Castle Fraser is off the B993 at Kemnay

Castle Fraser is one of the most impressive of the north-east castles. Its trademark massive round tower was admiringly copied in many nineteenth- and early twentieth-century 'revivalist' buildings, including Aberdeen's main Post Office (see p.159)! Most of what we see today was built between 1565 and 1635 but, like Drum, Castle Fraser has a simple early core. Here the tower is much reduced but was probably originally built by Thomas Fraser in the middle of the fifteenth century. The entrance can still be seen in the north wall of the hall on the first floor, since for security it would have been entered at a higher level. In 1565 the fifth laird, Michael Fraser, built a square tower at the north-west corner along with a round tower diagonally opposite. This was a typical way of extending accommodation, with a series of linked towers, in this case making a 'Z'-plan tower-house. This house was a fairly modest affair. How to aggrandise it? This was spectacularly done in the late sixteenth and early seventeenth century by Andrew Fraser with the architect-mason John Bel. The original hall was widened but the main expansion was upwards, with the round tower heightened by no fewer than four storeys and topped by a balustrade. Fraser also added an exuberant display of stone detailing and a coat-of-arms on the north front. As at Huntly, this panel would originally have been painted, with the strawberry leaves picked out in green. (The reference is a play on the French word *fraise* meaning 'strawberry'.) Having suitably enlarged the profile of the castle, Fraser then saw to the practicalities, putting up the 'laich biggins' (low buildings) with stores, a brewhouse and a bakehouse at the base of the structure. The crow-stepped, unharled buildings were constructed in the 1820s.

The house was much altered internally in the nineteenth century but this work is not without interest. The best rooms are the Laigh Hall, with its early vaulting, and John Smith's library, created out of the Long Gallery.

In 1921 the estate was bought by the multi-millionaire industrialist Lord Cowdray for his son. As at Dunnottar (see p.259), the aim was to restore the ancient building and this process was begun under the guidance of Dr William Kelly, the antiquarian architect of Aberdeen.

CRAIGIEVAR
National Trust for Scotland
Craigievar castle is 4 miles (7km) south of Alford on the A980 Alford–Banchory road. Viewing of the castle takes place in groups led by very good local guides. You may have to wait a few minutes but it is well worth it.

The little castle of Craigievar is one of the most perfect houses open to the public. It is a 'must-see' and worth the extra drive.

In 1610 William Forbes ('Danzig Willie'), a wealthy Baltic trader, bought the unfinished house, a six-storey tower, from the Mortimer family and employed John Bel, of the celebrated Bel family, to create this romantic masterpiece, which was completed in 1626.

Craigievar is much smaller than Castle Fraser and Huntly but uses all

Craigievar Castle

the same architectural 'language' of corbel table and bristling castle sky-line. Originally enclosed by a small courtyard, it still followed the late medieval principle of cellular planning, with a great hall, 18 other apart-ments and interlinking upper-floor staircases fitted ingeniously into a confined, verticalised envelope; but its exterior was ornamented with a typically Scottish Renaissance mixture of corbel table, pediments, turrets and balustraded viewing platform. On the garden side of the building, and (read diagonally) on its splayed side, the castle is roughly symmetri-cal. Inside, Craigievar's great hall features a vault with heavy strapwork plaster decoration, and a fireplace with large plaster royal arms above.

THE TOWN AND CASTLE OF HUNTLY

Huntly Castle is well signposted in the town of Huntly, 33 miles (53km) from Aberdeen via the A96.

Huntly is a wonderful small planned town of the type that the north-east specialised in during the eighteenth and nineteenth centuries. The grid was laid out in 1775 by the dukes of Gordon, but the town's roots are much deeper. It took its name from the Gordons of Huntly, who came originally from Berwickshire in the Borders. (The family take their name from the land of Gordon in Berwickshire.) The first earl of Gordon was created in 1449. The third earl, Alexander, received a charter of the Huntly lands in 1506. This charter decreed that his castle be 'named the Castle of Huntly' as it still is, even if it is now a beautifully preserved ruin.

The hub of Huntly is the Square. This was the creation of the dukes of Gordon in the 1770s but many of the simple granite buildings of that

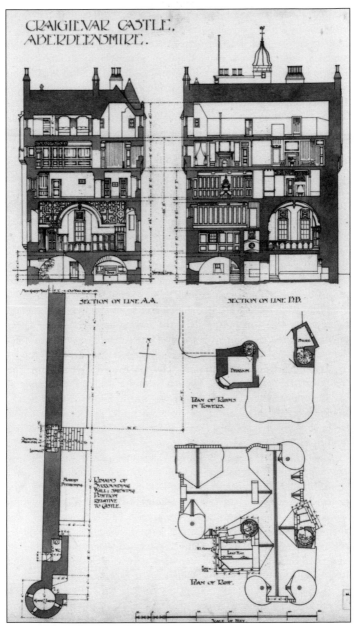

CRAIGIEVAR CASTLE,
ABERDEENSHIRE.

SECTION ON LINE A.A.

SECTION ON LINE B.B.

PLAN OF ROOMS
IN TOWERS.

REMAINS OF
SURROUNDING
WALL: SHEWING
POSITION
RELATIVE
TO CASTLE.

PLAN OF ROOF.

SCALE OF FEET.

Craigievar Castle: plan and section through the castle

time have been demolished or altered as the character of the town changed. 'By 1900,' one account goes, 'Huntly had four woollen mills, a hosiery factory and a large agricultural implement manufacturer. It served a wide area as a market and shopping centre attracted many holiday visitors, and enjoyed the patronage of the Dukes of Richmond and Gordon.' (The statue in the centre of the square, a memorial to Charles Gordon Lennox, fifth Duke of Richmond, was designed in 1862 by Alexander Brodie.) This was a flourishing town, which needed public buildings: Archibald Simpson's bank is at no. 2 the Square. This was built for the 'farmers' bank', the North of Scotland Bank, by their favoured architect. Their principal branch was on the Castle Street–King Street corner in Aberdeen (p.147). There is a large post office of 1934 in square-cut granite at no. 15, which also attests to the importance of the place. The rather out-of-place Gothic of the Brander Library was built in 1883 by a grateful son of Huntly, William Brander, who went on to great things in London. The design was by John Rhind and the building includes an impressive staircase and a library.

At no. 18 is the Huntly Hotel with its controversial use of sandstone and very lavish appearance. The fountain in the Square was put up in memory of James Robertson, a bank agent of Huntly who died in 1877. Fountains were often erected as memorials to teetotallers as a constant reminder to others of the perils of the hard stuff. There was a whole building erected in Huntly as an abstainers' rest. This was Gordon's Temperance Hotel, a tall building on the corner with Deveron Street. This building is now gone, but the Gordon Arms Hotel remains. The 'French roof' with its cresting reminds us of the Second Empire style of the later nineteenth century, which was much associated with hotels. Looking straight down Gordon Street, we see s big swaggering tower rising above its neighbours. This belongs to Stewart's Hall, which was built in 1875 by James Anderson.

The large and imposing St Margaret's Church reminds us that Huntly was one of the last redoubts of Catholicism in Scotland. The present church was built in an ornate Spanish Baroque style in 1834 by the Rev James Kyle. Inside there are seven contemporary paintings given by John Gordon of Wardhouse who had a Spanish connection. St Margaret's was an answer to the nearby Church of Scotland, which had been built by Alexander Laing in 1805 in Church Street. It is interesting to contrast these two buildings: one is a great 'shed' which revels in plainness and huge size; the other is a wilful attempt at the exotic.

The Castle
The Gordon family first made their mark by supporting the winning side in the power struggle between the Stewarts and the Douglases. James II's crushing of Black Douglas finally established his authority over all of Scotland and the loyal Gordon family prospered as a result.

Royal support continued and the castle played host to the marriage of James IV's favoured claimant to the English throne, Perkin Warbeck, and the 'White Rose of Scotland', Lady Catherine Gordon. The family went from strength to strength – perhaps even too much strength, in the eyes of certain jealous nobles. The change in fortune for Huntly came very soon afterwards. The Reformation in 1560 introduced Protestantism into Scotland. From this point on, Huntly became a redoubt of Catholicism and the Gordons temporarily became enemies of the state. Mary Queen of Scots, although a Catholic, found herself officially at odds with Huntly. Her army, led by Huntly's rival the earl of Moray, defeated Gordon at Corrichie on the Hill o' Fare on 28 October 1562. One of Huntly's sons, Sir John Gordon, was executed in front of Mary at Aberdeen (see p.135 for a description of this event). In the aftermath of Huntly's defeat, the castle was looted and the plunder used to furnish the house of Kirk o' Field in Edinburgh, where Mary's husband Lord Darnley was later blown up.

For forty years the house of Huntly had been on the wrong side, but now they made their peace with the state. In 1597 the earl confirmed his loyalty and two years later was created Marquis of Huntly. It was this man, George Gordon, and his son the second marquis, who created the spectacular palace block we see today. The family soon found themselves again in political difficulty: the second Marquis supported Charles I and suffered execution at the hands of the Covenanters for his beliefs. The Marquis's last words were: 'You may take my head from my shoulders but not my heart from my sovereign.' Huntly Castle thereafter fell into decay and disrepair until it was finally taken into the care of the state.

Tour of the Castle

The present-day entrance to Huntly is via the south front, which is the great glory of the palace. The house was elevated to palace status by the first marquis who added the spectacular series of oriel windows, dedicated to himself and his wife, Henrietta Stewart, whose names are inscribed. The couple's names are inscribed in a stupendous frieze, the likes of which had never before been attempted. The windows are probably inspired by the Château of Blois in France. Standing to the rear of the main building you can see the 'motte', a timber tower protected by a ditch or moat; the late thirteenth-century tower, of which little more than the foundations remain; and the great castle or, more correctly, palace.

The rest of the buildings of the courtyard were probably brewhouses and bakehouses but they are largely ruined beyond recognition. The formal entrance to the castle is on our left. The entrance is not particularly large or grand, in keeping with the castle tradition and the practicalities of life. There is a typical overdoor, a heraldic panel which is the best example in the country: the heraldry of the Gordon family is heaped, honour upon honour. The panel is arranged according to status: the greater the honour, the higher it is placed. First, there are the arms of the lord and his lady, above them are those of King James VI and his Queen Anne of Denmark, feudal overlords. Above again is Christ in Glory, and above all a figure of St Michael the warrior archangel, victorious over Satan. We should bear in mind that this entire panel would have been elaborately painted and gilded. It would have been set against the harled walls of the palace, which may also itself have been painted.

On the ground floor, with the prison below, was the steward's lodging in the round tower. This gave direct access to the master's rooms above. Note the *en suite* lavatory, issuing into the ditch. On the same floor was the huge kitchen with its associated cellars. On the floor above was the master's apartments: three 'reception' or public rooms which could form a sequence when entertaining guests. The hall was the most public of these spaces, equivalent to a modern dining-room. Then there was the great chamber, like the modern sitting-room. Favoured guests would 'withdraw' to this room, hence the term 'withdrawing-room' (shortened to 'drawing-room'). Beyond is the inner chamber, which was a bedroom, complete with a servant's bell. The sequence of rooms is repeated on the floor above, for the earl's wife. This arrangement is a version of the layout of the royal apartments at Holyrood and Stirling. All these rooms would have been richly painted and decorated, probably by the royal painter John Anderson. From the seventeenth century, furnishings and painting of the highest quality would have been introduced.

Ascending the stair leading off the great chamber you can access the turret room or *belvedere* right on top of the palace. This was built purely for the purpose of taking in the magnificent view of the surrounding countryside, including the summit of Cabrach in the distance.

LEITH HALL
National Trust for Scotland
Leith Hall is 6 miles (10km) south of Huntly, off the B9002 Insch–Huntly road.
Leith Hall is a curiously plain but fascinating building in the context of the area's spectacular, exuberant castles. The home of the Leith Hay family for three hundred years, the north wing is the oldest, built in 1650 as a plain block with turrets at the angles in the symmetrical style of Sir James Murray's work in Edinburgh of thirty years earlier. The house is only a generation younger than Huntly or Castle Fraser but the dynastic image is reduced to diminutive angle turrets. The house was successively added to and later mildly 'baronialised' with matching turrets. A curved stable bock was also built away from the house in a typical 'improved' eighteenth-century manner.

PITMEDDEN GARDEN AND MUSEUM OF FARMING LIFE

National Trust for Scotland

Pitmedden is 4 miles (7km) east of Oldmeldrum off the A920 Oldmeldrum–Ellon road.

The garden was originally laid out in 1675 by Sir Alexander Seton and was recreated by the NTS in the 1950s. Connected with the garden is a very good museum of farming life that has all the usual implements and devices but which also gives a clear picture of the social as well as the extremely hard-working lives of the farm workers. There is a recorded presentation of genuine 'bothy ballads', the folksongs of the north-east. These songs were influential in the folk revival of the 1960s and brought many artists to the area.

With the growth of the towns from the seventeenth century, we also see a corresponding interest in the escape from the town – the garden. The formal Renaissance garden, with its statues, fountains and shaded walks, started to appear attached to the greater houses or villas from the 1600s onwards. Being of such a transitory nature very little survives today from this period. The celebrated formal garden of Drummond Castle in Perthshire, for example, is a complete reconstruction of 1839 following the revival of interest in this stately age of landscape design. At Seton Palace, a 'turreted' walled garden was recorded in 1603. The most notable surviving Renaissance geometrical garden is that added to Edzell Castle in 1604 by Sir David Lindsay, Lord Edzell. Lindsay was a cosmopolitan lawyer and great 'improver' who carried on large-scale tree-planting on his estate. His garden was surrounded by walls originally decorated with pilasters, pediments, Stuart unionist royal symbols and carved panels depicting the planetary deities, the Virtues and the Arts (Geometria, above). It is important to bear in mind also that gardens were also perceived as 'philosophers' groves' and theatres of science.

FYVIE CASTLE

National Trust for Scotland

Fyvie is 7 miles (11km) south of Turriff off the B9005 Fyvie–Ellon road. The road to Fyvie is something of a detour and can be omitted. However, it is a stunning house which should be visited if you have time. Afterwards, you can return to the main Aberdeen road via Haddo House or carry on straight back to Oldmeldrum and on to Tolquhon.

From the later sixteenth century, the small-scale 'politeness' of Rowallan, Edzell or Tolquhon was largely forgotten as the major powerbrokers and landowners rushed into vast architectural projects. As a direct result of the aristocracy's new status, there was a dramatic rise in the country house as a building type, along with the 'demilitarising' of the landed classes who were its patrons. In post-Reformation Scotland, the Renaissance attribute of militarism was played down in favour of the liberal arts: music, painting, philosophy and architecture. As Scotland moved into a phase of peace with its old enemy, England, the time was ripe for the cultivation of the arts of peace. Lawyers and administrators were now more in demand than generals. This hundred-year period also saw the end of the virtual state monopoly on architecture. The new buildings and reconstructed setpieces continued throughout the century to take their cue from the court but, especially after 1603 and the Scottish king's departure for London, the aristocracy took on an unusually powerful role through a circle dominated by a few 'great' families: the Maitlands, Argylls and Setons in a series not of new houses, but of lavish reworkings of earlier Baronial architecture.

Chancellor Seton's Fyvie Castle is the one of these 'revived' castellated houses, but there was another side to Seton, as there was also to the seventeenth-century Scottish character. The staircase-hall at Fyvie was full of heraldic display, Lord Seton having 'quite a passion for that science', but at his Edinburgh villa, Pinkie House, European cosmopolitanism and liberalism flourished. The house and garden were conceived together as a place of peace: in Seton's own words, 'no place of warfare, designed to repel enemies'. Between 1560 and 1660 the 'high' architecture was becoming the 'property' of the nobility as opposed to the crown, but the nobles had no sooner taken control than it was passed to the burgesses, and even eventually to the town councils.

In none of the building projects of the aristocracy in the later sixteenth century was the scale of the works undertaken in the time of James IV and James V works even approached. However, near the end of the sixteenth century Alexander Seton set about the aggrandisement of his newly acquired house at Fyvie Castle. Working with a member of the famous Bel family of masons, Seton spectacularly extended an old house which probably dated from the thirteenth century. Seton's new frontage comprised flanking corner towers and a huge centre block consisting of linked round towers with a central arch. Inside, a spectacular new ceremonial approach was constructed in the form of a stone staircase contained within a 20-foot-square space. The staircase is built on a series of arches springing from the newel (the central pier) and resting on the decorated consoles (brackets) of the outer wall. The whole space is therefore carried on barrel vaulting, in contrast to the elaborately ribbed vaulting of French examples such as Château de Chaumont.

HADDO HOUSE

National Trust for Scotland

Haddo is 6 miles (10km) north-west of Ellon off the B999 Aberdeen–Methlick road.

Haddo House is by no means a castle, but it represents the type of house that generations of Aberdeenshire magnates were building. Too small to be a 'stately home', yet much larger than a conventional villa, the original

Haddo House was designed by William Adam for William Gordon, the second Earl of Aberdeen, in 1732. It was designed in a simple and restrained Palladian style and can be contrasted with Adam's design for Duff House further up the road at Banff, which is a much bolder Baroque composition. The house has 'quadrants' leading to wings, which were heightened by the Aberdeen architect Archibald Simpson in 1822. There were much larger-scale alterations in about 1880 carried out by Wardrop & Reid who brought the entrance down from the original position at the first floor *piano nobile* to the ground floor. This happened in a lot of eighteenth-century houses which had been built according to an older Scottish and French tradition of living on the first floor, derived ultimately from life in castles on the trail like Fyvie or Craigievar. The chapel was designed between 1876 and 1881 by the London Gothic Revival master G.E. Street, architect of the Law Courts in the Strand. The interior is important as it is one of the first of the Adam revival style, which is rather confusing at a house originally designed by William Adam. The decorative style being revived is that of William Adam's son Robert. The only room with original William Adam panelling is the anteroom. The rest are lavishly and comprehensively decorated and furnished. There are paintings by Van Dyck and Domenichino deliberately placed within the general decorative scheme.

Notice the wonderful sweeping landscape in which the house is set. Most of what we see was laid out between 1805 and the 1850s. The landscape artist and architectural adviser James Giles (see p.173) was involved in the creation of the magnificent afforested setting of the house. During his time 14 million trees were planted. Much of this landscape is now incorporated into a country park, open to the public free of charge.

The moment of historical glory for Haddo came in the nineteenth century with the political rise of George Hamilton-Gordon, the fourth Earl of Aberdeen. Gordon was orphaned at the age of 11 and brought up by his guardians William Pitt the Younger and Viscount Melville, who was a kind of Scottish viceroy. With guardians like these, 'Dody' as he was known, was bound to succeed in politics. Gordon, who later added his first wife's name 'Hamilton' to his own, became Britain's most assured diplomat and finally settled a long-standing border dispute between Canada and the United States through the Webster-Ashburton Treaty of 1842 and the Oregon Treaty of 1846. In 1852 the Earl of Aberdeen became prime minister, heading a coalition of supporters of Sir Robert Peel, Whigs and a Radical. His downfall came after the military disaster of the Crimean War and he resigned on 29 January 1855.

TOLQUHON CASTLE

Historic Scotland

Tolquhon Castle lies 4 miles (6km) east of Oldmeldrum and 1½ miles south of Tarves. The castle is reached by a minor road off the B999 Aberdeen–Tarves road.
Tolquhon Castle was one of two principal seats in the ancient thanage of Formartine between the rivers Ythan and Don. The other was Fyvie (p.247). In the thirteenth century the thanage was held by the Prestons who were also lords of Craigmillar near Edinburgh. When Sir Henry Preston died without a male heir, the thanage was split between the husbands of his two daughters. Tolquhon thereby came into the possession of Sir John Forbes who had married Sir Henry's second daughter Marjorie in 1420. Sir John's castle is the ruin in the north-corner of the courtyard known as Preston's Tower.

Tolquhon is one of a group of houses which includes buildings as far apart as Edzell in Angus and Rowallan in Ayrshire. At Edzell, the plan was palace-like in its courtyard form and complexity with its separate ranges of residential, hall and ancillary accommodation. There was also a beautiful formal garden, which is still in existence. These houses represented a rejection of communal living in tower-houses. This was a gradual process, which would continue throughout the following four centuries, eventually spreading to all other social classes. But for the moment, it was the nobility alone who had the wealth and taste to follow the royal fashion for 'family' privacy, which we now take so much for granted. What we see at Tolquhon today is almost entirely the work of the colourful character Sir William Forbes who rebuilt the entire complex between 1584 and 1589 when he was quite advanced in years. He was a minor example of this new class of wealthy and pretentious laird. He was probably brought up under cramped conditions in Preston's Tower which had been built by his ancestors nearly a century before. Sir William's plan was to create a new more civilised modern residence like the royal palaces (see Dunnottar, p.259) grouped around a courtyard.

Tour of the Castle

We enter the castle through an outer gate, a mere archway in a boundary wall, but notice the triple gun loop: an ostentatious feature of the whole complex. We see the remains of the doocot (dovecote) immediately to our left and then we walk over the spacious outer court. The area is now under grass but it would originally have been laid out as a formal garden, very probably in the manner of Edzell Castle. As we approach the twin towers of the gatehouse, we should think 'display' rather than 'defence'. The towers were miniature versions of the Stewart house style of architecture seen at Stirling, Falkland and Linlithgow. The gatehouse is richly decorated with armorial panels and sculpture. Notice the carved panel advertising the date of the 'new wark'. One of the sculptured figures on

Tolquhon Castle

the gatehouse may represent Forbes himself. Now walk through into the inner court. To the left is all that remains of Sir William's boyhood home, Preston's Tower. Next you will see the deep well, the castle's main water supply. Again to your left is the east range with a bakehouse and pit prison. In front of you is the main house with its turreted tower bristling above. To your right is the west range with its brewhouse below and a gallery above, connected to the main accommodation. The gallery would be hung with pictures and connected to a study or library in the adjacent tower.

Around the Walls of Tolquhon

When I was walking round the building with my family during the preparation of this book I saw a Twix wrapper lying at the base of the wall, directly below a latrine outlet. I knew that the children had all been eating these chocolate bars so I was pretty sure that one of them had dropped the paper. Very naughty! It did, however, remind me that in all the comparative luxury and home comforts of Tolquhon arrangements for the disposal of human waste was still quite basic. A stroll round the wall on the east side could have been hazardous in the late sixteenth century, but on the other side there was a 'pleasance' – a wooded walk adjacent to the castle walls. Remnants of the planting are still there to see and the area is very beautiful. On the outer courtyard wall you will see 12 square recesses. These are bee-boles, which originally housed skeps (beehives), to provide the household with honey.

Stonehaven

Stonehaven is a resort town 15 miles south of Aberdeen in a sheltered position where the Carron Water and the Cowie Water reach the North Sea. It was formerly the county town of Kincardineshire, so there are fairly large public buildings as well as a thriving central area. Stonehaven lies adjacent to a deeply indented bay surrounded on three sides by higher land between Downie Point and Garron Point. The harbour, consisting of two basins, was improved in the 1820s by the engineer Robert Stevenson and became an important centre of the nineteenth-century herring trade.

During the twentieth century the town changed from being predominantly a fishing settlement and turned into a holiday resort with a variety of recreational and sporting facilities including a leisure centre, swimming-pool and 18-hole golf course. Stonehaven is on the main railway line to Aberdeen and is linked to the city by the A92 road. Visitors should not miss the Stonehaven's excellent examples of the built and the natural heritage: the town and harbour; Dunnottar Castle, the most stupendous monument in the country; Dunnottar Woods; and the Fowlsheugh Bird Reserve.

STONEHAVEN PEOPLE

Stonehaven has been home to many important people. Among the most celebrated of these are Lewis Grassic Gibbon, Lord Reith and Robert William Thomson, inventor of the pneumatic tyre, as the town's sign proudly explains.

Lewis Grassic Gibbon, the pseudonym of James Leslie Mitchell, is one of Scotland's most celebrated writers. He was born in 1901 at Seggat of Auchterless in Aberdeenshire but at the age of eight the family moved to a farm near Drumlithie in 'the Mearns', the rural hinterland. He was educated at the local school in Drumlithie and then at Mackie Academy here in Stonehaven, leaving at the age of 16. He became a journalist, working on the *Aberdeen Journal* and the *Scottish Farmer*. After returning to the family farm due to illness he enlisted in the army and later served for eight years in the RAF as a clerk, spending some time in the Middle East.

Mitchell left the RAF in 1928 and embarked on his literary career, writing 16 books and many short pieces during the next seven years. The trilogy *A Scots Quair* is his most renowned work. The three parts of the book, *Sunset Song* (1932), *Cloud Howe* (1933) and *Grey Granite* (1934), tell the story of Chris Guthrie as she grows from being the daughter of a tenant farmer in the Mearns through to being a farmer's wife and then a rural minister's wife and finally a widow and mother in the 'Grey Granite' city of Aberdeen. The hard-hitting and highly realistic description of the prevailing social system of the times was not flattering. Mitchell had a great feeling for the countryside of the north, believing that civilisation was at its peak during the stone circle era of the Bronze Age.

After a brief literary career, during which his books were not at first appreciated, Mitchell died in 1935 at the age of just 34. It seems fair to suggest that had he lived longer he would have exerted an even greater influence on Scottish and international literature. Today his work is highly regarded (*Sunset Song* is included in the National Curriculum) and his life is commemorated by the Lewis Grassic Gibbon Centre at Arbuthnott, off the A92 south of Stonehaven.

Lord Reith (1889–1971), another famous son of Stonehaven, was the first chairman of the British Broadcasting Corporation (BBC). His full title was Lord Reith of Stonehaven, John Charles Walsham Reith, the first Baron. He was born in July 1889, a son of the manse, whose stern authority was influential until very recently in the world of broadcasting. As director-general of the BBC from 1927 to 1938 he laid the foundations of the Corporation's patrician attitude: its mission, as he put it himself, to 'educate and entertain'. Reith was also chairman of Imperial Airways.

The achievement of **Robert William Thomson** (1822–73) was the crucial invention of the pneumatic tyre. Solid rubber tyres had been fitted to London Hansom cabs by 1881 but these were very hard on the road surface, to say nothing of the passengers. Many people at the time were experimenting with air-filled tyres but Robert Thomson was the first inventor to be issued with a patent, in 1845. This was for a hollow leather tyre filled with air. Thomson aerial wheels ran for 1,200 miles on a brougham, a one-horse closed carriage. He then went on to invent a rubber version of the same tyre.

STONEHAVEN'S FISHING HERITAGE

Fishing is one of mankind's oldest known industries, and the many inlets and havens on the Kincardineshire coast have provided shelter for fishermen for centuries. Some of the finest examples of fishing villages in Scotland can be seen in the Grampian area, many of them dating from

The harbour at Stonehaven

the seventeenth century (although some are even earlier). Since the traditional methods of fishing have now died out, the industry in nearly all these smaller villages has declined too. And although Stonehaven is a flourishing town, with agricultural, manufacturing and holiday interests, the sea fishing involves only small craft and is mainly recreational. In its harbour and the surrounding area can still be found traces of the town's rich fishing heritage.

Stonehaven's Art Deco open-air heated swimming-pool is the last of its kind in Scotland. It was built about 60 years ago in controversial circumstance, many of the locals objecting to such an extravagance when the pool was originally proposed. The argument raged on and the council took the unusual step of carrying out a referendum. The vote was carried and the pool has been a huge success ever since. It has also been the training ground for several famous international swimmers. The pool attracted as many as 65,000 people a year in the early 1970s. Despite the building and opening in 1985 of a games hall and smaller indoor pool, numbers attending the superb outdoor facility have been increasing. The very warm summer of 1999 drew about 35,000 people compared with 1990's previous top figure of 25,000. One of the pool's great attractions is the midnight swim, held once a week in summer. Try it out but bear in mind you won't be gliding blissfully in the moonlight. With all the splashing and shouting in the darkness I'm afraid I was reminded of the sinking of the *Titanic*! It's great fun, though.

There are a variety of places to eat in Stonehaven. The Tolbooth Restaurant is said to be one of the best fish restaurants in the north-east and it's right on the harbourside. Have an aperitif sitting outside in the

Ship Inn or the Marine Hotel and then saunter down the harbour. Alternatively, try the excellent Tandoori Haven in the main street. This is a restaurant with a southern Indian theme, whose flavours are much more delicate than the usual experience. The service is wonderful. The big Inverbervie fish-and-chip restaurant is also good.

The Tolbooth Museum is one of the best small museums in the area. In it can be seen artefacts from Stonehaven's fishing past as well as the original 'Thief Hole' where condemned prisoners were held before being led to 'Gallows Hill' half a mile south of the town. There is no doubt that as long ago as the sixteenth century, when the Tolbooth was built, 'Stonehyve' already had some form of fishing community. The natural harbour of Stonehaven and nearby Cowie Village provided shelter from the harsh North Sea. Eventually settlements rose up around these areas that were suitable for landing the small craft of the time, and towards the seventeenth century stone piers were constructed in the more prosperous districts.

FISHERS' COTTAGES AT COWIE

These houses are at the opposite end of the town from the harbour, just beyond the outdoor swimming-pool and caravan park. The earliest houses for the fisherfolk were very simple, similar in appearance and layout to these cottages today at Boatie Row. When originally built they were very like the homes of agricultural workers, many of whom were forced into fishing because of 'improvements' in farming carried out from the eighteenth century. The villages were generally laid out in rows, usually with their gable-end to the sea for protection from the wind. The most famous example in the north-east is at Pennan, which was used as the location for the film *Local Hero*. The fishermen's houses were crowded together near the shore and often so close to the sea that they were just above the high-water mark. Others were sited close to the edge of hazardous cliffs, as at Catterline, a few miles south of Stonehaven.

The homes were built of rocks and stones gathered from the shore and in some cases from nearby quarries or ruined buildings. The roofs were normally thatched with heather broom or earth 'dyvots'. Usually there was only one door, with one small window opening to each room. These would be shuttered rather than glazed. External wooden shutters would cover the opening at night. There was an earthen floor sprinkled with sand or gravel. A large open fireplace with the crook hanging down from the 'rantle tree' above the fire provided cooking facilities. The inner roof was always blackened with soot from the open fire. The home of the fisher could always be identified by the hakes hanging outside and inside by 'hairs for tippens', hooks and, in later years, herring nets. The old houses, although still standing, are nowadays all modernised. Just beyond the cottages is the net-repair green where you can still see fishing nets strung over poles for repair. There is a coastal walk beyond the net-repair green. Be careful here and follow the signposts. A little further on you will see the remains of the castle of Cowie.

DUNNOTTAR WOODS AND DUNNOTTAR CHURCH

There are extensive, well-signposted walks through beautiful mature trees on a wooded slope at the back of the town. Within the woods is the Gallow Hill, the traditional site of executions. You will also see the 'Shell House' or 'Shell Hoosie', a kind of small ornamental hermitage, probably of eighteenth-century origin. The idea was that an estate would employ a hermit to live in the house, a sort of resident Diogenes, for the amusement of the estate owner and his family. The internal walls are decorated with sea shells.

The walk by the road will take you up to the beautiful little Dunnottar Church. Follow the signs and keep to the right with the Carron River on your right. Stay on the pavement, and when it runs out at a 'V' junction, keep to the right and you will soon be at the church, with its manse opposite. Sir Walter Scott stayed at this manse. He was inspired to write his novel *Old Mortality* when he saw an old man restoring the grave of a Covenanter in the churchyard opposite. The information board in the churchyard guides the visitor around this important burial place. Among the monuments is the burial aisle of the local landowner of Dunnottar, the Earl Marischal. The little building was erected in 1582 and restored by Aberdeen University in 1913 as a mark of respect to the founder of Marischal College. We might consider why this 'aisle' sits in isolation. In 1560 Scotland's ancient system of patronage was reformed as a parish-based system. From then on, there were no architectural requirements other than a 'preaching box', focused on the minister. In spite of attempts to bring the Scottish Church into line with English practice, the consequences for new architecture were minimal. However, the consequences for existing churches were considerable, as the Reformers set about reorganising them internally for the new service, with the pulpit and the communion table at the centre. Many churches, split into separate areas and chapels, had never been designed to accommodate congregations. Churches were also 'cleansed' of ornament and much was lost in the process, although a greater loss seems to have been sustained during a second, far more severe phase of iconoclasm carried out by sixteenth-century Covenanters.

The simplest way of accommodating the new Protestant order was by the addition of a new wing, making the church T-shaped. This wing was often of two storeys with a burial aisle and/or a patron's loft. The parish church thereby entered into its new, eventually contentious, role of ancillary power centre of the local laird. The most interesting laird's 'aisle' (range or wing) of this period was the Dunfermline Aisle, added around 1610 by Alexander Seton, first Earl of Dunfermline, to St Bridget's Church in Dalgety Bay. Seton was also the patron of Fyvie. At first glance his building hardly looked like a church building at all. It is very much the 'office' of Seton as powerful local landlord, architecturally representing its patron as a man of scholarship and classical learning with its monumental exterior and expensive stone-panelled interior. The Earl Marischal's aisle has a similarly plain grandeur.

The church itself in its original form was of the simple, reformed 'preaching box' with a bellcote at one end. You see these all over the country, often lying in ruins with a churchyard around them. Here the church was adapted and increased in size rather than abandoned altogether. The result is very pleasing. Look at the lovely 'cherry cocking' of the church's original stonework opposite the Earl's Aisle.

MEARNS FOREST WALK

Four miles south of Stonehaven is Drumtochty Glen, which used to be part of the Drumtochty Estate. There are a number of very pleasant woodland walks here with wildlife ponds and picnic areas. A short distance up the glen is the 'Shakin Brigie' – supposedly built by the local minister to permit his parishioners to cross the river for Sunday service. At the top of the glen is the very impressive viewpoint known as Cairn o' Mount overlooking the Mearns to the east and Royal Deeside to the north and west.

FOWLSHEUGH RSPB RESERVE

The Fowlsheugh RSPB reserve is just to the south of Stonehaven. 'Fowlsheugh' means 'bird sanctuary' (a 'sheugh' in Scots is a ditch or a crevice). The best way to see the reserve is by boat, and trips are available from the pier at Stonehaven during the summer months. The reserve supports one of the largest seabird colonies on mainland Britain. Tens of thousands of auks and kittiwakes return here to nest each spring, attracted by the shoals of fish (especially sand-eels) off the eastern Scottish coast and by the geology of the cliffs with their abundance of nesting sites. Most of the white birds you see swarming around the cliff-tops are kittiwakes. Nearly 60,000 pairs nest here, about 12 per cent of the entire British population. The name 'kittiwake' is an imitation of the cry of the birds. Like most of the other seabirds here they eat mainly sand-eels. The herring gull also makes its home here – about 3,500 pairs nest here (though only 500 or so of these are on the reserve). They choose relatively flat areas on which to nest, and they feed on a wide variety of foods, including the young of other species here.

The soaring birds with the stiff little wings are fulmars. The fulmar, a kind of tiny albatross, nests singly near the top of the cliff, where it lays its one egg. There are nearly 2,000 pairs here now, but before 1914 there were none at all. In fact until the end of the twentieth century St Kilda was the only place in Britain you could find them. Now they have spread all around these islands. The fulmar's nest is made of grass and seaweed and is stuck onto the narrowest of ledges, and the two or three young are instinctively motionless, staying firmly in the precariously placed nest.

The eider duck is another species of seabird which is common here. They are seen best on the flat rocks and rocky islets at the bottom of the cliffs, where the smart black-and-white appearance of the mate contrasts with the seaweed colours of the female. These birds feed on shellfish, which they prise off the rocks underwater using their strong bills.

STONEHAVEN TO DUNNOTTAR CASTLE

To visit Dunnottar Castle we can take a relatively arduous but very satisfying walk up the steep coastal road or drive up via the A92 to Montrose and Arbroath, following the signs and leaving the car at the castle carpark. Alternatively, you could take a taxi up and have a gentle stroll back down. The coastal road turns inland at Black Hill, which is the site of Stonehaven's unusual temple-like war memorial, featured in Grassic Gibbon's *Sunset Song*. You can meet this road from a very rough and even rather dangerous track leading from the shore. Whether or not you climb the hill, it's worth taking this newly boardwalked path and looking back at the town's mighty harbour. The path can be reached by walking right to the end, south of the harbour.

DUNNOTTAR CASTLE

Dunnottar Castle is one of the most spectacular castles in Europe, an 'impressive ruined fortress' as the sign here says. It is much more than a fortress, though, in the same way that Stirling and Edinburgh were built for a great deal more than simply defence. Its cliff-top setting is reminiscent of Brittany's Fort Lalatte. It is a familiar profile, yet Dunnottar is strangely one of the lesser known buildings in Scotland even although it has been used as a setting for films such as Mel Gibson's *Hamlet*, in books such as the old French *Romance of Fergus* or in the twentieth-century Lewis Grassic Gibbon's *Sunset Song*, which was later televised. Most recently Dunnottar has featured as a backdrop for the Scottish Tourist Board's European campaign. The reason why Dunnottar has been popular and why it is so photogenic is its dramatic outline and its cliff-top setting on top of one of these craggy rocks that have become detached from the mainland. The prefix 'Dun' suggests that the castle existed as a fort or place of retreat in Pictish times.

In May 1276 William Wishart, Bishop of St Andrews, consecrated a parish church of Dunothyr on the site but the church was also dedicated to St Ninian (360–432), the first known Christian apostle of Scotland, who pre-dated St Columba by two hundred years. It is possible that Ninian founded a branch of his Candida Casa in the neighbourhood. The castle has changed hands many times. In 1297 Dunnottar was captured by the English but was stormed and taken by William Wallace.

The Scottish leader, according to Blind Harry the patriot's biographer, then burned the entire garrison alive in the chapel where they had sought sanctuary. In 1336 during the time of Balliol the castle was again occupied by the English but they were ejected, this time by the Regent Moray who 'passand forthwart on this wise, he brint Donnotir'.

The most famous incident in the castle's action-packed history was the rescue of Charles II's crown jewels. The regalia had been deposited at Dunnottar to be looked after during the Civil War by the castle's owner Earl Marischal, Hereditary Warden of the Regalia. The king's private papers were also kept here. At the same time the ceremonial maces of St Andrews University, Scotland's oldest seat of learning, were also deposited for safe-keeping during these uncertain times. Cromwell's army advanced north and, by 1652, Dunnottar was the last redoubt of royalism in the country. Rumour spread that locked away inside the castle, besides the sceptres and regalia 'ther are all the King's rich hangins and bedds, plate and other furniture'. Cromwell was determined to grab this loot and to receive the state regalia. Meanwhile, inside the castle the small garrison of 69 men waited in vain for a friendly invasion from 'the men of Norway'. The English troops arrived and immediately decided that the castle could not be taken by storming and so they waited for six months for their heaviest field artillery to arrive. The huge assault began and ended almost on the same day when the garrison surrendered under the 'havock of bombs and the shoaks of thundering canon'.

Having finally got inside, however, the English did not find what they were looking for. Much earlier, the regalia had been lowered over the castle walls to be received by a serving woman 'on pretence of gathering dulse and tangles [edible red seaweed and course seaweed, Laminaria]'. The regalia were taken to the parish church of Kineff where they were hidden below the floor until the Restoration in 1660. The king's papers were very cunningly smuggled out of the castle by Anne Lindsay, a kinswoman of the castle governor Sir George Ogilvy. Lindsay had stitched the papers into a flat belt, which she wore around her middle on her way through the lines of the besieging army. Angered at their loss, the troops demolished as much of the building as they were able and destroyed Dunnottar's famous library.

The castle had many more adventures in its long existence but the end came with the Earl Marischal's support of the Old Pretender in the Jacobite Rising of 1715. The Earl's lands and possessions, including Dunnottar and all its contents, were forfeited and the castle dismantled. it began a slow decay which continued until its rescue in 1925 by the widow of Baron Cowdray (see p.104), Annie, Viscountess Cowdray.

One of the really charming things about Dunnottar is the fact that it is almost completely uncommercialised. This is one of Scotland's most important castles, yet there is no shop selling souvenirs, no 'Dunnottar Experience'. The only thing available to buy is the wonderful guidebook by the late Douglas Simpson, an Aberdonian and one of Scotland's great historians.

As we look at the castle from the neighbouring rock we can appreciate why the site was described as 'the fiddlehead' from its narrow neck giving on to a broad platform on which the castle is built. (The tunnel cut through this neck at ground level is modern.) There is literally no way of approaching the castle without being seen by the watchman at his post on the cap house. The oldest surviving part of the castle is the fourteenth-century keep, a rectangular tower 41 feet by 36 feet and 50 feet high. The walls of the keep are more than five foot thick. This is the building that dominates the tiny arched entrance to the castle. Early in the sixteenth century, a new block was built east of the keep and in 1574 the larger accommodation block known as the Priest's House was put up. The west wing of the quadrangle was added in 1581 along with the chapel, and two further wings were built to make a courtyard or quadrangle on the flattened base of the rock. The whole site thereafter took on the appearance of a royal palace like Stirling with its various blocks arranged around a central 'square'. The monarch had taken the lead in introducing the quite recent modern notion of privacy in a form we can recognise, with its segregated bedrooms, dining-rooms, and hallways. This desire for comfort and privacy led to a movement towards more specialised planning, including self-contained blocks of lodgings, as at Dunnottar, where guests could be accommodated away from communal areas. This is what gives Dunnottar the appearance of a royal palace. The quest for comfort was now taken up by the aristocracy, as was the architecture of power such as the towers and battlements as we see on the Castle Trail. The aristocracy also followed the monarchy's example in adding to existing buildings rather than building anew.

3

Cruden Bay

Cruden Bay is a little holiday resort to the north of Aberdeen on some dramatic but accessible coastline. There is just enough of a break in the continuous cliffs of this very rugged stretch of coast to have permitted the creation of a small harbour. There is also a famous golf course in a superb setting, and the wonderful Slains Castle: a sombre and exceptionally creepy ruin which teeters on the edge of the cliffs. The castle was the inspiration for Bram Stoker's *Dracula* when he visited the Earl of Erroll in 1895. Visit the castle, especially around dusk, and you will soon see why. BUT KEEP AWAY FROM THE CLIFF EDGE – IT IS VERY DANGEROUS!

The easiest way to reach Cruden Bay is by car but there are also buses out of Aberdeen. Take the A92 for about ten miles then the A975 for Peterhead. Cruden Bay is another 12 miles along this road but you should go at a leisurely pace and enjoy the strange but beautiful land scape of the Ythan. The name Cruden Bay derives from '*croujo-dane*', meaning 'slaughter of the Danes'. In 1012 the plain behind the bay was the site of a bloody battle between the Scots of King Malcolm II and the Danes under the leadership of Canute, who later became King of England. After the Scots' victory, the Danes evacuated all their forces from Scotland, undertaking never to return as foes. It was perhaps this defeat which persuaded Canute to turn his attention to England, which he conquered four years later.

Prior to the nineteenth century Cruden Bay existed only as Ward of Cruden, a tiny fishing hamlet perched under the shadow of Slains Castle. Between 1875 and 1880 the Earl of Erroll, the owner of the castle, built a harbour and, to mark this, Ward of Cruden was renamed Port Erroll. The harbour failed to attract the herring industry to the extent expected, however, as it was tidal and virtually dry at low water. Consequently, it was used almost exclusively by small boats catching white fish and shell-fish.

As you arrive, notice Old Church of Cruden Bay. It is given great prominence in this windswept landscape. Built in 1776, it was enlarged in 1834 and renovated in 1913. The surrounding graveyard contains many evocative family stones.

EPISCOPAL CHURCH OF ST JAMES

Situated 1½ miles south of Cruden Bay, it was built in 1765 by the Earl of Erroll. Its font is said to have originated from a church built by Malcolm II on the battlefield of Cruden to mark his victory over the Danes. Set on the ridge of Chapel Hill and visible for miles it is open daily.

CRUDEN BAY BEACH

The beach consists of more than 2 miles of soft sand in a crescent shaped bay and is included in a guide to the best 100 beaches in Britain. Access is from Harbour Street. The Water of Cruden flows into the sea at Cruden Bay. It once provided power for seven mills which made thread-making an important local industry. The remains of some of the mills still stand and one, at Hatton, has been converted into a bar.

SLAINS CASTLE

Slains Castle can be easily reached by footpath from Cruden Bay. Paths run from Castle Road and the carpark on Main Street. The paths are used by youngsters on mini-motorbikes so beware.

VERY GREAT CARE MUST BE TAKEN WHEN WALKING ON THE CLIFF-TOPS. DO NOT ALLOW CHILDREN NEAR THE EDGE.

The castle was first erected in 1597 by the ninth Earl of Erroll. It replaced an earlier family seat some six miles to the south which was

Slains Castle

THE DRACULA CONNECTION

There are two rather macabre connections with the brooding remains of Slains Castle. In 1895 Bram Stoker visited the house and was immediately inspired to write his novel Dracula. When you see the village below and the mysterious, massive house teetering on the rocks above, you can easily call to mind the fictional bloodsucking count. It is popularly believed that Stoker began writing Dracula in Cruden Bay in August 1895. It is thought that he had been planning a novel with a vampire theme for some time, and a number of critics have argued that much of the plot comes from Shakespeare's Macbeth (which Stoker had previously researched for a Lyceum production). There is no doubt, though, that Slains Castle was the model for the lonely, desolate castle which Dracula occupied. Early drafts of the story had the vampire count coming ashore to Britain at Slains (though this was later changed to Whitby in Yorkshire). Bram Stoker (1847–1912) was born in Dublin, and spent much of his life working as manager of the Lyceum Theatre in London. His published works are extensive, ranging from children's stories to a reference book based on his experience as a clerk in the Dublin courts. It is for the Count Dracula story that he is most remembered, of course. Many of his earliest works had a horror theme but his writing became considerably more horrific after he discovered Cruden Bay while on holiday in 1893. The area's towering cliffs, jagged sea rocks, wild shores and landscape of swirling 'haar' inspired him, as did local tales and superstitions of ghosts and evil spirits. As in most 'remote' places, local superstitions persisted and travellers were interested to hear them. Stoker returned to the area every summer, taking rooms at the Kilmarnock Arms Hotel until he eventually occupied a summer cottage at Whinnyfold. Immediately after his first visit, Stoker began publishing novels and short stories which were set in or inspired by Cruden Bay. The Man from Shorrox's, Crooken Sands and The Watter's Mou were all full of local character and superstition. Dracula was the work which most thrilled the public. It was an immediate success and the story has been filmed many times.

Slains Castle had been the childhood home of Josslyn Hay, twenty-second Earl of Erroll. Hay was the victim of an infamous murder in Happy Valley, Kenya, in 1941. A film, White Mischief, based on James Fox's book of 1984, was made about the affair. Erroll's home in Happy Valley was called 'Slains' after the family home here at Cruden Bay.

destroyed by James VI as punishment for Erroll's part in a revolt of Catholic nobles. Subsequent earls rebuilt and added to the castle, the last great reconstruction being completed in 1837. Dr Johnson and James Boswell visited Slains during their travels in 1773, Johnson describing how 'the walls of one of the towers seem only a continuation of the perpendicular rock, the foot of which is beaten by the waves'.

Slains reached its height at the time of the nineteenth earl, who built the harbour at Port Erroll and created what has been described as a 'mini-welfare state' in the district. During the early twentieth century Slains often played host to actors, writers, musicians and singers of the day, including Dame Clara Butt who organised and performed in a fundraising concert of patriotic songs in neighbouring Peterhead following the outbreak of the First World War. The nineteenth earl's beneficence, coupled with death duties and taxation, so reduced the family's wealth that the twentieth earl was forced to sell the castle in 1916. The new owner, an absentee landlord, allowed Slains to fall into disrepair until it was unroofed in 1925 and left abandoned to the elements.

GOLF AT CRUDEN BAY

As long ago as 1791 the Port Erroll Golfing Society was established at Cruden Bay. The club is just a bit younger than the Society of Golfers at Aberdeen, which was founded in 1780. Golf was at first very much a 'links' or coastal game and Port Erroll was perfectly placed for this type of game.

In August 1897 the Great North of Scotland Railway opened a branch line from Ellon to Boddam which passed alongside Cruden Bay. The company saw potential for developing the little village as a luxurious holiday resort and built a large, 55-bedroom hotel with its own tennis courts, croquet lawns and bowling green. A championship-standard golf course was also created and an electric tramway, half a mile in length, was built to transport guests to the hotel from the railway station. The new course was opened with a star-studded tournament featuring the golfing legends Harry Vardon, James Braid and Ben Sayers. The Cruden Bay Hotel, as it was named, was the ultimate in luxury. It was the kind of set-up that had succeeded at Gleneagles and Turnberry, both of which had dedicated railway stations. But Cruden Bay was a little bit more out of the way and, although it did very well at first, it soon began operating at huge losses. Its isolated position was heightened when the railway closed in 1932 and, after being requisitioned by the army and used as a hospital during the Second World War, it was closed and demolished between 1947 and 1952. Today no sign of it remains but it was perhaps instrumental in the renaming of neighbouring Port Erroll as Cruden Bay in 1924 and it certainly encouraged the development of other visitor facilities in the town. Cruden Bay is now a popular resort town whose two miles of sandy beach attracts day-trippers and holidaymakers alike. The golf course is superb and continues to flourish. It is widely recognised as one of the top courses in Britain. The Cruden Bay Golf Club is at Aulton Road, Tel: (01779) 812285.

Just to the south of Cruden Bay is Whinnyfold, an old cliff-top fishing village. During the mid-nineteenth century 24 boats fished out of here even though there was no harbour. Boats were drawn up and fish laid out to dry on the shingle beach below the four rows of cottages. Off-shore lie the jagged rocks of the Skares of Cruden. They have caused many shipwrecks. Legend has it that at certain times of the year the bodies of those who perished on the rocks could be seen coming out of the sea to join their spirits in heaven or hell. This was the story that inspired Bram Stoker to write his tale *Mystery of the Sea*.

BODDAM

Boddam lies on the coast between Peterhead and Cruden Bay at Buchan Ness, the most easterly point on the Scottish mainland. It was once a thriving herring port with 85 boats and 13 curing yards, but it lost its fishing industry to Peterhead. The old parts of Boddam have a nineteenth-century character and the village is dominated by the huge Buchanness Lighthouse, built by Robert Stevenson in 1827, and the more modern structure of Peterhead power station. There is a tradition that during the Napoleonic Wars the people of Boddam discovered a monkey, which had survived a shipwreck, and hanged it as a French spy. The same tale is told about other places, probably by rival villages, and most famously of Hartlepool in England.

BULLERS OF BUCHAN

The Bullers of Buchan are famous sea cliffs located just off the A975 three miles north of Cruden Bay. There is gigantic sea chasm some 200 feet deep where the sea rushes in through a natural archway open to the sky. The cliff scenery here is among the most spectacular in the country and seabirds of many species can be seen. There is a carpark and a small village at the Bullers. A rough footpath leads to the very edge of the chasm.

GREAT CARE MUST BE EXERCISED AT ALL TIMES.

Index

Abbotsford Place 170

Abercrombie, Charles 41, 51

Aberdeen Art Gallery 101

Aberdeen Arts Centre (former North Church) 42, 150

Aberdeen Central Bakery 156

Aberdeen Combworks 153

Aberdeen Football Club 211

Aberdeen Grammar School 72, 95, 104, 117, 153

Aberdeen Land Association 172, 224

Aberdeen Market 127

Aberdeen Royal Infirmary 42, 107

Aberdeen Trades Council 98

Aberdeen–Inverurie Canal 143

Adam, Robert 42, 53, 102

Adam, William 100, 249

Adelphi 51, 58

Advocates' Hall 55, 62

Albert (Prince) 36, 62, 64, 104, 111, 215

Albert Basin 207

Albert Terrace 231

Albyn Place 221

Albyn Terrace 224

Alexander II 16

Alford Lane 221

Allan, J. Ogg 155

Anderson, Sir Alexander 178

Anderson, David, of Finzeauch 16

Anderson, John, 'Wizard of the North' 91

Anderson, Sir Robert Rowand 110, 162

Argyle Crescent 229

Argyle Place 119, 229

Assembly Rooms 30, 42, 66, 67, 134

Athenaeum 56

Back Wynd 96

Baird, Sir Dugald 221

Baird, Lady Mary 221

Barbour, John 134

Barclay, Robert 83

Beach Ballroom 211

Beach Bathing Station 210

Beach Boulevard 210

Beattie, James Forbes 176

Bel family 238

Belmont Street 98

Berry Street 156

Betjeman, Sir John 49

Billings, Robert 54

Birch, G.B. 225

Blind Harry 108, 260

Boddam 266

Boece, Hector 17, 182

Bon Accord Centre 88

Bon Accord Crescent 168

Bon Accord Free Church of Scotland 112

Bon Accord Square 166

Bon Accord Street 166, 173, 176

Bower, Walter 182

Braehead House 213

Braid, James 265

Bridge of Dee 167, 176

Bridge of Don 212

Brig o' Balgownie 214

Broad Street 16, 55, 56, 57, 77, 78, 80, 81, 96, 150

Broadford Works 21, 132, 154

Broadgate 16, 18 177

Brough, Robert 37

Brown, Captain Samuel 171

Brown & Watt 112, 120, 156, 220

Bryce, David 239

Buchanness Lighthouse 266

Bullers of Buchan 266

Burleigh, Lord 167

Burn, James 41, 135

Burnett family 240

Burwel, John 185

Butt, Dame Clara 264

Byron, Lord 95, 100, 116, 117, 214, 239

Cadenhead, James 36
Caledonian Place 169
Cameron's Bar 97
Campbell's Ltd, Post Horse Masters 165
'Canny Sweet Pots' 212
Capitol Cinema 70
Cardan, Jerome, of Padua 229
Cardan's Well 230
Carden Place 230
Carden Place United Presbyterian Church 231
Castle Fraser 240
Castle Street 18, 133, 142, 143, 144
Castlegate 139, 143, 144
Castlehill Barracks 140
Castlehill Court 140
Cathedral of Our Lady of the Assumption see St Mary's Church
Causewayend Primary School 153
Cementarius, Richard 214, 239
Central Library 111
Chalmers, George Paul 36
Charles I 141
Charlotte Street 154
Cheere, John 101
Chilton, Margaret 195
Christ's College 219
Church of St Nicholas 61, 87, 89
City Hospital 210
Cluny's Garden (Cruikshank Botanical Garden) 197
Clyne, Arthur 33, 65
Codona Fun Park 208
Collison Aisle 29, 94
Comper, Sir John Ninian 33, 151
Concert Court 55
Congregational Church 47, 63, 98
Correction Wynd 60
Corrichie, Battle of 135
Cottier, Daniel 194
Cottown of Balgownie 213
Coutts, George 33, 162, 228
Cowdray, Viscount (Weetman Dickinson Pearson) 104, 241
Cowdray, Viscountess Anne 260
Cowdray Hall 65, 103
Cowie, James 38
Cowie (village) 256
Craigievar Castle 241
Craiginches Prison 171
Crathes Castle 240
Cromwell, Oliver 141, 142

Cromwell's Tower 187
Crown Street 162
Cruden, Alexander 55
Cruden Bay 97, 262
Cruikshank Botanical Garden 197

Dancing Cairn quarry 67
'Danzig Willie' of Craigievar see Forbes, William
David I 49
'Davie dae a' thing' see Anderson, David, of Finzeauch
Dee, River 16
Dee Street 16, 165
Dee Village 173
Deeside Railway Company 105
Denburn Viaduct 104
Devanha Gardens 172
Devanha House 172
Devanha Terrace 171
Diamond Street 66
Don, River 16
Donmouth Nature Reserve 212
Drum Castle 214, 236, 239
Duke of Gordon statue 67
Dun, James 101
Dunbar, Bishop Gavin 173, 176, 193
Dunbar, Sir William 125, 133
Dunnottar Castle 259
Dunnottar Church 257
Dunnottar Woods 257
Durnin, Leo 116
Duthie, Charlotte 174
Duthie Park 17, 172, 173
Duthie Ropeworks 205
Duthie Shipyard 204
Dyce, William 35, 103, 137

Eardley, Joan 103
East Green 127
Edward VII statue 64, 65, 104, 111
Elliot, Archibald 221
Ellis, Alexander 30, 168, 169
Elphinstone, Bishop William 17, 92, 185, 187
Epidemic Hospital see City Hospital
Episcopal Church of St James, Cruden Bay 262
Erroll, Earls of 263
Esplanade 212
Esslemont, Peter 56
Esslemont & Macintosh 56

Façade, the 61
Ferryhill Parish Church 24, 170
Ferryhill Place 170
Ferryhill Road 169
Fever Hospital see City Hospital
Fittie Wynd 140
Fletcher, Thomas 51
Footdee 16, 201, 202
Forbes, Sir William 250
Forbes, William ('Danzig Willie' of
    Craigievar) 18, 238, 241
Fordun, John of 108, 182, 193
Foresterhill Hospital 39, 107
Forsyth, Alexander John 187
Fountainhall Road 226
Fowlsheugh RSPB Reserve 258
Franche, Thomas 176
Fraser, Alexander 187
Futtie's Port 149
Fyvie Castle 247, 236, 237

Gaelic Chapel 98
Gaelic Lane 98
Galleria 165
Galloway, Alexander 176
Gallowgate 152
Garden, Mary 165
Garden Nook Well 111
Gardner, A.B. 116
Gawpuyl 16
General Post Office 159
George Street 60, 68, 153
Gibbon, Lewis Grassic (James Leslie
    Mitchell) 39, 253
Gibbs, James 11, 29, 92, 93
Gilcomston Park 112, 115
Gilcomston Primary School 120
Gilcomston South Church 70
Giles, James 34, 42, 173, 223, 249
Gill, Sir David 120
Girdleness Lighthouse 199, 211
Glover, Thomas Blake 213
Golden Square 66
Gordon, Catherine, of Gight 95
Gordon, George first Marquis of Huntly
    245
Gordon, George, second Marquis of Huntly
    245
Gordon, Harry 208
Gordon, James, of Rothiemay 76, 202
Gordon, Sir John 240
Gordon Highlanders 66

Gordon Highlanders Museum 232
Gordon of Khartoum statue 100
Grampian Television 229
Grandholm Works 21
Grant, Duncan 38
Great North of Scotland Railway 112, 143
Green, the 126
Gregory, Professor James 212
Greyfriars Church of Scotland 25, 56
Guest Row 56
Guild Street 157

Hadden Street 129
Haddo House 248
Hall, Sir William 176
Hall Russell Shipbuilding Yard 202
Hall & Co, Alexander 203
Hamilton Monument 91
Hamilton, David 52
Hamilton-Gordon, George, fourth Earl of
    Aberdeen 249
Hamilton Place 119, 228
Hardgate 70
Hay, Josslyn, Earl of Erroll 264
High Street, Old Aberdeen 186, 188
His Majesty's Theatre 107
Huntly 242
Huntly Castle 237
Huntly Street 68
Huxley-Jones, T.B. 116

Imperial Hotel 33, 128
Irvine, Hugh 239

Jackson's Garage 166
James III 185
James IV 133
James V 136
James VII 139
Jamesone, George 35, 86
Jasmine Place 145
Johnson, Dr Samuel 39
Jopp, James 156
Justice Mill Lane 70
Justice Port 144

Keith, George, Earl Marishcal 79
Keith, James Francis Edward 140
Kelly, Dr William 30, 63, 65, 153, 164, 232
Kemp, Marjorie 195
Kilgour, Robert, Bishop of Aberdeen 149
Kincorth 175

King Street 147
King's College 17, 183
King's College Chapel 183
King's Gate 228
King's Links 212
Kittybrewster 143

Langstane Place 162, 165
Langstane Place Church 69
Lavery, Sir John 102
Laws, Dr Robert 71
Leith Hall 246
Lennox, Annie 203
Leslie, Alexander J. 117
Leslie, Provost 143
Leslie, William 33
Little Belmont Street 97
Loch Street 156
Lochlands 151
Lorimer, Hew 195
Lorimer, Sir Robert 149, 195
Lorne Buildings 177
Lower Denburn 106

Macadrews Bar 162
McBey, James 37, 103
McCombie's Court 57
MacDonald, Alexander 232
McElvie, W.R. 173
Macfarlane, Walter 119
MacGillivray, Pittendreigh 116
MacGillivray, William 190
MacGregor, Rob Roy 138, 212
McGrigor, Sir James 81
McInnes, Shona 94
Mackenzie, A.G.R. 32, 132, 166, 194
Mackenzie, A. Marshall 31, 70, 80, 102, 104, 107, 111, 112, 130, 164, 175, 188, 219
Mackenzie, J. Russell 31, 172, 220, 224, 232
Mackenzie, Thomas 31, 164, 219
Mackenzie & Matthews 222, 223
Mackie Place 120
MacKinnon, A.H.L. 196
Maclennan, Harbourne 164
MacMillan, Duncan 31, 120, 170, 172
McRobbie, Alexander 71
Ma Cameron's 97
Maberly, Sir John 154
Maberly Street 154
Margaret Tudor (Queen) 133, 185
Marine Terrace 172
Marischal Street 21, 41, 134, 137

Marischall College 79
Maritime Museum 130
Market Street 129
Marochetti, Baron 111
Martin, Samuel 57, 59
Mary, Queen of Scots 135
Matcham, Frank 107
Mathieson, Robert 80, 187
Matthews, James 31, 55, 117, 118, 169
Mearns Forset 258
Mears, Sir Frank 175
Mechanics' Institute 129
Medico-Chirurgical Building 148
Menzies of Pitfodels 98, 134, 188
Mercat Cross 136
Mernes, Barons of 193
Migvie House 68
Mitchell, Dr Charles 80
Mitchell, Sydney A.G. 65, 162
Mitchell Hall 80, 150
Mitchell Hospital 196
Monaghan & MacLachlan 163
Montgomery, John, of Old Rayne 139
Montrose, James Graham, fifth Earl and first Marquis of 167
Morgan, John 227
Morrocco, Alberto 82
Mounthooly 152

Narrow Wynd 56
Nash, Paul 102
Netherkirkgate 57
New Inn 147
New King's, Old Aberdeen 188
New Pier Road 206
Newhills Church
Norco House 156
North Church (Aberdeen Arts Centre) 150
North of Scotland Bank 42
North of Scotland Fire and Life Insurance Company 148
North Pier 207
North Silver Street 66
Northern Co-operative Society 156
Northern Hotel 166
Northfield Place 116

Odeon Cinema 71
Old Aberdeen Town House 190
Old Church of Cruden Bay 262
Old Town School 97
Oldrieve, W.T. 163

Our Lady of Aberdeen 179

Palace Hotel 125
Patagonian Court 98
Peacock, Francis 147
Peddie & Kinnear 53, 113, 134, 223
Petrie, Arthur, Bishop of Moray 149
Phillip, John 'Spanish' 36, 127
Phipps, Charles 157
Pirie, John 33, 175, 224
Pirie & Clyne 224, 228, 229
Pitmedden Garden 247
Pocra Quay 206
Polmuir Road 170, 172
Poultry Market Lane 150
Powis Lodge 187
Provost Ross's House 131
Provost Skene's House 76, 132
Putachieside 129

Queen Elizabeth Bridge 171
Queen Street 95, 150
Queen's Cross 224
Queen's Cross Church 220, 224
Queen's Links 208
Queen's Road 226

Raich, the 206
Regent Quay 130
Reid, Sir George 37, 232
Reith, Lord 254
Rennie's Wynd 125
Richards & Co 154
Riverside Drive 175
Robert the Bruce 19, 144, 227, 240
Robert Gordon's Hospital 95
Rosemount Square 114
Rosemount Viaduct 114
Row, John 187
Royal Blind Asylum 68
Rubislaw Den North 226
Rubislaw Den South 227
Rubislaw Terrace 173, 222
Ruskin, John 228
Rust, Provost James 210
Rust, John 210
Ruthrieston 175
Ruthrieston Terrace 175

St Andrew Street 155
St Andrew's Episcopal Cathedral 25, 33, 42, 148

St Clement's Church 142, 202
St Columba's Parish Church 25
St James the Great, Stonehaven 26
St John's Episcopal Church 31, 164
St John's Place 164
St John's Well 221
St Machar Bar 190
St Machar Drive 191
St Machar's Cathedral 192
St Margaret's, Huntly 244
St Mark's Church of Scotland 25, 107, 111
St Mary's Church (Cathedral of Our Lady of the Assumption) 53, 68, 95, 169
St Mary's Episcopal Cathedral ('Tartan Kirkie') 231
St Nicholas Centre 53, 88
St Nicholas' Church see Church of St Nicholas
St Nicholas' Churchyard 61
St Nicholas' United Free Church 71
St Nicholas' West Church 61, 93, 97
St Paul's Chapel, Gallowgate 156
St Peter's Church 146
Salvation Army Citadel 144
Sandilands 206
Sandness 206
Sayers, Ben 265
Schoolhill 89, 100
Scott, Sir Walter 55, 128
Seabury, Bishop Samuel 149
Seaton Park 18, 195
Seton, Chancellor Alexander 248, 257
Shiprow 129
Shoe Lane 150
Shore Porters' Society 138
Silver Darling Restaurant 207
Simpson, Archibald 28, 42, 43, 80, 92, 127, 129, 147, 148, 167, 172, 221, 230
Skene, Alexander, of Newtyle 54
Skene, Provost George 18, 162
Skene Place 119
Skene Street 119
Skene Terrace 120
Skinner, Bishop John 149
Slains Castle 97, 263
Smeaton, John 206
Smith, James 19
Smith, John 30, 42, 61, 68, 90, 97 147, 177, 184, 187, 194, 241, 149
Smith, Trevor 34
Smith, William 30, 120, 137, 153
Smith, William Robertson 220

Snow Churchyard 188
South Silver Street 66
Souttar, James 33, 98, 129, 228
Springbank Terrace 169
Stead, Tim 94
Steill, John 110
Stevenson, Robert 211, 253, 266
Stevenson, W. Grant 108
Stewart & Co, R.S. 153
Stoker, Bram 98, 264
Stonehaven 253
Strachan, Robert Douglas 37, 194
Street, G.E. 249
Sutherland, T. Scott 34, 71, 100

'Tartan Kirkie' 231
Taylor, Rachel Annand 221
Telford, Thomas 53, 207, 212
tenements 113
Theroux, Paul 11
Thomas the Rhymer 214
Thom's Court 189
Thomson, Robert William 254
Thornton, William 29
Tillydrone House 195
Tivoli Theatre 157
Tolbooth 54
Tolquhon Castle 250
Torry 225
Torry Battery 207
Town House (municipal buildings) 26, 37, 47, 50, 54, 59, 134, 145, 225
Trinity Hall 62
Trinity United Free Church (former) 164
Triple Kirks 62, 104, 219

Union Bridge 51, 62
Union Street 41, 42, 50, 57

Union Terrace 64
Upperkirkgate 82

Vardon, Harry 265
Victoria (Queen) 143, 225
Victoria Place 233

Wallace, William 108
Wallace Statue 108
Wallace Tower 195
Ward of Cruden 262
Waterhouse, Paul 163
Waterloo Basin 143
Watt, George 33
Wellington Bridge 157, 171
Wellington Street 202
West Church 92
West Craibstone Street 43
West North Street 150
Whinnyfold 265
Willett, John 64
William the Lion 16
Williamson, Gavin 166
Williamson, Peter 125
Wilson, Harry 184
Wilson, R.G. 30, 71
Windmill Brae 162
windows 230
Wishart, William 259
Woolmanhill 107
Wrights and Coopers Place 190
Wyness, J. Cumming 163

York Street 202
Young, Provost William, of Sheddochsley 137

Zoffany, Johannes 102